The Essential Walt McDonald

The Essential Walt McDonald

WALT McDONALD

TEXAS TECH UNIVERSITY PRESS

This book is typeset in Baskervville. The paper used in this book meets the minimum requirements of ANSI/NISO Z39.48-1992 (R1997). ♾

Designed by Hannah Gaskamp
Cover photograph by Wyman Meinzer

Library of Congress Cataloging-in-Publication Data

Names: McDonald, Walter, author. Title: The Essential Walt McDonald / Walt McDonald.

Description: Lubbock: Texas, Tech University Press, [2022] | Summary: "A lifetime collection of poems by esteemed Texas literary voice Walt McDonald, as selected by the poet himself."—Provided by publisher.

Identifiers: LCCN 2021030488 | ISBN 978-1-68283-121-2 (cloth)
Subjects: LCGFT: Poetry. Classification: LCC PS3563.A2914 E87 2022 | DDC 811/.54—dc23
LC record available at https://lccn.loc.gov/2021030488

Printed in the United States of America
22 23 24 25 26 27 28 29 30/ 9 8 7 6 5 4 3 2 1

Texas Tech University Press
Box 41037
Lubbock, Texas 79409-1037 USA
800.832.4042
ttup@ttu.edu
www.ttupress.org

This publication is a work of fiction. These are poems, made things. The names, titles, places, and events come from the author's imagination. Any similarities between these poems and the real lives of persons living or dead are unintended and coincidental.

Publisher's note: Walt McDonald published over 2,300 poems in journals large and small. Some citations in this book are incomplete, and certain pieces of information could not be verified. As much of the available original publication information as was available has been included.

Punctuation has been standardized throughout; some poems may differ slightly from previously published versions.

For Carol, who married a pilot, not a poet.

Contents

Part 1

Part 2

Part 3

Part 4

Foreword

These poems require no introduction. None of the ordinary tribute paid to poetry collections, by blurbs and reviews and forewords such as this one, can do justice to the extraordinary accomplishments of this poet, whose work of a lifetime you now hold in your hands. We, his readers, are the ones being honored. By Walter McDonald's poetry. By his vision. By the respect he's shown us with this offering. Given his gifts—musical, narrative, epiphanic, intellectual—Walter McDonald might have left some work undone. He might have chosen to repeat himself, to rely on tricks and techniques, or to have turned to trends, made use of the many easier devices and practices of our era. Instead, he's given us the praise we should give to him.

Over all the years and through all the drafts of his days, Walter McDonald has paid tribute to us, to poetry, and to the human experience. With unwavering empathy and generosity, this poet has lived and listened. He's looked hard at things we might never have seen had he not done so. To read this poetry is to understand what a life lived with such openness and attention might offer the poet himself, and also what it might cost, and what his readiness to pursue such a vision offers the rest of us and will go on offering his readers for generations to come.

I met Walter McDonald when I passed briefly through West Texas many years ago and, familiar with his work and thrilled to know he was teaching a workshop that he was willing to let me take, I had the privilege of learning from him. Our workshop met once a week, and after each session I needed a week to process all he'd shared in order to prepare myself for the next meeting. I left that season with a notebook full of insights, suggestions, lines of poetry he'd memorized and recited for us. His casual brilliance was like nothing I'd before encountered. The man seemed to have read everything, and everything he'd read had taught him something he wanted to share with us. He showed me by example what it was to be humbled by poetry—the reading of it and the writing of it—and how such humility must be the way one approaches something as magical and sacred, ancient and dangerous and miraculous as a poem. You come to the practice of writing poetry on your knees. You come to the reading of a poem with your eyes wide open, prepared to be blinded by its power. You don't rely on easy solutions. You must have too much reverence for language and line, repetition, rhythm, and for all the poets who came before you to leave your choices to chance, to leave any stanza you might've written better unrevised, to claim to be a poet until, like Walter McDonald now, after so many years spent paying such devoted attention to poetry, he gives here us the tangible (and auditory, and visual, and spiritual) evidence of the significance of such devotion.

As a poet, I will never reach such heights, perhaps. But as a reader, I am ever conscious that Walter McDonald has taken me to them. His poems reveal to all of us that if we could be as disciplined (while also as unguarded), as full of acceptance and as sincerely excited to be surprised, to be changed, to be ready, to be honest, and to be made as unafraid—by other people, by the world and its creatures, by love, by violence, by self-scrutiny, by loss, and by joy—as he has been, we might one day see as clearly and write as memorably and with as much force as he has. In the meantime, he's given us the incredible gift of this introduction to ourselves, which he sends to us, selflessly, from the heights he's reached, as a promise and a kind of protective charm, an encouragement to us (keep looking, keep living) in this book of poetry that needs no introduction.

LAURA KASISCHKE
DECEMBER 29, 2020

Editor's Note

Walt passed away during the final stages of production of this book, when most of his work on it was complete. There do remain a few textual aspects that I would have asked Walt to explain in his preface. Since he could not, I will do my best to enumerate those here.

The book is organized into four parts. The first part includes poems from these books: *After the Noise of Saigon* (1988), *Blessings the Body Gave* (1998), *All Occasions* (2000), and *Climbing the Divide* (2003). Part 2 encompasses: *The Flying Dutchman* (1987), *Night Landings* (1989), *Counting Survivors* (1995), *Great Lonely Places of the Texas Plains* (2003), *A Thousand Miles of Stars* (2004), and *Faith Is a Radical Master* (2005). Part 3 comprises: *Anything, Anything* (1980), *Burning the Fence* (1981), *Witching on Hardscrabble* (1985), *Rafting the Brazos* (1988), *The Digs in Escondido Canyon* (1991), *All That Matters* (1992), *Where Skies Are Not Cloudy* (1993), and *Whatever the Wind Delivers* (1999). Part 4 contains poems that were published in journals but not in books. Sometimes Walt snuck poems into a part where they did not technically belong. While it is possible he did this as an oversight, I prefer to honor the result, because the new placement is itself a form of composition.

Walt thought a great deal about arrangement and progression, selecting poems that feed off one another while giving the reader a narrative-like sense of mood, language, and scene. As he assembled these, he revised and updated some of them. He told me that poems are never finished, only published. After he died, we encountered a select few poems where it was difficult to tell whether some aspect was a deliberate change or an error he would have adjusted in proofs. Walt was a deliberate and exacting editor, especially of himself. We did our best to leave his poems untouched and to hew to his distinctive grammar and sound when we had to make decisions on his behalf. We did not change words, but we did add some clarifying commas and delete some extraneous punctuation, mostly quotation marks.

Throughout, our north star was adhering to Walt's most recent updates. If there was a conflict between two versions of a poem, I included the one that most closely aligned with the book version of that poem. In one case, we substituted a poem that appeared twice in proofs. "Flicking Its Tongue at the Sun" on page 172 had also featured on page 137, where it had a different title, "Balance" (which was how it was published in *Southern Poetry Review*). We inserted "Backpacking the San Juan" in its stead. I am tremendously grateful for the work of Walt's longtime editor Judith Keeling, who looked at proofs with an expert knowledge of Walt's grammar and style, and for that of Janice Whittington, whose deep familiarity with the poems' provenance also aided with these decisions.

Walt wrote without ego or pretension, typifying instead the unadorned essence of poetry, invoking beauty through clarity and precision. Anyone can read a Walt McDonald poem and find something with personal resonance. I have the pleasure of knowing, also, that he was a good friend. He worked tirelessly on this manuscript for as long as he could, and when he could not continue he told me simply that he trusted us to do our best. We exchanged emails near daily for the first two years of the COVID pandemic, working on the manuscript and talking about our families, current events, and books we like. In every note, he was as generous and openhearted as his poems. Any errors that remain in them are surely ours.

TRAVIS SNYDER
TEXAS TECH UNIVERSITY PRESS

Preface

Each spring, after I retired from the Air Force, my wife Carol and I drove from Texas to Estes Park, Colorado, to our favorite lodge just east of Rocky Mountain National Park—the top rooms with fantastic views—for two to five weeks. There, without telephone or daily papers, I wrote first drafts of more than half of my 2,300 published poems. (I didn't count them, but from the start, I numbered each first draft—1, 2, 3—to keep track of them, in case I later changed the titles.) Carol and I had the rest of each day to hike, watch wildlife with friends or on our own, delight in mountain food, visit each church nearby, write letters to our children in Virginia, Texas, and Montana, and drive mountain roads to the top of the world, when snow allowed—often, twenty to twenty-four inches of snow—some of the best hours snowed in by the fireplace, together, for a while.

I came to poetry late, as a retired middle-aged pilot. I also taught English for three tours of duty at the US Air Force Academy, with a PhD from the University of Iowa. I love flying, but a good story or poem gives pleasures I find nowhere else. Not as much joy as holding hands with my wife on the patio at dawn or bending to lift one of our granddaughters and twirl her around and feel her hug my neck. I know the difference between a poem and a person.

Reading and writing can be richly entertaining, though, a "moveable feast," as Hemingway said of Paris—stunning, sometimes, and wonderful. Robert Frost claimed poetry at its best can be "a momentary stay against confusion." I like that. Even the everyday has splendors that we strain to capture and save, or at least share by emails or iPhones—or in films or on canvas, in melodies, or in writing what we call poems.

I wrote out of a paradox of needs: the enormous delight of discovery and the continual pleasures of play. What kept me going back to the keyboard was a simple faith that words would show me the way. When I sat down to write, I felt totally ignorant. I had no idea what was coming. I liked that silence. When I typed a first word or phrase that intrigued me, I felt a sense of immediate complicity, as if the words and I were up to something.

After his conversion, the poet John Berryman wrote this about the hard, happy work of writing: "Father Hopkins said the only true literary critic is Christ. Let me lie down exhausted, content with that" (Berryman, #10 of "Eleven Addresses to the Lord").

On his weekly TV show a half century ago, Dean Martin sang a song made popular by Jim Reeves: "Welcome to my world. Won't you come on in." I believe that's what every poem says to every reader. If not, why bother.

WALT MCDONALD
2021

The Essential Walt McDonald

Part 1

Praise

It's four, Montana cabin cold.
I lift a blanket past her arms
and slip outside with coffee,

valley so still I hear the Amtrak
to Seattle miles away. No breeze
or stars, the deck so cold

steam rises like a rope trick
from the cup. The moon plays poker
with a deck of clouds, and folds.

Last week, a pack of wolves downwind
raised muzzles to the moon and howled,
prowlers of mountains back in Montana.

Praise dark before the dawn.
Praise God who made the dawn
and water tumbling down from snow,

the tap I'll turn today. Praise God
for sleep, for grizzlies
wild in the mountains, and massive.

For breath that puffs away,
for this dark day, the sun
we're spinning around, the moon

I believe is out there past the clouds.
For my wife's closed eyes
I need to open once more, soon.

[Previously published in *Bellowing Ark* 15, no. 6 (1999): 25 and *Climbing the Divide* (Notre Dame, IN: University of Notre Dame Press, 2003).]

My Father on His Shield

Shiny as wax, the cracked veneer Scotch-taped
and brittle. I can't bring my father back.
Legs crossed, he sits there brash

with a private's stripe, a world away
from the war they would ship him to
within days. Cannons flank his face

and banners above him like the flag
my mother kept on the mantel, folded tight,
white stars sharp-pointed on a field of blue.

I remember his fists, the iron he pounded,
five-pound hammer ringing steel,
the frame he made for a sled that winter

before the war. I remember the rope in his fist
around my chest, his other fist
shoving the snow, and downhill we dived,

his boots by my boots on the tongue,
pines whishing by, ice in my eyes, blinking
and squealing. I remember the troop train,

steam billowing like a smoke screen.
I remember wrecking the sled weeks later
and pounding to beat the iron flat,

but it stayed there bent
and stacked in the barn by the anvil,
and I can't bring him back.

[Previously published in *The Kenyon Review* and *Blessings the Body Gave* (Columbus: The Ohio State University Press, 1998–winner of the 1997 Ohio State University Press *The Journal* Award in Poetry).]

The Waltz We Were Born For

Wind chimes ping and tangle on the patio.
In gusty winds this wild, sparrow hawks hover
and bob, always the crash of indigo
hosannas dangling on strings. My wife ties copper
to turquoise from deserts, and bits of steel
from engines I tear down. She strings them all
like laces of babies' shoes when the squeal
of their play made joyful noise in the hall.

Her voice is more modest than moonlight,
like pearl drops she wears in her lobes.
My hands find the face of my bride.
I stretch her skin smooth and see bone.
Our children bring children to bless her,
her face more weathered than mine. What matters
is timeless, dazzling devotion–not rain,
not Eden gardenias, but cactus in drought,

not just moons of deep sleep, not sunlight or stars,
not the blue, but the darkness beyond.

[Previously published in *First Things* (1998), *The Best Spiritual Writing 1999* (ed. Philip Zaleski, San Francisco: HarperCollins, 1999), *Blessings the Body Gave* (Columbus: The Ohio State University Press, 1998–winner of the 1997 Ohio State University Press *The Journal* Award in Poetry), and *Great Lonely Places of the Texas Plains* (Lubbock: Texas Tech University Press, 2003).]

Baptizing the Dog at Nine

I heard puppies have no souls,
but I loved that mongrel with a bulldog mom.
Behind the barn, I preached that dog's head
down until he dozed. His stubby tail said "Yes, I believe
whatever you say." Crows in the arbor cawed like scoffers.

I staggered with thirty grunting pounds, shoved him
to the stock tank and huffing said the words
and dumped him. He splashed and came up paddling,
head up and wholly dunked, shock of pond scum
in his eyes. The startled crows swirled off,

a flutter of black hosannas. I thought he'd rise
and talk like Balaam's donkey, but he thrashed
as if drowning. Slick-haired, he never barked.
I had to drag him out, his glazed eyes hopeless,
fat crows in the arbor cawing.

[Previously published in *Seneca Review* and *Blessings the Body Gave* (Columbus: The Ohio State University Press, 1998—winner of the 1997 Ohio State University Press *The Journal* Award in Poetry).]

Crossing the Road

What's a boy to do, both shoes caught in the tar,
the road past our house turning to street,
and me, a chicken trying to reach the other side.
Men burly as my uncles swore and shook their shovels,

laughing. My mother waited on the porch,
drying her hands in her apron. My big sister teased,
her gawky girlfriends howled, and someone screamed
"Tar baby!" I swear I tugged, cursing the only words

I had learned, squashed down in July asphalt
like a bug, like Captain Marvel in the comics
turned into a tree, unable to budge. And of all days,
on my birthday. Carl would see me soon, and Mary Jane,

all kids I knew pointing on the curb and dancing.
Like a god roaring up on his motorcycle, my older brother
dismounted and stared. Tucking a Camel in his lips,
he lit and flipped the match away, came strolling down,

fists doubled, snorting smoke, not smiling.
Massive, towering above me, he jerked me up
without my shoes and hauled me like a sack of oats
back to the grass, his own boots ruined.

I remember him that way, not the box of belongings
they brought from Okinawa, not the flag Mother hung
in the window for all cars to see speeding past
the four-lane street, pounding my sneakers down.

[Previously published in *The Sewanee Review* 104, no. 1 (1996): 40 and *Blessings the Body Gave* (Columbus: The Ohio State University Press, 1998—winner of the 1997 Ohio State University Press *The Journal* Award in Poetry).]

Hosanna in the Family

Uncle Earl rolled his eyes over Aunt Bernice
and winked. Aunt Bernice was a honey,
curvy and plump. Earl deeded her parents
a section of his ranch, a dowry she didn't have,

sweetheart so lovely he didn't mind,
would have signed his sunburned soul
on the dotted line. Before Vietnam,
before my cousin Bobby died at Da Nang,

I worked eight summers on the ranch,
their only nephew. Uncle Earl taught us
to ride, to rope and hold a calf down
for branding, to jab and burn its hide

and step back while it flounced and ran.
Aunt Bernice heaped biscuits on our plates,
and yellow butter, my cousin's creamy mother
who worshiped sunburned Uncle Earl,

who drawled raw jokes and stabbed his fork
in the air like pitching hay. What simple days
before the war, hard work and horses
I thought I'd ride forever with Bobby,

Aunt Bernice spoiling us all, forking sausage
and biscuits on our plates, winking
at Bobby and me, leaning toward Uncle Earl
and humming, patting his big-boned fists.

[Previously published in *The American Scholar* (Phi Beta Kappa magazine) 60, no. 3 (2000): 99 and *Climbing the Divide* (Notre Dame, IN: University of Notre Dame Press, 2003).]

The Night of Rattlesnake Chili

Only the lure of a rattler kept us
jerking dry tumbleweeds back
from the bunkhouse. Already, cook
had chili boiling, peppers and beef
convincing us all we were starving.

Cursing, throwing empty bean cans
at our horses, cook swore he'd douse
the fire and dump our dinner to the mules
unless we brought him a long dry tail
of rattler. I used to hear of cooks

crazy enough to grind rattles
like chili powder, a secret poison
to make a pot boil darker than whiskey.
Kicking and calling each other names,
we scoured the range for an hour,

a ranch so cursed with snakes
jackrabbits weren't safe while mating.
At last, I grabbed one by the tail,
the writhing muscle trying to escape
down a burrow, and Billy Ray shot it.

Cook cut off the tail and grinned,
held up the ticking rattle, then
crushed and ground it in his fists.
Hulls floated down into red steam,
and simmered. That night, we ate

thick chili redder than fire
and griped about the dust and hulls,
but begged for seconds. Even our beer
was cold and sweeter than most
and steel spoons melted in our mouths.

[Previously published in *The Seattle Review* 10, no. 2 (1989): 51 and *After the Noise of Saigon* (Amherst: University of Massachusetts Press, 1988–winner of the 1987 University of Massachusetts Press Juniper Prize).]

Uncle Earl's Wind River Ranch

It's salt, not rain, fat elk cows need.
Uncle Earl hauls salt blocks up from town
and dumps them, wedged by boulders
licking tongues can't tumble.

Elk wander down to graze his slopes.
Wild elk often nod, big bellies swaying,
calves on their way, most snow
melting that far down in gusty winds

that wild. Uncle Earl looks up
once a day, takes elk for granted
and boulders above him,
a million years of mountains

balanced, except stones
that tumble, an avalanche
of chance. Like that one
massive by his barn, a stone

he built his wide corral around.
Look at those up there, thousands
of boulders propped on slate
and sand that slide, erode,

steep ledges cracked and tilted
where cougars make their homes,
scratching gravel to widen cracks for caves,
arching their wide big-muscled backs.

[Previously published in *London Review of Books* (UK) 19, no. 2 (1997): 30 and *Blessings the Body Gave* (Columbus: The Ohio State University Press, 1998—winner of the 1997 Ohio State University Press *The Journal* Award in Poetry).]

Driving at Night Across Texas

Her arms held all the songs I longed for,
and four tires took me there.
A pilot on the base at Laredo, I spent
more hours on the highway than flying,
driving at night across Texas,

humming the same old songs.
We keep losing our heroes,
grandparents and singers, friends
missing in action. Car wrecks take them away,
or drugs, planes that crash in mountains

or winter fields, or plain old death.
I think of Glenn Miller in World War II,
Patsy Cline and Billie Holiday, and a boy
from my hometown named Buddy Holly.
Nine grandchildren after a war,

Vietnam is always a fact—"there it is,"
even at night. Some go on
in hospital beds or wheelchairs,
some so boldly brave I'm stunned.
I rock with my wife under stars

on the lawn swing, stroking the same hair dark
as it was those nights in Austin
when the world seemed like a dance hall
and we had coins enough forever,
the jukebox full of songs.

[Previously published in *The Gettysburg Review* 14, no. 3 (2001): 498 and *Climbing the Divide* (Notre Dame, IN: University of Notre Dame Press, 2003).]

The Dark, Hollow Halo of Space

Rock of all, my marble, stone of my tomb
and my stairs. More firm than granite in mountains,
You are older than diamonds and gold.

My body is putty, a tiny brief dot in the dark
hollow halo of space. Billions of stars are specks
in your eyes, maker of fabulous galaxies far

from earth, and all burning. My heart burns slowly,
unnoticed, as gold burns, even novas I've never seen.
I'm numbed by the buckshot of stars, trillions of tons

in each one. When the flesh I'm made from is ash,
only dust I'll become, and go when You call,
where You are, stone of my tomb and my stairs.

[Previously published in *Christianity and Literature* 50, no. 1 (2000): 14 and *Climbing the Divide* (Notre Dame, IN: University of Notre Dame Press, 2003).]

Faith Is a Radical Master

God bats on the side of the scrubs.
With a clean-up hitter like that, who needs
to worry about stealing home, a double squeeze,
cleat-pounding triples? If nothing else works,

take a walk, lean into the wicked pitch
careening inside at ninety miles an hour.
At bat, just get on base and pray the next nerd
doesn't pop up. When someone's already on,

the coach never calls me "Mr. October," seldom
signals "Hit away." If Johnson with the wicked curve
owns the strike zone or the ump, I'll bunt. No crack
of the bat, no wildly cheered Bambino everyone loves.

Lay it down the line like the weakest kid in school,
disciple of the sacrifice. Some hour my time will come,
late in a game, and I'm on third, wheezing from the run
from first after a wild pitch, and Crazy Elmore

waving like a windmill by the third-base line.
Hands on my knees, I'll watch the pitcher
lick two fingers, wipe them on his fancy pin stripes
and try to stare me dead. I'll be almost dead,

gasping, wondering how I'll wobble home if someone
bunts or dribbles a slow roller and the coach yells
"Go!" But there, there in the box is God,
who doesn't pound home plate like an earthquake

but slowly points the bat like the Babe toward
center field, and all my family in the clouds go wild,
all friends I've loved and lost, even the four-eyed scrubs
in the dugout slugging each other and laughing,

tossing their gloves like wild hosannas, and why not—
it's bottom of the ninth, two outs, a run behind
and a hall-of-fame fast baller on the mound,
but I'm on third and leaning home, and look who's up.

[Previously published in *Windhover* 4 (1999): 110 and *Faith Is a Radical Master: New and Selected Poems* (Abilene, TX: Abilene Christian University Press, 2005).]

One Night Before Saigon

The second cellist rubbed pure resin on her bow,
knowing songs were hard to find in times of war
and climates made for cactus. South Texas natives
boiled sweet jelly from sap of prickly pears,

risking wasps and scorpions, squeezing amber drool
into jars. Near the Rio Grande on the air base,
an orchestra from Austin played Bizet, the school's
packed auditorium breezy with ceiling fans

like World War II propellers. Two nights
before I flew to Vietnam, my wife and I
sat close on bleachers built for children,
knees bent, fists locked on an armrest.

The maestro's wildly sweating brow
couldn't drown jet roar of night flights taking off.
Both cellists bowed and vowed with elbows flying,
"What joy this is, wish you could hear!"

The Wing Commander's wife approved it all,
sitting with widows while her colonel flew,
leaving next week himself for Vietnam. Chin up,
she led us all in applause, kept smiling "Yes, oh yes!"

[Previously published in *Michigan Quarterly Review* 43, no. 4 (Special Issue, "Viet Nam: Beyond the Frame," Fall 2004): 618.]

The Food Pickers of Saigon

Rubbish like compost heaps burned every hour
of my days and nights at Tan Son Nhut.
Ragpickers scoured the edges of our junk,
risking the flames, bent over,
searching for food. A ton of tin cans

piled up each month, sharp-edged, unlabeled.
Those tiny anonymous people could stick
their hands inside and claw out whatever
remained, scooping it into jars, into their mouths.
No one went hungry, we said. At a distance,

the dump was like a coal-mine fire burning
out of control, or Moses' holy bush,
that was not consumed. Watching them labor
in the field north of my barracks, trying
to think of something happy to write my wife,

I often thought of bears in Yellowstone
our first good summer in a tent. I wrote
about the bears, helping us both focus
on how they waddled to the road and begged,
and came some nights into the campground

so long ago and took all food they found.
We sat helplessly naive outside our tent
and watched them, and one night rolled
inside laughing when one great bear turned
and shoulder-swayed his way toward us.

Through the zipped mosquito netting
we watched him watching us. Slack-jawed,
he seemed to grin, to thank us for all
he was about to receive from our table.
We thought how lovely, how much fun

to be this close to danger. No campers
had died in that state park for years.
Now, when our children eat their meat
and bread, and leave good broccoli
or green beans on their plates,
I call them back and growl,

I can't help it. It's like hearing
my father's voice again. I never tell them
why they have to eat it. I never say
they're like two beautiful children

I found staring at me one night
through the screen of my window
at Tan Son Nhut, bone-faced. Or that
when I crawled out of my stifling monsoon
dream to feed them, they were gone.

[Previously published in *TriQuarterly* 67 (1986): 122–23 and *After the Noise of Saigon* (Amherst: University of Massachusetts Press, 1988—winner of the 1987 University of Massachusetts Press Juniper Prize).]

Out of the Stone They Come

My son hung a framed painting
on his wall. Head down, a man my age
leans on black granite. A soldier
holds out a ghostly hand to touch him.

Others beyond the wall look out,
young as my son in their helmets.
Out of the stone they've come
with incredibly young arms

because he's here, head bowed, surviving.
They don't seem to envy
his graying hair, black attaché case
or vest. He knows their names

and leans alone in sunlight.
Beside this frame in smaller frames
are shots of my boy's own friends
who'd never gone to war

until the Persian Gulf. One night,
we parked in blowing snow
and hunched a half mile slowly
to the wall, not talking about a war

he can't recall. While I looked for names
he waited, a soldier as old as those.
I rubbed my fingers on the words,
black granite cold as a mirror.

I saw my son's own image in the stone
but found no other face,
only a wide black wall
and names, names blurring together.

[Previously published in *New Texas* (1992) and *Counting Survivors* (Pittsburgh: University of Pittsburgh Press, 1995).]

After the Noise of Saigon

If where we hunt defines us,
then stalking this steep hillside
dark with spruce makes sense,

more than dreams I foundered in
for years, trying to fathom signs
for hours and wading ashore

disgusted. Switches dripping sap
keep flipping me when I glance
over my shoulder for spoor

I might have missed. Evergreen
needles sting when I swing my head
face-forward for clues. Isn't this

the strangest nightmare of all,
knowing my aim with a bow
is no better at twenty yards

than forty? But here I am, alone
with a cougar I've stalked all night,
climbing until I'm dizzy.

These blue trees have nothing
and all to do with why I'm here
after the noise of Saigon,

the simple bitter sap that rises
like blood I need to spill out here
alone in silence of deep woods,

far from people I know who see me
as a friend, not some damned
madman stumbling for his life.

[Previously published in *Poet Lore* 81, no. 13 (1986): 191 and *After the Noise of Saigon* (Amherst: University of Massachusetts Press, 1988—winner of the 1987 University of Massachusetts Press Juniper Prize).]

Counting Survivors

I'm stunned to see so many of us home.
I drive downtown to shout hosanna quietly,
pipe organ booming. The padded church bench
shudders like a med evac jet on takeoff.
Saigon falls often in my dreams.

I see sad others on TV on cycles
roaring toward the Wall, or leaning down
in greens and jungle boots. Most friends I knew
are back in body. I miss good friends
who earned this service. I've faced the Wall

and placed my fingers on their names.
I wish for Easter all year long.
I watch parades in person from the curb
and wonder how do survivors live?
How do the dead arise?

[Previously published in *Maryland Poetry Review* 9 (1990): 45 and *Counting Survivors* (Pittsburgh: University of Pittsburgh Press, 1995).]

What If I Didn't Die Outside Saigon

"So what do you want?" he growled inside the chopper,
strapping me roughly to the stretcher
as if I were already dead. "Jesus," I swore,
delirious with pain, touching the hot mush of my legs.
"To see my wife. Go home, play with my kids,

help them grow up. You know." His camouflaged face
was granite, a colonel or sergeant who'd seen it all.
He wore a parka in the rain, a stubby stale cigar
bit tight between his teeth, a nicked machete
like a scythe strapped to his back. He raised a fist

and held the chopper. He wore a gold wrist-watch
with a bold sweep-second hand. The pilot glanced back,
stared, and looked away. Bored, the old man asked,
"Then what?" his cigar bobbing. I swallowed back
morphine and choked, "More time. To think,

plant trees, teach my kids to fish and catch a ball."
"Yeah?" he said, sucking the cigar, thinner
than he seemed at first. Through a torrent of rain,
I saw the jungle closing over me like night.
"And travel," I said, desperate, "to see the world.

That's it, safe trips with loved ones. Long years
to do whatever. Make something of my life. Make love,
not war." I couldn't believe it, wise-cracking clichés,
about to die. He didn't smile, but nodded. "So?
What then?" "What then? Listen, that's enough,

Isn't that enough?" His cigar puffed into flame,
he sucked and blew four perfect rings
that floated through the door and suddenly
dissolved. Without a word, he leaned and touched
my bloody stumps, unbuckled the stretcher straps

and tore the "Killed-in-Action" tag from my chest.
And I sat up today in bed, stiff-legged, out of breath,
an old man with a room of pictures of children
who've moved away, and a woman a little like my wife
but twice her age, still sleeping in my bed.

[Previously published in *The Dalhousie Review* (Canada) 69, no. 1 (1990): 80 and *Counting Survivors* (Pittsburgh: University of Pittsburgh Press, 1995).]

Cascading Down McDonald Creek

Clouds entangle in snowcapped mountains
bulging above us. Heads back, we revel
and we stare. Clouds rise and clash,

should echo back like boulders.
How can such vapor swirls keep silence?
The Lord's in His holy temple, here,

although signs in Glacier Park warn
"Here there be grizzlies." Plaques along
park roads explain the fossils, plate tectonics.

A month in Glacier Park's a blink,
a glimpse of switchbacks, a million rocks
not even scratched. Nights under blankets,

we lie with curtains wide and watch the stars.
Hiking, we lean over thousands of feet
where trickles start, tumbling to a stream

we've picnicked by, cascading down
McDonald Creek to rivers, the Pacific, back
as snow over glaciers, high in hosanna clouds.

[Previously published in *Ellipsis: Literature and Art* 37 (2001): 93 and *Climbing the Divide* (Notre Dame, IN: University of Notre Dame Press, 2003).]

The Digs in Escondido Canyon

The clues are here like dominoes
pulverized in sand—a tusk,
the heel bone of a wolf, the spine
of a dinosaur, a few dots of fossils

that must have had a sea.
Nothing about these plains
predicts a river in this dry canyon.
Comanches watered here for years.

Shards of pottery centuries ago
wedge up like skulls. Trees grow
from their bones, the only native bark
on plains too dry for roots.

How many nights did people
wandering deserts lie down together,
fearing all evil under the stars,
guarding their firelight from fangs

and others on two feet, sleeping
with blunt tools and spears all night
in this valley of the shadow of water,
dry now, nothing but white caliche

and bones, measured and staked,
each century an inch, each of us kneeling,
troweling and brushing the dust,
praising the slightest sign of life.

[Previously published in *After the Noise of Saigon* (Amherst: University of Massachusetts Press, 1988—winner of the 1987 University of Massachusetts Press Juniper Prize).]

To the Tribe

"That jerk"
–customer, leaving the counter

I believe in jerks
who throw fast food together,
who pop the corn
for horror shows,
who pump the gas. At eight,
I walked home after work
splattered with house paint,
breathing the smoke
of buses, saving my dime
for a Hershey halfway home.
Outside Saigon
I sweated in jungle boots
and trudged with buddies,
all of us "jerks"
who wanted only
the love of someone
and heaven
and the grace of breath.

[Previously published in *New Texas* (1995): 121 and *All Occasions* (Notre Dame, IN: University of Notre Dame Press, 2000).]

Adoption

We took them in our arms, those washed,
donated blankets and weeks-old babies,
bare facts scratched on tablet paper—
their foster-parents' chronicles
of formula and colic, their bottles
and pajamas, their oddly temporary names.

Three babies in different years, the lightest loads
we'd ever hold. That was the Sixties
before I flew to Vietnam and back, branded
vicious, baby killer. Such hope would happen
again, the whole world's peace at risk.
Those wise case workers knew about loss,

half trauma nurses, half Santa Claus.
Joyful, we took the babies they gave,
miraculous heartbreak, each almost weightless,
shockingly small, almost too delicate to take
from the arms of a nurse who knew how to bring
and let go. I can still feel the cling

of fingers wrapped around mine,
the charm of tiny eyes open wide.
We held each baby in the neon gaze
of the state's agency, helpless, tall,
heart-pounding strangers these babies came to—
voices they'd never heard, might never

have picked—big-fisted, dazed,
throat-choked and humming lullabies,
blur-eyed, not caring who might see.
We were only a couple holding a baby,
giddy and trembling with questions, and clumsy,
but parents, and our baby was hungry.

[Previously published in *The Christian Century* 115, no. 13 (1998): 432 and *Blessings the Body Gave* (Columbus: The Ohio State University Press, 1998—winner of the 1997 Ohio State University Press *The Journal* Award in Poetry).]

One Morning Between Wars

The girl in the purple robe
tangled like a bath towel
lolls on the couch and laughs,
some pre-school song or clown trick
bouncing in her mind. Will she

years from now recall this Sunday morning
on the coast, up before Mommy
and her brothers, the lazy, purring world
all to herself? Will she remember
this hour of lounging, twisting,

turning and humming, her daddy
bringing breakfast on a tray,
the brittle bacon, the tiny tub of syrup,
hot strips of sweet French toast?
Will she miss the months he wasn't home,

the TV chant of "Desert Storm"
most grown-ups found exciting? He's back,
and now she lolls and rolls the bacon
on her lips, and nibbles, dips the toast
and dribbles sticky syrup on her tongue.

Her own real daddy brings more
bacon strips. He says she makes him
happy when she eats so well. Twisting
bacon like a rotor blade, she sings
about her daddy days ago, descending

from the sky like Santa Claus,
leaves swirling circles up and down,
the whole crowd waving at her daddy's
helicopter, a real, brave daddy
finally back. She sniffs the bacon,

lips it, sucks it like a lollypop
and hums, God up in Heaven,
her daddy close enough to hear her
when she calls, another strip
of French toast in her bowl.

[Previously published in *National Forum* 78 (1998): 47 and *All Occasions* (Notre Dame, IN: University of Notre Dame Press, 2000).]

Blessings the Body Gave

All week the river rolled
down a fancy rickrack of stones,
a mountain roar. Even the dog heard music,
static of a battery radio. Sprawled,
the dog kept time with worried eyes.

He believed that mountain cabin was home,
if we said so, the air so thin it froze.
Last week we stuck in mud, slick-spinning
down to stone until wet rubber smoked.
Nothing could turn us back from our A-frame

high in the San Juan. We waded the last half-mile
to blue spruce dwarfing a red asbestos roof.
All night the dark clouds rained a roar
and far from telephones. All week, we tamped
pine needles and leaned back, propping pads

on laps of drawn-up legs. Sunlight sliced
through vinegar-sweet pine needles, our fingers
sketching nothing tame, the leaves so still
we heard tapping and scratching like two
of everything approaching to be named.

Last night, I dragged our chairs to the hearth
and scratched a long-stemmed match. Music
hummed and buzzed, static as the searching
dial spun slow. Her hands knew all the songs
I needed, and she twisted distant stations off,

our last hours alone before summer.
I leaned my rawhide chair to hold her,
the pine logs popping sparks. She smoothed
my flannel sleeves and we locked hands and rocked,
the cabin cold unless we faced the fire.

[Previously published in *Maryland Poetry Review* 9 (1990): 43; title poem of *Blessings the Body Gave* (Columbus: The Ohio State University Press, 1998—winner of the 1997 Ohio State University Press *The Journal* Award in Poetry).]

Autumn in Our Hands

When I open both fists wide, my God!
what wrinkles, like a pond rippled
on a windy day, seen from a thousand feet
in a chopper. Squeezed into fists again,
the skin tries to lie about my age,
betrayed by creases like canals on Mars.

I've seen these hands on Grandfather
in the hospital, an IV needle
taped like a tire patch, my hero
who carved robins and hawks from blocks
of mahogany and oak, feathers so real
I swore he could make the buffed wood fly.

How fast my skimpy lifeline aged
in these palms, old knuckles stiff
and broken. This thumb can't flex
without snapping, bone on bone,
a clicker for Halloween. So this
is how we hold autumn in our hands.

Held wide, my fingers tremble, the fist
I pitched with, that held the stick
in Air Force jets, that slipped the ring
on my wife's finger, fists that held
three babies up to the world as if to beg
"Be good, be careful with these kids."

[Previously published in *All Occasions* (Notre Dame, IN: University of Notre Dame Press, 2000).]

Old Pets

Hawks in wide, hardscrabble skies track mice
in fields we say we own. We feed too many pets
our children raised by hand and abandoned.
Old bulls aren't worth the hay to save them,

but I don't throw away a glove because it's ugly.
Look at them, old goats and horses fat in the pasture.
That palomino's lame, the oldest mare on the plains,
drools when I rub her ears, can't hear unless I whisper.

Leans on me like a post, slobbering oats from my gloves,
swishing her tail. This abandoned barn was weeds,
the padlock missing. Thieves hauled good metal off,
nothing but someone's dream holding a roof over stalls,

the cows long slaughtered. Owls watched the plunder
of doors in silence. A man with children built this barn
to last, but not one stayed to carry on his herd.
We had to track them down to sign, and now the barn is ours,

and pastures fenced by barbed wires dangling from posts,
and most of those are broken. We might as well breed wolves
or trap for bounty snakes that kill our calves.
We could sell the rattlers' venom for research,

and wolves are bred for national parks in Montana
so why not here? Dawn, I shake my head at my schemes
and saddle up, time for rounding strays
and dumping hay to old pets bawling at the barn.

[Previously published in *Poetry* 172, no. 5 (1998): 276 and *Blessings the Body Gave* (Columbus: The Ohio State University Press, 1998—winner of the 1997 Ohio State University Press *The Journal* Award in Poetry).]

That Child Abandoned on the Porch

In that child in tonight's newscast
I see our son, wandering Montana.
With luck, he'll find what he's after,

hunting for gold or answers. What odds
brought him to us, a million to one,
ten million? The darkest hair, his eyes

squeezed tight in the agency's bright lights.
That nurse must have swaddled babies
a thousand times, but to us she was an angel

and we mere shepherds in from the cold.
There, near the gold-domed Denver capitol, star
on a highway map, there where they gathered taxes

in mountains, there we had come with nothing
but a note telling us the birth hour,
not even the baby's weight, only that he

was the one, all of our luck in one boy,
and when we held him, he was,
he was the child in our arms.

[Previously published in *Christianity and Literature* 47, no. 1 (1997): 75 and *Blessings the Body Gave* (Columbus: The Ohio State University Press, 1998–winner of the 1997 Ohio State University Press *The Journal* Award in Poetry).]

The One That Got Away

In time the bleeding stops.
Puddles of mud go back to sand
and blow away. The buck
can't shake it off, can't see

what knocked him down
and stings. Leap by leap
he quivers to shake the pain.

He runs with it upstream,
the dry bed solid, flies
swarming the blood.

For days he'll wander,
avoiding the others,
wondering what to do,
what to do.

[Previously published in *Stand* magazine (UK) (Autumn 1987): 50 and *After the Noise of Saigon* (Amherst: University of Massachusetts Press, 1988–winner of the 1987 University of Massachusetts Press Juniper Prize).]

Stumbling to the Deck at Dawn

March, when Carol and I stumbled to the deck
with iced tea instead of coffee, or in the kitchen
with coats on and an opened freezer door

we knew it was time to go home to cold Montana
to climb, to walk on ice, collapse exhausted and happy
on snow drifts deep as a house, to breathe that rare

and heady air. We raised three babies on the plains,
shared a few swift years of hugs with them and slept,
and suddenly they were gone. Packed for a drive

of a thousand miles to the mountains, we talked about
their pets, and how they lost them, the dogs and cats
that died of old age, the goldfish and gerbil someone

flushed down the commode. Floating on radial tires
on the highway, we knew all survivors are Noah,
whether we have two dogs, two cats, or only each other.

Blink, and ten more years are gone. Our cattle graze
and fatten even at night, and nothing, not even power
knocked out by storms, will stop the clock.

[Previously published in *Prairie Schooner* 75, no. 3 (2001, 75th anniversary issue): 82 and *Climbing the Divide* (Notre Dame, IN: University of Notre Dame Press, 2003).]

Halfway Between the Gulf and Mountains

We memorized each other's eyes before Saigon,
casting for bass after dark, hearing the splash
and battle in the shallows. Last week, driving back,
we watched hawks glide over piñon and spruce

and disappear. I rode the brakes around steep
switchbacks. Centuries slid past the last wide turns,
black granite cracked by juniper roots, the bark
sloughed off, stumps twisted by winds.

Woodcarvers rub for weeks to groove the grain
that smooth–rings around wounds
grown perfect, curves no lathe could turn.
Years, and no more pilot friends come back.

We've been to the wall and rubbed our fingers
on their names. Now, the sun sustains us
halfway between the Gulf and mountains.
Nothing on these flat plains seems like war

except sometimes asleep. Good neighbors offer fruit
from gardens on rationed water. Even our dogs
feel at home. They raise wet muzzles to the moon
and howl at stars so far away they stare.

[Previously published in *The Kenyon Review* 18, nos. 3–4 (1996): 184 and *Blessings the Body Gave* (Columbus: The Ohio State University Press, 1998–winner of the 1997 Ohio State University Press *The Journal* Award in Poetry).]

Watching Dawn on Padre Island

From the deck, sunrise splashes the Gulf,
glistens like highways paved with gold.
The condo's garden sprawls like seaweed
flattened by the breeze. Salt sprays the balcony,
chairs sticky with brine. Lazy as Lazarus,

I lounge with my wife, weeks after doctors
sawed my chest bones wide and lifted out my heart.
Holding hands, we watch the waves, the sandhill cranes,
beaks to the wind like weathervanes. Last month,
I listened to neighbors telling fables of near-death,

as if those would console me—a light so bright
pain wouldn't matter. Like this blazing stairway
to the sun, glittering over millions of sharks
and dolphins. The glare's so bright I'm blind,
and flip sunglasses down from my scalp and blink.

Dying makes surgery easy—a silly, giddy relief,
a straw to grab for, touch of the master's hand—
easy, wheeled down the hall to a bright-lit room
that dazzles, forbidden to friends, to family.
I remember counting back, then odd confusion

in a recovery room, like waking dazed in a cave
or casket, bright light and voices, but whose?
And what were they saying, what happened
and where is this, wondering why can't I rise
and throw off these winding sheets and walk?

[Previously published in *JAMA: The Journal of the American Medical Association* 282, no. 21 (1999) and *All Occasions* (Notre Dame, IN: University of Notre Dame Press, 2000.]

Gardens of Sand and Cactus

My wife took salt for starters, and rusted strands
of barbed wire, the iron Grandfather left.
Chipped chunks from a salt block mired in sand,
that tongue-rubbed marble artwork of the West,

anywhere cows roam—not buffaloes that lick
their salt from cactus and the bones of coyotes.
Took bones, a skull, when she saw one. Took snakeskin
like twisted strips of film. Looked under yucca

for the best, six feet at least. But fierce
grandfather snakes don't rattle until they're sure,
so she listened before she stooped. Found horseshoes
to pitch, any flint or curved stones shaped like tools.

Tugging our child's Radio Flyer in the pasture,
she brought pigments home, even the burnt sienna bolus
of owls. Scraped umber from banks of the Brazos,
however dry, gold dust where bobcats marked the stumps.

Packed, stacked it all. Took time, fanned with her hat,
then hauled that wagon wobbling to our house.
Amazed that she made gardens of cactus and sand,
I mitered frames to hang whatever she found

and salvaged as art, even rocks she cut and tumbled
in a barrel grinding like sweet, hand-cranked ice cream,
turning that desert we called home into babies' mobiles,
wind chimes and swings, bird feeders in every tree.

[Previously published in *Blessings the Body Gave* (Columbus: The Ohio State University Press, 1998—winner of the 1997 Ohio State University Press *The Journal* Award in Poetry).]

Dark as the Plains Out There

High Lonesome tipped back his hat
and his horses snorted. Maybelle nodded,
her teacher's smile a wild azalea
in miles of cactus. Uncle Rollie's buckboard

groaned to a stop, in town for flour
and grease and beans. All that, decades ago,
before he taught me how to cowboy. In summers
we broke broncs, patched fences cut by hunters,

shot coyotes hobbling and starved.
He never married after Maybelle died, no one
to carry on the herd but me, a summer nephew.
Uncle Rollie taught me to rope and brand,

step back when the calf jumped up.
Rollie taught me to shoot, a mile-long whine
across the plains. His ribs were gaunt,
an old bull alone on a winter range.

Before I flew back from Vietnam, he died.
His saddles and gates were still the same.
My wife and I moved out to the ranch,
both windmills whirring, the same bad drought.

Our own children left home years ago,
leaving us rocking at night under stars,
far from the wall in Washington
where Don's and Roy's and Warren's names

are carved in granite dark as the plains
out there–no moon, tonight, no one but us
to hear the coyotes, the squeal of a field mouse
caught by an owl, flapping back to the barn.

[Previously published in *Ploughshares* 26, no. 1 (2000): 96 and *Climbing the Divide* (Notre Dame, IN: University of Notre Dame Press, 2003).]

In Gusty Winds That Wild

Hawks don't hunker down in burrows
when it blows. Their claws dig
hard on posts against stiff wind.
Sand gashes the skin like glass.
People pop their contacts out
and weep the scratches clean.

Hawks on barbed wires bob
and ride it out, beaks to the wind,
wings tight as if diving. In March,
wind pounds down daily from the west.
Nothing flies in gusty winds
that wild, not even hawks.

Like that one across the road,
caught by our mailbox. Here,
squeeze these binoculars
and watch those feathers flounce.
Watch the claws, that splendid head.
Her eyes don't even blink.

[Previously published in *Poet Lore* 9, no. 1 (1996): 36 and *Blessings the Body Gave* (Columbus: The Ohio State University Press, 1998—winner of the 1997 Ohio State University Press *The Journal* Award in Poetry).]

What Old Pilots Say

Play with it, say it out loud
when you're alone, if that will help.
Gnaw horror like a bone, suck blood
and marrow out. Reach behind your face
and turn it off, like lights-out on the base.
Someone will die today, tonight.
Rockets fall, some posts get overrun.

That's what guards and body bags are for.
You can't fly safe without sleep.
Tell your sergeant, "Wake me if they break
through the lines. Otherwise let it lie."
Home won't come by holding your balls
and breath too tightly in your fist. Jog,
play handball, cut back on booze and fats

after you're back. Look five ways
in Asian skies, swivel your crash-helmet head.
When your wingman spots a missile, break
any way he says. Take it one flight at a time.
Go back to the world, your only wife,
breed lots of kids and tell your lies.
Or not. Some of us have to die.

[Previously published in *Stand* magazine (UK) 39, no. 3 (1998): 34 and *Blessings the Body Gave* (Columbus: The Ohio State University Press, 1998—winner of the 1997 Ohio State University Press *The Journal* Award in Poetry).]

Squall Line at Sixty-five

Sloshing through soggy bogs,
we leave the trees balled up in the truck
and jog to the porch swing,

slinging holy water from our hats.
Tonight, the cloudbursts will all be gone,
soil almost a crust by dawn.

By noon, even the holes we dug will drain,
foam on the bottom ready for roots.
Saplings in the pickup tilt and bend

in the breeze, and thunder booms.
Cows in the pasture wait, wet muzzles
turned to the wind, eyes almost closed.

The horses are downwind by the barn,
hogs clean at last, flicking their snouts
and squealing as if they'll never eat again.

Rocking, we watch the storm and wonder
if grandkids 400 miles away are home
from school, if maybe they'll call tomorrow.

[Previously published in *New York Review of Books* 50, no. 6 (2003): 26 and *Climbing the Divide* (Notre Dame, IN: University of Notre Dame Press, 2003).]

For Friends Still in Vietnam

When I take my meddling friend for coffee, he picks
at paper napkins, shredding them all like warnings.
Before Mary Jane pours refills, Joe asks how long
I've been up, how many empty beer cans

I've recycled, how many skunks and crows
I've shot. He knows whose daughters are overdue,
whose son's gone overseas. Squeezing his mug,
he gripes about lawyers, tells me which

older widows he's seeing, which of the younger
have money, which ones seem faithful
to their holy ghosts. Like this, week by week,
even when other old vets from Vietnam

drop by, the booth full of elbows, aisle blocked
by extra chairs. Only Earl smokes, ash trays
banished. Earl paces in the parking lot,
puffing, staring at nothing. Joe asks Ray

about Earl's work, his jitters and weight loss.
Ray looks away, and Joe falls back and frowns.
I read Joe's scowls as signs, those folded arms
as a warning. When Earl returns, I catch his eye,

and Earl stares back and nods, as if he's seen
the clues I saw, bamboo nicked by a flicked
machete, the oozing stalks and swarms of bees.
Flicking his eyes between us, scooping the lint

and squeezing, Joe leans close. "What's up?"
he pumps. He stares past us at something far away,
angry if one of us says "Nothing" or only smiles.
Nothing we could say would be enough today.

[Previously published in *JAMA: The Journal of the American Medical Association* 280, no. 5 (1998): 396 and *All Occasions* (Notre Dame, IN: University of Notre Dame Press, 2000).]

Killing Nothing but Time

Snakes slither under rich milk cows all day,
hunting mice and lizards, cows and cactus the only shade
for rattlers that thrive on prairies made for drought.
When these are the plains you ride, you bow to the sky

in a hat. Neck and ears burn anyway, skin cancer
bounced from sand to your eyes no matter how wide
the hat. Granddaddy taught me to waddle and ride
while Daddy slogged in Pacific swamps, shot dead

on Okinawa. His dog tags dangle from my neck,
my own tags stashed after Vietnam in the attic.
I've fenced these fields so many years I'm brown,
chaps and Stetson my disguise. Often at dawn

I see old neighbors in the distance, other vets
back from the jungles, guns slung low and hats
tugged down. I meet them past the corral, or wait
by the windmill grinding its clatter. I see it in their eyes

sometimes, the way snakes go their own way, alone,
not fearing a man or his rifle. Today, we're awake
after steaks and biscuits, ready to patch barbed wire
and brand, to break strange colts with words,

"easy, easy." Maybe something came back to them
last night, watt-faced and haunting, nothing else
on these wide plains like Vietnam. But here
together we're fine in boots and Stetsons, men

of the sunburned eyeballs, riding high over rattlers,
taking turns yelling jokes and shouting with laughter,
twisting and creaking in saddles, killing nothing
but time, riding home to our wives after dark.

[Previously published in *The Sewanee Review* 107, no. 4 (1999): 525 and *All Occasions* (Notre Dame, IN: University of Notre Dame Press, 2000).]

All We Do Is Already History

We're all on a speeding Amtrak,
one-way tickets toward glittering
far-off events, no turning back.
Whatever we do, it's already history.

Queue up in a gilded terminal
and board when they call our names,
it's all over—the thrill of "All aboard,"
wine and roses we could almost taste.

Pastures and valleys we glimpse
are Switzerland clacketing by,
Swiss cheese, ski slopes we'd like to try,
but railway warnings flash by,

cars waiting, people waving in their fields,
then gone. We're pulling emergency cords
and calling, hauling the conductor here
to our window, "There, those resorts

are our stop!" He jerks away and scowls.
We look back, frantic, but it's gone,
the end of our holidays, our foreheads
mashed against the glass. For days,

for years, we taste the legendary cones
of Cornish cream, hear the crack
of the bat in Yankee stadium, peanuts
and crackerjack at the ballgame,

boyish, broad-shouldered Mickey Mantle
rounding the bases, doffing his cap
as he jogged home and down
into the dugout, another man at bat.

[Previously published in *Southern Poetry Review* 37, no. 1 (1997): 28 and *Blessings the Body Gave* (Columbus: The Ohio State University Press, 1998—winner of the 1997 Ohio State University Press *The Journal* Award in Poetry).]

Learning How in the Southwest

Bring nothing clean. Fossils of coyotes and hawks
have burned, and soot is king, a fat voyeur that pries
through your bags, smudges your calling cards.
This town is not Montana—no native trees,

no mountain streams, no mountains. People here
are restless and loud for hours in bars with greasy steaks
and friends. Hardhats from seven counties drop by
and brag how many gushers they've drilled

since Christmas, baby's little booties encased in gold,
not bronze. Any five best women here know something
no one wrestling derricks cares for, except after hours,
down in motels or trailers after the last bar closes,

the last dull darts have missed the target zone,
the last fast women with freckles and bleached hair
have staggered off with drunks who were their husbands
after all. That's when some mother's songs drift

softly at midnight, alarming tunes not taught
in oil fields, an ache for chords that come from more
than guitars, like honey and homemade bread
learned when young, commotion in hearts

stronger than cactus and black shale, scattering of sparks
before the gas is capped—music from church or school,
memories only such women give singing lullabies
to babies that cry and, cuddled, go back to sleep.

[Previously published in *The Windsor Review* (Canada) 29, no. 1 (1996): 32 and *Blessings the Body Gave* (Columbus: The Ohio State University Press, 1998—winner of the 1997 Ohio State University Press *The Journal* Award in Poetry).]

Diamonds in the Carnegie Museum

Our guide was blind and kind,
chatting about diamonds we circled
like wagons in box canyons,

no way out, but united for the night,
bound for Montana. She was thirty-five,
without a ring. Her dazzling eyes rolled back

and blinked. She was singing, prattling
about diamond mines and dreams, but singing,
her voice charming us to see. She loved these halls

she never saw, loved all of us she had touched
in the lobby, touched each one only once
but knew us, or made us believe she did.

I marveled at wonders she sang about
and saved. She turned and tapped her way
with a penlight-thin retractable pole

to bulletproof transparent glass,
and sighed. She was a bride among diamonds
and we mere cousins in from the cold,

sharing what she held at arm's length every day,
too precious to wear, crushed coal and fire
in the heart of earth too radiant to see.

[Previously published in *Chelsea* 65 (1998): 29 and *All Occasions* (Notre Dame, IN: University of Notre Dame Press, 2000).]

Boiling Shells at Kitty Hawk

Back home, my wife will lace them into wreaths,
glue-gun the shells as bouquets for neighbors–
Scotch Bonnets, conches, glossy moon snails curled
like custard cones. Boiling, they smell like lobster,

the condo opened to a gale that cracks the breakers back.
No dolphins leap and pirouette today, no swans.
Gulls flap and sidle, laws of yaw and roll as old as wings.
Orville rode two pusher props twelve seconds over dunes

a mile from here, nine decades ago today. At noon,
I measured the path of his flight, takeoff to touchdown,
no farther than hop-skip-and-jump when I was a boy.
Four decades ago, I soloed, when Saigon and Da Nang

were distant, exotic towns. The Wrights launched me
to madness. Hurtling down that track at twenty knots,
did Orville worry about war, the rubble bombs would cause?
Or was he giddy like me that first roll down a runway,

ready for anything, anything? Firewall the pistons, nose up
and feel it lift. All roads led to Rome, but runways
started here near the beach of my father's boyhood.
All my father's friends from World War I are dead,

the Wrights are dead, many friends I flew with.
I've touched their names in granite on a wall.
Retired, I don't fly, except at night in orbits that won't stop.
Turn out the fire and let the boiled pot cool.

Lay out the mussels, slipper shells, the angel wings
and let them dry, then pack them like bone china
in paper towels. Even periwinkles last if padded,
enough for a wreath for some good neighbor's wall.

[Previously published in *Shenandoah* 49, no. 2 (1999): 46 and *All Occasions* (Notre Dame, IN: University of Notre Dame Press, 2000).]

Hardscrabble, Tooth and Claw

Packs roam the plains,
attacking abandoned pets.
Caught in the fields,
most cats survive. They scratch
the eyes of dogs,
the pack maddened by blood.

We've come across cats
before buzzards found them,
and blind dogs stumbling
and whining. I pack a rifle
even for bobcats. Owls don't ask
who did it. My wife's green eyes

glean kittens from the fields,
like picking lint off cashmere.
Last night, we found another
sack-full by the road, a litter tossed
from a car, scraps for the buzzards.
When we're in time,

my wife nurses cats
with eyedroppers, milk
from a Holstein. They grow up
gladly in our barn, stalking mice
on claws grown perfect,
their purring mouths all fangs.

[Previously published in *The Windsor Review* (Canada) 27, no. 2 (1994): 22 and *Counting Survivors* (Pittsburgh: University of Pittsburgh Press, 1995).]

When Children Think You Can Do Anything

Living on hardscrabble, a man is less
than a wolf and knows it, carries a rifle
in season or not. Out here, killing's
always in season, time enough for scruples
sweating in bed with the windows raised.

I hear my kids kicking their sheets.
Good kids, they blame the heat.
I feel my wife's heat inches away.
They sleep with only me to protect them,
nothing outside I haven't tracked for years,

bobcats and wolves, rattlers that coil
under our trailer like tribal gods.
I'm paid to patch fences around a range
nothing but goats and cows could graze.
I keep the stock tanks full, the buzzards hungry.

When cows stray down arroyos, the wolves
are sure to follow, circling a calf too weak
to waddle. If I can drop one wolf by moonlight,
the others tuck-tail and run. If I'm late,
next morning I drive the cow out

wide-eyed and frothing, her full bag tight,
mesquite and cactus wedging us apart. That night,
I splash my face a long time at the pump
and comb my hair and shave, roll down my sleeves
and go inside as if nothing's happened.

[Previously published in *Poetry* 149, no. 5 (1987): 280 and *After the Noise of Saigon* (Amherst: University of Massachusetts Press, 1988—winner of the 1987 University of Massachusetts Press Juniper Prize).]

The Dust We're Made Of

On summer nights, we stroked the dirt
with hand trowels under bright klieg lights.
Those digs could disappear, vandals
and idle boys playing plunder—
an arrowhead wedged in a Levi pocket,

a jawbone mocked and tossed away
like a corncob, a hand-smoothed bowl
crushed to dust by a boot. We peeled back
sand like tapestries, layer by layer down
to mammoths and bears the size of bulls.

We found bronze kernels never baked,
like golden ears hung up to keep
on adobe porches. We've eaten tortillas
of such crushed corn. Here, people like us
lay down in darkness. We sifted dust

we're made of. What did they fear?
Near midnight on our knees,
we cataloged clues for regional museums,
the signs of modest toil, evidence of hope
not seen, the kernels not consumed.

[Previously published in *Poetry* 160, no. 4 (1992): 187, *Counting Survivors* (Pittsburgh: University of Pittsburgh Press, 1995), and *Poetry* magazine's *The Poetry Anthology*, 1912–2002.]

Dazzling Montana Dawns

Bring back that rabbit that hopped
over rocks and stopped. It crouched,
not moving even its eyes, as if shifting
might lure the shock of fangs,
the least unique act in Montana.

Praise hawks and bald eagles,
coyotes, even wolves brought back
to Glacier Park, stalking flocks of sheep.
Praise tents for two, green Coleman stoves
and gloves. Bring back a year that seemed

a year, not four brief months and gone.
How quickly we cleared the calendar
and drove back to mountains, buffet style–
a glimpse of rabbits and sheep, memories
heaped with dazzling mountain dawns.

But we're too stiff for tents and hikes
at midnight, so let the rabbits hop,
let buzzards starve, or waddle paunchy
from the bones. Let wolves survive,
let ranchers stalk them all,

let winter come. Let elk herds
breed and nearly freeze in drifts.
Let grandchildren hike Montana range
and mountain peaks someday, let weeks
fly by, whatever we can't change.

[Previously published in *Appalachia* 54, no. 2 (December 2002): 19 and *Climbing the Divide* (Notre Dame, IN: University of Notre Dame Press, 2003).]

After His Apache Crashed

Now, out past the breakers, dolphins pass,
dark bodies glistening, arching in perfect curves,
single file like an honor guard. For months
our son's helicopter flew down the Outer Banks
past Kitty Hawk, back up the coast and home.
Daily he saw dolphins graceful past the breakers,

their mile-long hunting habit. Later, when his crew
went down, we waited by the phone for hours,
nothing on TV but scandals, the rise and decline
of stocks, death of a princess and an aged saint.
This year, we're here to grieve on the beach
of Kill Devil Hill, to watch the dolphins

that never knew our son, don't honor him at all
in solemn, dignified review. We're here
because they're here, because he said they're here
that's enough, that's not nearly enough
to take back with us to the plains where dolphins
and starfish haven't lived for a million years.

[Previously published in *The Christian Century* 116, no. 24 (1999): and *Climbing the Divide* (Notre Dame, IN: University of Notre Dame Press, 2003).]

The Winter They Bombed Pearl Harbor

All winter peacocks showed off, strutting the same slow
pose. At dawn, I smashed ice with a hammer, dumped pots
of boiling water steaming into troughs for peacocks preening
and screaming. They shoved each other off like cousins

bunched at the only mirror at church. Our logger father
whittled a forest with buzz saws, the whine and buzz of steel
and mosquitoes the songs my ears were tuned for.
Sisters and I played keep-away with feathers, dazzling

the surly turkeys and peacocks with footwork, lobbing
frozen dirt clods like grenades, until our father called us.
When roads were frozen, I jockeyed the throttle of a tractor
rusted before the war, hauling hay bales to farmers miles away.

The war was almost lost when my brother enlisted,
Pearl Harbor bombed, the fall of Bataan and Guam
what we heard mostly on the radio, our mother talking softly
with us at bedtime and peacocks screaming in the dark.

[Previously published in *The Kenyon Review* 18, no. 3 (1996): 185 and *Blessings the Body Gave* (Columbus: The Ohio State University Press, 1998—winner of the 1997 Ohio State University Press *The Journal* Award in Poetry).]

Rocking for Days in the Shade

In another parched summer,
Comancheros gone, we rock
on the back porch, fanning,
watching buzzards circle like clocks,

calling their lazy cousins to supper.
We sip iced tea, rolling cold glasses
on our skin. Not one thick cloud
for months, the weeds so brittle

goats snap them off like sticks.
We wonder, are we here by choice?
Great-grandfather left the cavalry
for this? After renegade bullets and arrows

he stayed in Texas where topsoil was sand
and free. He said he needed sun to heal.
The only blood he lost in forty years
dried on rocks already red.

These goats are not his goats.
Imported rams he bred were sterile,
cotton the way he kept from starving.
When he stumbled on this canyon

in smelly blues on horseback,
chasing the last straggling
Comanchero raiders
off the plains of Texas,

he retired—a hidden range,
enough water to bathe in,
far enough from town
to build a shack with a back porch

and do whatever he wanted, rocking for days
in the shade, watching buzzards
thirsty for his blood, daring anything
to make him leave.

[Previously published in *The Paris Review* 115 (1990): 53–54 and *Counting Survivors* (Pittsburgh: University of Pittsburgh Press, 1995).]

Wishing for More Than Thunder

Mirages hover like angels fanning the fields,
we see them in summer, a shimmer of wings.
Our stubborn steers ignore them, wading dry acres.
They hook their horns in invisible robes,

shaking their heads to graze. For them
the sky is falling, the grass is manna.
Having lost all hope when they entered
the round corral as calves, they stuff themselves

even in drought, as if all pastures
on the plains are theirs. They never wonder
if God's in His heaven. Stubble is fodder enough,
alfalfa paradise. Watching steers graze

in a lake of shimmering light, seeing angels
fanning themselves, we wonder if even they
could make it rain, how many spin on a windmill,
how many squeezed would make a decent cloud.

[Previously published in *Poetry* 160, no. 4 (1992): 188 and *Counting Survivors* (Pittsburgh: University of Pittsburgh Press, 1995).]

Climbing the Divide in Montana

Stub of a month, so many crags and valleys
 and nothing but old legs to climb them.
Light as moleskin, even our boots are cracked,
backpacks stitched again, again. Loaded

and hoisted up, they snug the small of our backs
like hands we know and never tire of.
We don't throw away old gear because it's brittle.
We've come a thousand miles for wild Montana.

Next month, we'll go home to cattle neighbors watch,
to debts and telephones. Even after fifty years
of coming here, we're giddy, tongue-tied
like on our honeymoon, but panting now,

stopping more often, binoculars wobbling
as we stare past fir and aspen, sweeping past
snowcapped timberline, always another cave
in a cliff. Dazzled, we're out of breath.

We could live here all year, we could.
Even a million acres of huckleberries
still taste sour. Give them a week or two,
let them ripen. Out there, bighorn sheep

nibbling tundra, another grizzly rising up
a thousand yards uphill to sniff and stare,
maybe a cougar hungry under a ledge of shale,
blinking, flicking its dark-tipped tail.

[Previously published in *JAMA: The Journal of the American Medical Association* 285, no. 12 (2001): 1550 and *Climbing the Divide* (Notre Dame, IN: University of Notre Dame Press, 2003).]

Fishing with Uncle Walter

Uncle Walter led me to a tub of red racers in a shed
in Arkansas, down by the Ouachita. "Worms," he said,
"big worms long as your arms!" I stopped nose level
with the tub, nothing but fifty pounds of dirt and straw.
Daddy leaned down to sniff, his big-knuckled fists
on the nicked and rusted rim. Here was rot, real stink

in a back-swamp bait shop, a dozen wash tubs
of rotting crawdads, fish heads and eels, the hot shed
squishing as I ducked under cobwebs long as nets.
The one-armed man who owned it all reached
around my back and tapped the tub with a hammer.
Dozens swanned, enormous worms twelve inches long,

slicing up and out of black dirt, swarming each other,
gone in the blink of an eye, zipping and squirming
out of the muck of the tub to disappear like eels.
His nub still around me, the old man banged again, and out
they zipped and slithered, red racers slimy and fat.
I wondered what fish these could catch, the sharks

or alligator gar it would take to swallow worms, meat hooks
we'd have to squish and impale them on, if any of us
could hold them whipping, slipping around. I don't know
how many gar and big-mouthed bass we caught that night,
what bait worked best. I remember my uncle weeping
against the wall, dim light on his bald head in the bait shop.

I remember Daddy clearing his throat and staring at worms
with unusual interest, big knuckles white on the tub.
The next day, driving home, Daddy said Uncle Walter
lost his only son at Pearl Harbor. I thought we came 500 miles
over bumpy roads to fish. I didn't know Uncle Walter
had already lost a son in the war, the reason we came,

to grieve again with Dad's brother and sister-in-law.
Now that I've gone to war, now that I've watched TV
around the clock and worried about my own son
under Iraqi rockets, I remember my uncle beating his fist
against the wall of the bait shop. That day, Daddy's face
sunburned. Out on the lake, I sipped my first half bottle of beer.

I got to pee from the boat, standing up, a long-arched splash
and ripple my uncle promised would draw fish. We portaged
a canoe over boulders and a mushy crust of mud that shuddered,
and fished that river past midnight. I remember my uncle cursing,
beating gars to death with his oar, trash fish he hated, head down,
shaking, smashing them to pulp in the moonlight with his fists.

[Previously published in *The Missouri Review* 20, no. 3 (1997): 45 and *Blessings the Body Gave* (Columbus: The Ohio State University Press, 1998—winner of the 1997 Ohio State University Press *The Journal* Award in Poetry).]

When It Seemed Easy

Booze and a dance band swore we were bold,
crepe-paper streamers wrapped around all
who soloed that night, hands whacking our backs
and buddies shouting. Bachelor instructor pilots
slouched and watched our wives, sunglasses

nudged down from their eyes, white scarfs dangling
twice around their throats, heroes we worshipped
but swore we could beat in the air one on one,
someday. Maracas and trumpets blasted so loud
we shouted, tossing down blue flames of brandy

and aroused by our wives' sweet arms until lights
went out all over Georgia. Before dawn, we climbed
into cockpits and strapped in, a drama of checklists
and oxygen, all dials and gauges in the green,
crash helmets on and controls working fine for takeoff.

Down east, dark skies turned golden as the sun rose,
the magical tone for cameras, one more mystery seen,
now back into the blue. I longed for peace, good will
to all, knowing wars are fought by pilots like us
and others with enemy symbols on their wings.

[Previously published in *Connecticut River Review* and *Blessings the Body Gave* (Columbus: The Ohio State University Press, 1998–winner of the 1997 Ohio State University Press *The Journal* Award in Poetry).]

Uncle Earl's Last Ride in Dallas

Uncle Earl's blue suit hangs like a rustler's,
four pairs of boots lined up like a posse's
in the closet. We did what we must
with his will's stipulation—Levi's
and long-sleeved shirt unbuttoned,
his best beaver Stetson, back brim cut flush

to let his head lie flat. A chaw of Red Man
in his jaws, stitched tight and natural,
except no ooze, no chewing. Dress boots
were under there somewhere, although
no coffin would show them, polished or not.
But when they rolled the casket in, everyone

heard the jangle of spurs, muffled by the fluff
and satin. Old Earl would have been the first
to chortle, the way he hobbled off with his hat,
gored by the only bull to toss him in years,
a glove over his throat to hide the blood,
as if patting his chest pocket for a smoke.

[Previously published in *The Seattle Review* 26, no. 1 (2003): 90 and *Walt McDonald: Selected Poems*, Texas Poets Laureate Series (Fort Worth: Texas Christian University Press, 2016).]

Witching on Canvas

With horsehairs dipped in oils
 she scatters our lean cattle
deep into pebbles of canvas,
witching mesquite and cactus
from hardpan caliche white.

I've watched oil borders dry
while she draws babies' baths
and irons real clothes in summer.
In times of mumps or fever
she goes without sleep,

without a brush in her hand for weeks,
and then like cracks in the crust
of last year's drought,
she draws windmills and streams
and makes cold water flow.

[Previously published in *Crosscurrents* 7, no. 2 (1997): 93 and *Counting Survivors* (Pittsburgh: University of Pittsburgh Press, 1995).]

The Hairpin Curve at Durango

Where the road dips back on itself
downhill, I slow the rig
so I won't jackknife

or sail off into space.
That turn kills runaway trucks
smashed on the stones below,

convertibles and fast sports cars
careening smartly out
and tumbling. Truckers I know

don't dread crashing head-on
with drivers who fall asleep
on the straightaway,

don't mind running sassy pickups
off the road, the devil
and bar ditch take them.

But icy roads that curve
and slide us helpless into air
are trouble. Dieseling downhill,

I bluff oncoming traffic
to the rails, no way I'd risk the edge
for courtesy. Climbing home,

groaning with a load of calves,
I grind uphill, my right wheels
safe on asphalt,

making poor guys creeping downhill
hug the centerline.
Knowing the gray sky twists

and disappears inches away
below them, I glance
at their wide eyes, their fists

white-knuckled on steering wheels,
I see their clenched teeth yelling
at their kids, "Shut up! Shut up!"

[Previously published in *The American Scholar* (Phi Beta Kappa magazine) 61, no. 1 (1992): 107–8 and *Counting Survivors* (Pittsburgh: University of Pittsburgh Press, 1995).]

Watching for Ships off Padre Island

Bring back the days of waves slapping the shore,
gulls hovering over us all day, and sailboats
bobbing in the bay. Here where it rains two times
a year, we watch dry clouds on wide horizons

and pretend they're ours, puff balls that blow away
like smoke. Coronado crossed here out of breath,
his polished armor strapped to a mule, clanking,
his soldiers grumbling, begging aid of the Indians,

begging news of Eldorado, begging for rain.
Even his priest faltered, spitting dry wads
and coughing. Clutching a skull, he declared
God was dead in the desert. "These are His bones,

behold the eyes like sockets! Turn back,
or join the Indians: they own the water."
He howled at night and wet the sand
while sleeping. Coronado watched his eyes,

the wild hair stiff under his cowl.
Coronado called these plains a dead sea
turned to sand. We don't know where he rode.
There are signs on every highway claiming

his route crossed here, right here. Nights,
my wife and I pretend we go away by writing
French love notes in sand on the nightstands.
We think of beaches and promise we'll go back.

What if Coronado didn't stumble home to Mexico
broke, but found all he needed and sailed to Spain?
Let's pretend we're Coronado and his new-world bride
lying on the beach, waiting for ships, nothing gained

from exploring but his wife's gold deerskin
dress and his priest's surprising self-immersion
in the Gulf, splashing, screaming to white gulls
wheeling and gliding his undying love of God.

[Previously published in *After the Noise of Saigon* (Amherst: University of Massachusetts Press, 1988—winner of the 1987 University of Massachusetts Press Juniper Prize).]

Before the Glaciers Melt

Montana dawn holds up the moon,
Off-white and umber, the last
half nugget found above ground
in the Rockies. I pitch the tent flap back
and it crackles: I'm twenty again,

watching my bride in the bedroll.
Montana geese honk past,
gliding to the lake. Honeymoon,
the dew so cold the fall grass snapped
when I stepped out, wildly in love with a girl

I thought would be young forever.
Now we're back in Montana at 65,
and here come the geese. Next year
will be 2000, glaciers melting fast
this side of the ice age. Another

hundred years, they'll all be gone.
Tourists then may come in sleek,
electric cars and wonder
why it's called Glacier Park,
like fossils in the park's museum.

They'll see eagles mounted in glass,
stuffed grizzlies rearing up
from the '90s, beasts they've read about
like dinosaurs. They'll pass a tent
like ours, and camp stools, a propane stove

and bedrolls, the quaint way
others like us camped long ago.
Crouched, I pump the Coleman stove
and put the coffee on, strike a match
and watch the flames turn blue.

Inside the tent, my wife
unzips her sleeping bag, sits up
and brushes her gray, lovely hair,
and I duck inside and kneel
with both mugs steaming in my fists.

[Previously published in *The Christian Century* 117, no. 3 (2000): 95 and *All Occasions* (Notre Dame, IN: University of Notre Dame Press, 2000).]

Barter

A blue-healer pup nuzzling my toes
meant more than silver dollars. "Saucy,"
I called her, hard for Uncle Ray to show
four dozen pups a year and name each

before weaning, sold to hunters who drove
all night for his hounds. All summer,
I churned Aunt Edna's butter, dug post holes,
milked the herd. One dawn, milk sloshed over

on my feet, and one fat puppy lapped my toes.
I put both buckets down and picked her up.
Her tongue wouldn't stop, popping as she poked
and licked, tail like a wind-up pup's.

Daily she followed while I squeezed the teats,
missing the bucket on purpose, the stream
hissing on my feet, then back with a splash
in the bucket. Saucy licked my dusty feet

in the barn and all the dawdling way
to the house. I confess, Uncle Ray
warned me, each pup worth more than my pay—
the best hunting season in years. I swore

I'd work free until Christmas, skip school,
weed his fallow pastures and pick the corn,
but that fat litter sold in June.

[Previously published in *American Literary Review* 10, no. 1 (1999): 118 and *All Occasions* (Notre Dame, IN: University of Notre Dame Press, 2000).]

Boys and Their Fathers' Shotguns

Carl hugged the gun
he sneaked from his father,
shaking his head and sobbing.
What madness made him whirl
and shoot both barrels

at Billy Ray, what angel
shoved Billy's head
seconds before the blast?
Squinting, Billy Ray sprawled,
head cocked as if seeing visions.

Carl offered the shotgun
with both hands, begged Billy Ray
to take it, shoot it all day,
but please don't tell.
Billy Ray held his head,

still on his knees between echoes
as if looking for contacts.
Carl's crotch and eyes darkened,
the stain spreading wide
on his Levi's. We didn't laugh,

not even when Carl tried to hide it,
the shotgun trembling in his fists,
thunder we'd carry forever,
the cold blue metal of barrels
more dangerous than snakes.

[Previously published in *Illinois Review* 1, no. 1 (1993): 28 and *All Occasions* (Notre Dame, IN: University of Notre Dame Press, 2000).]

In the Shallow Molasses

In months of drought like a hammer,
the ranch parches like Kalahari summers.
Hippos snort and waddle off through dust.
Elephants with babies starved for water
and slopping in sticky clay remember a river
miles away and turn there for salvation.

Frog ponds swallow the sun like salt,
and prawns turn back to clods. Geese
sip the last brown sap and flap, flap to rise.
The warthog flounders, the least beast
of creation, half-finished, formed
of the mud of the fields. In tar pitch

between corpses of monkeys and snakes,
foul flesh of half-eaten gazelles, frogs
hold their breath, wedging their skulls
deep, deep into holes until it rains.
Here, the lung fish wallows and thrashes,
gills shut, thick lips like a bass

gulping air, in the shallow molasses
of mud. Bubbles like news rise up
from the breath hole. Mud hardens
over its mouth, the earth's own throat.
This fish, dried flat as death, turns stiff,
but if it rains even an inch, it lives.

[Previously published in *Weber Studies* 17, no. 3 (2000): 63 and *All Occasions* (Notre Dame, IN: University of Notre Dame Press, 2000).]

Harvest All Year Long

No dogcatchers ride by, only cars
with pets like rejected hearts. Our stock tank
blesses dogs abandoned by cars with city tags.
Dogs starve if they aren't born hungry for blood,
part wolf, or cute as Disney dogs some farmer's daughter

begs him to adopt. Stray cats survive on birds and mice
prowling somebody's barn. Stiff winds spread fires
to fields where pheasants risk the rattlers.
The sun leads cows to pasture, time for windmills
to spin their rapture, turning grass to milk.

Sometimes I squeeze a squirt to a row of cats
waiting with tiny mouths with fangs. The farm
is harvest all year long. At night, rattlers
that survive the fires move rippling over rows,
and silent barn owls dive to pluck their evil eyes.

[Previously published in *Manoa* 2, no. 2 (1990): 12 and *Counting Survivors* (Pittsburgh: University of Pittsburgh Press, 1995).]

When the Children Have Gone

What could we say, for they heard rumors:
something was out there that shouldn't be,
futures only they must own.
They rose on silver wings and disappeared,
far from summer sun on prairies.

Driving back after a week with grandkids,
we pass the asphalt hours by naming pelts
of flattened rattlers, coyotes,
crushed armadillos. What needs a meal
clacks its beak and staggers oddly off

into the sun, fat belly sagging,
black wings flapping a tight
possessive spiral back to bones
belly up under the thump of tires
with nothing better to do than swerve.

Back home, we listen to coyotes howling
the song we've sung for years. We live on beans
and fajitas braised over mesquite,
red peppers that scald our tongues. At dusk,
we carry chairs outside and watch the sundown.

My wife believes in the peace of dark,
the burning stars. I watch light shimmer
on her face, her flashing eyes. Now it begins,
the golds and purple of the plains. Blink
and miss it, like flecks of silver in her hair.

[Previously published in *The Nation* 250, no. 2 (1990): 66 and *Counting Survivors* (Pittsburgh: University of Pittsburgh Press, 1995).]

The Summer Her Family Moved to Houston

"Don't ask," Uncle Earl scolded,
"you don't want to know." Oh,
but I did, Aunt Emma bursting
with secrets I should know.
What happens when a body rots,
when cancer eats the lungs?
What did she mean, "exquisite pain"?
At nine, I tasted fire when I swallowed
with my tonsils gone, saved by a fire
brigade of nurses with ice cream.
I'd seen dead pigs, found my brother's

old dog stiff behind the barn.
What could be worse than watching
Barbara ride off in her family's packed
station wagon, waving goodbye
from the tailgate and weeping,
moving to Houston a thousand miles
away? If anything could ever
be worse than watching their house
for hours across the road, no one
to ride with across a mile of meadow,
Barbara forever gone, I had to know.

[Previously published in *JAMA: The Journal of the American Medical Association* 281, no. 6 (1999): 494 and *All Occasions* (Notre Dame, IN: University of Notre Dame Press, 2000).]

Grandmother Bankhead's Lake

Sprawled on our bellies, we clawed through muck
and Irish potatoes under Grandmother Bankhead's shack
on stilts. We turned the loam with pitchforks,

lifting fat worms writhing on tines. Copperheads
lived there, and waterdogs, black widow spiders.
I felt them crawl, and slapped, smacking my skull.

My brother hissed "Shut up!" as if worms had ears.
Our great-grandfather dammed that pond in the Civil War,
birthright for boys with fishing rods and bait,

the coolest shade in Alabama. Later that month,
our older brother died on a battleship near Okinawa,
island hopping with MacArthur. But now, catfish and bass

hungered for our worms, dug up near graves of uncles
in magnolia groves, their oddly familiar names on plaques.
Bodies of boys and horses had washed down to the dam.

Wading to cast past tangled vines and mosquitoes,
I imagined corpses bobbing in the spring-fed lake,
their skulls and ribs nibbled by fish along the bank.

[Previously published in *All Occasions* (Notre Dame, IN: University of Notre Dame Press, 2000).]

Backpacking with My Bride in Montana

A flicker uphill, chipmunk or robin, or larger.
Outside the tent, the coffee's hot, my bride inside,
asleep. I reach for black binoculars and watch.

Nothing, then frantic signals start,
ground squirrel soprano hitting a high note.
At once, the green slope's littered with lookouts

stretched tall as a dozen inches can see
past boulders and a thousand pines. A fox
or coyote prowls, not black bear or puma,

too haughty or cunning for us with nothing
but hard tack and water, beef jerky sealed
in air-tight plastic and hung a hundred yards

downhill. My wife of five nights lifts
the tent flap and winks, still in her robe.
It's there, red fox or coyote wily and starved.

I pour a cup that steams at 10,000′ and hold
it for my wife. I marvel at her lips, the tilt
of her throat when she swallows, the taste

and curve of her, a perfect world. Ground
squirrel babies play and tumble by their holes.
The guard shrieks thin, ear-piercing screams,

tucking her gut and thrusting a tufted head
like a coach, a game they play to the death
every day, real bogeymen with fangs

that stalk and test the wind, and even
if the fox and coyote pass by, detected
and warned away, tomorrow they'll be back.

[Previously published in *Staple* (UK) 41 (1998): 20 and *All Occasions* (Notre Dame, IN: University of Notre Dame Press, 2000).]

Songs of Country Girls

Who are these singers with sequined eyes
and paste-on nasal twangs? Wild horses
couldn't make these girls look plain.

They pinch the mikes with scarlet nails,
flashing rings like peacocks. Bring back the days
of faithful girls so homely they hurt.

They moaned old songs in smoky halls,
strong-jawed women choking back real tears.
Where are they, now that we need them?

When their hearts broke, we swayed
and held sweet darlings close, humming
softly to ourselves and waltzing home.

[Previously published in *The Missouri Review* 17, no. 1 (1994): 68 and *All Occasions* (Notre Dame, IN: University of Notre Dame Press, 2000).]

Cousin Billy and the Weather

Spinning his wheelchair, he'd rise up suddenly
for air and fall back, yelling old gospel songs.
No one loved noise like Cousin Billy, deaf
and crippled in the war. He kept radios
blasting in all rooms, on different stations,

battles of empty decibels. I turned them down
so I could hear, but found them twisted loud
when I came back with liniment and magazines
and bullets, items he scribbled on lists.
He kept pistols on each window ledge,

sat up some nights alone in moonlight,
best hunter I knew before the war.
He shot coyotes and buzzard from his room,
and rattlers, skunks and turkeys fool enough
to waddle close. At dawn, he wheeled his chair

outside to find and clean whatever he could eat,
jerking the wheels in ruts. He hated rain,
sticking in mud and falling, shouting "Help,"
yelling "On Jordan's Stormy Banks I Stand,"
cursing and crying. I'd find him outside

or naked in the tub scrubbing turkey blood,
his shoulders bulging. He broke V.A. appointments,
dates I made for him with girls he'd known
in church or college, nothing but songs and rockets
on his mind after the noise of Da Nang. He cursed

jolly game shows and commercials on TV,
radar and weather charts all he would watch,
spinning channels to find the warnings, the rise
and fall of the jet stream, the stalled squall lines,
the highs and lows of regions under siege.

[Previously published in *CutBank* 27/28 (1988): 69 and *After the Noise of Saigon* (Amherst: University of Massachusetts Press, 1988—winner of the 1987 University of Massachusetts Press Juniper Prize).]

Bull

Purple-faced, like old plumbers
standing on their heads to shove
a snake down through a sewer,
my uncles and father argued

Saturdays away about anything
that moved or didn't move.
They never budged, never conceded
the world wasn't flat, the weather

the same, the kids my age wiser
and wilder. Facts like barbed wires
fenced them in, old bulls snorting
at each other. They huffed

and pawed up curses like dirt,
daring each other to find
a logical gate they hadn't tried.
My aunts and mother left them alone

in the den, and weaved their own
pleasant way through pastures
of laughter and gossip, secrets
I thought they whispered about girls

I needed to know, things more urgent
than battles my father and uncles
kept bringing up like cud
and chewing over and over.

[Previously published in *The Fiddlehead* (Canada) 148 (1986): 12 and *After the Noise of Saigon* (Amherst: University of Massachusetts Press, 1988–winner of the 1987 University of Massachusetts Press Juniper Prize).]

Goat Ranching

I could let go and live with the goats
that forage our mesquite and cactus,
browsing on grass, salt blocks

and cardboard boxes that tumble by.
Goats saunter to the tank and drink.
They've never killed a kid by kindness

or neglect, never had to put their kids'
old dogs to sleep, close friends
that drool and quiver, and stumble

hobbling to our hands. I've never
seen a goat afraid of trouble. Horny,
they strip the bark off cedar posts

and stand for hours in moonlight,
butting fence posts, whetting their horns
like sabers on barbed wires.

[Previously published in *After the Noise of Saigon* (Amherst: University of Massachusetts Press, 1988—winner of the 1987 University of Massachusetts Press Juniper Prize).]

Bulls, at Sundown

He's alone, the old bull
hump-shouldered by the barn,
scars on his back and neck
like braided whips. His snout

puckers in the cold, and younger bulls
back off. He snorts, and flicks his tail.
Night coming on, he walks
stiff-legged and swaying to his stall,

no longer tossing his horns,
no longer expecting one of his herd
to be there waiting, her narrow back
and barrel turned toward him

from habit, quivering. Always
a feast of grain is there in the trough,
and he goes for it now
without desire, without fighting

the pain in his nose, the ring
long a part of him like cramps in his legs
he takes with him everywhere.
Eyes glazed, he lowers his head

and chews, blowing the dust,
the hulls. Finished with all that
at last, he waits on four legs
in the dark and listens to his farm,

the fat hens clucking, the snort of horses
in the barn, the faint swishing
of his cows' tails, and farther off,
a dog's persistent barking.

He closes his eyes, leans
a few degrees for balance and feels
the barn, the weight of the farm
and the long day disappear.

[Previously published in *Cincinnati Poetry Review* 15 (1986): 59 and *After the Noise of Saigon* (Amherst: University of Massachusetts Press, 1988—winner of the 1987 University of Massachusetts Press Juniper Prize).]

In Green Pastures

It's grass, not bulls, spring cattle need.
The clink and creaking of gates alerts them.
The man who fed them silage and grain all winter

is calling. Riding high on his horse, he swings
the bars of a wide gate outward, out of packed
dust and splatter of the barnyard. Fields

fallow all winter beyond fences are ripe at last.
Alfalfa opens to dreams of pastures beyond
the fence. For weeks they sniffed a vinegar

sweetness in the wind, and trudged along
barbed wires, restless, mounting each other's backs,
desiring something other than a bull.

Surprised, they find a feast before them. Alfalfa
sways like the playa lake when it's full and flowing
in a storm. Aroused, almost dizzy, tails swishing,

they stagger through pastures rolling thick
and tender under hoofs. They bury tongues
in deep green hours they believe will last forever.

Their round eyes glaze, they never blink, they eat
as if they're waltzing. They follow the lead of lips,
and bells around their necks are ringing.

[Previously published in *The Massachusetts Review* 29, no. 1 (1988): 69–70 and *After the Noise of Saigon* (Amherst: University of Massachusetts Press, 1988—winner of the 1987 University of Massachusetts Press Juniper Prize).]

Lay Down the Battle Axe, the Halyard

It's done in wonder, like falling on ice
and rising, or finally reaching a high note,
shocked by a noise in the night
that would make white marble ring—

Saul, on Damascus Road, blinded
by light, and seeing. Blind Bartimaeus,
so simply healed he flinched,
blinking, needing no one to say

"That's Him!" Lay down the battle axe
and halyard, the six-mule plow.
Walk tall through the rocks and weeds,
hardscrabble leeched by years

of the same sad crops, fire-blackened
after harvest. Take off the cotton sack
you've dragged behind you for decades,
heavy with sorrows, mistakes, regrets,

burst clods to dust, kneel down in a row,
in the weeds, hold on to nothing you own,
let go, let faith thick as midnight
save you, believing "This is all I need."

[Previously published in *Climbing the Divide* (Notre Dame, IN: University of Notre Dame Press, 2003).]

October Compost

Leafrakes go back, go back and trees give up
more leaves than roots can use. Pack down
the pounds of locust twigs, the aspen gold
and fat catalpa bark. All summer we stacked
the pantry, hauled bushels of pears to neighbors
and the town's food bank. Now come the geese
from Canada, fields of loud flocks

pecking grain and corn. Our yard's a compost.
Take pitchforks and garden hose, turn
barrels of garbage for the garden, tumble,
churn it like sauerkraut steamy and damp.
All seasons whisper resurrection.
I need this gray decay. Since March,
I've wrestled bales of barbed wire,

bossed the herds, but fall brings cattle trucks.
Runt calves and old cows ride to slaughter.
Fall feeds the soil, and harvest saves
the stalks as silage to make cold cattle fat.
Fall saves migrating geese from freezing,
calls for our coats, tilling the earth
till springer cows give birth.

Christ saves us from decay. Soon enough,
we'll shove wheelbarrows of dark
October compost and watch the dry dirt
bulge, mulch of worms and beetles
making debris a kingdom in Spring.
Come, shirtsleeve months, come
bawling calves cavorting in corrals.

[Previously published in *Climbing the Divide* (Notre Dame, IN: University of Notre Dame Press, 2003).]

The War in Bosnia, the Beach at Kitty Hawk

Black, or mother of pearl, they snag on sand,
stranded till seagulls pick them clean.
We find seashells on restaurant walls
and sold as souvenirs, even above commodes,

glue-gunned to silk and plastic flowers
or wrapped into wreaths, clams and conchs
washed up at Kitty Hawk. We stroll packed sand,
bending to help grandkids picking shells.

Starfish tumble ashore in bubbles
washing our socks with salt. Granddaughters
splash and save sand dollars, moon snails,
hopping when waves ebb out and scatter shells

they run to save, and squeal when waves
rush back and splash their rubber boots. Tonight,
their father in Bosnia flies an Apache gunship,
patrolling more than ocean, firefights he can't stop.

I wonder if Wilbur and Orville thought of bombs
and rockets when they launched face down
a mile from here. Tonight, near Kitty Hawk,
my wife and I sip coffee on the condo's deck,

granddaughters finally asleep. We face the east
where our son flies, millions of stars from here,
hot coffee cooling as we sip, nothing to see
but miles of dark and white caps crashing down.

[Previously published in *The Christian Century* 117, no. 15 (2000): 548 and *Climbing the Divide* (Notre Dame, IN: University of Notre Dame Press, 2003).]

Stoking the Logs at Dawn

Ashes drift down like snow, smoke from the chimney
easy to breathe, split piñon from New Mexico.
Decades of nights come back on the breeze,

coils of memories like DNA–Son swinging a rope
from his pony, Daughter in bed with teddy bears
and mumps, teaching her pup ballet and tap

on a pillow stage. Now, from the porch, we watch trees
bloom before our eyes, and weeds the goats love
turning green. So many miles to Daughter's house,

an ocean between us and our Son's college, Seville
a city we learned meant "Spain," a foreign shore
where exotic others live. Grandchildren sleep

without us, now, holidays we treasure, any excuse
to call, to hear deep breathing in the receiver
and "I love you Mamaw and Pop," then teenage

giggles, call-waiting clicks and gushy love
goodbyes. Pockets of pine sap sizzle and pop
in the fireplace, the bittersweet aroma of smoke

like cabins in mountains long ago, our fingers
locked on sofas, like now, big-knuckled and stiff,
a coupling of fingers and lips that still fit.

[Previously published in *Westview* 18, no. 1 (1998): 9 and *Climbing the Divide* (Notre Dame, IN: University of Notre Dame Press, 2003).]

A Thousand Miles of Stars

I thought I needed a dozen sweethearts
when I rode bulls in rodeos, Palominos
to prance and nudge my fist for sugar cubes,

nibbling my palms, dogs to bark
and call me master with their tails, wagging,
dragging my slippers. I fancied monkeys

and leopards doing amazing tricks to please me,
red and blue toucans perched on my chair,
cooing, free to fly in and out, preened

and singing when I came home. What did I know,
straddling a brown, two-thousand-pound bull
twisting and bucking, a thousand fans

cheering the cowboy and the bull? Now
at sixty, stiff when I saddle the same fat gelding
I've fed for a decade, I miss our children

who bring their offspring yearly to the ranch,
wonders my wife and I hold to our hearts,
waving goodbye as they drive off at dawn.

When even the dust has settled, we close the gate
and hobble to the porch, old lovers who shake
our heads and laugh, recalling the fall the toddler took

but climbed back giggling to the porch,
how quickly they learned to rope, the giddy
long-distance calls the teenagers made to boys.

We rock and hold each other close. We listen hard
and hear dogs bark a mile away, the windmill
spinning fast, the far-off roar of stars.

[Previously published in *Clackamas Literary Review* 2, no. 2 (1998): 12 and *All Occasions* (Notre Dame, IN: University of Notre Dame Press, 2000).]

When I Glance Up

Buckets swing and jingle against her knees.
I could hobble out and help, but who'd do the math—
so many calves, so many bushels an acre,
so many days before it rains. When I glance up,
she's on the slope going slow, moccasins

swishing through tall grass down to the spring.
My hip has itched all week, fire from knee to the groin.
I slide a bent-wire hanger down inside the cast,
scratch all I can reach, like a dog in winter
clawing fleas, coat too thick to nip with his teeth.

I need to hang storm windows before blizzards
and patch the roof, my hammer there where I left it,
clumsy, falling like a tumbling act without a net.
We said if we build here, spring water always cool
would flow, the chimney would draw, the roof

swirled free of smog, no honking cars, no telephones.
And now she's back, hardly huffing, big buckets
bumping but not splashing the path from both pails,
shimmers of sweat on her cheeks, lips parted
and licked till they glisten like her eyes.

[Previously published in *The Acre* 1, no. 10 (2000): 10 and *Climbing the Divide* (Notre Dame, IN: University of Notre Dame Press, 2003).]

Batting Practice at Sixty

I slap five dozen balls back through the box,
grounders that hop to the shortstop's glove,
some sneaking through for singles, but not far.

Lately, I've gotten good at fly balls and pop-ups,
swinging too late, cutting under, eye on the ball
but jerking, forcing the bat. My turn to chase

somebody's flies, so I trot to third and flip
the padded hat, hoping for grounders, ready to scoop
and throw out my arm across the mound to first.

Old folks hoping to play should practice twice a day
to surprise our sons, not once a week for games
in the senior league. I taught our children to bunt

and run, hang tough and hit away when the sign's right,
and slide, be men, shake hands and come out fighting.
But those were days before Saigon, before parents died,

back when flying was easy escape for me on weekends,
before our son's battles in Desert Storm, when hopes
turned back to dread. By sixty, closets meant keepsakes,

videos we watch when the boys are here. Albums
of their games seem ancient, like honeymoon photos,
back when Whitey Ford controlled the mound, Yogi Berra

behind the plate, a kid in center field named Mickey
Mantle shagging every out, trying to match DiMaggio's
career in Yankee Stadium, Babe Ruth's bambino face

on the plaque behind him—my old fingers aching,
magic and grace in every field we saw, the whole
wide world before us, the Yankees in first place.

[Previously published in *The Sewanee Review* 107, no. 4 (1999): 525 and *All Occasions* (Notre Dame, IN: University of Notre Dame Press, 2000).]

All Dogs Are Pirates

All dogs are pirates, wild for an opened gate,
a different scent. At any jiggled leash,
Old Rollo stumbled to the door, begging
for plunder, wagging his bulldog butt.

I've seen dogs try to board others, sniffing,
tails up like flags, or down on their backs
like Blackbeard giving up. Dogs in Montana
tug their tourists uphill at Little Bighorn,

sniffing for clues, gobbling pretzels and bread
tossed for the crows, peeing on signs with fines
for stealing bones. Dogs rock the boat
of good manners, barking at startled guests

on the porch, probing with noses like hooks,
lifting up purses and skirts for inspection,
scratching, licking themselves before we cast them
adrift in the back yard black as a dungeon.

Armadas of dogs sail by, marking the alley fence
like treasure maps, to make them bark. Guests gone,
dogs lope inside and sniff the floor for gold
before bedtime, panting, holding no grudge.

For years, Old Rollo drooled and groaned
by our chairs, happy with any tidbit
we tossed, fat belly scratched until his leg
thumped, any pat like a ration of rum.

[Previously published in *Buffalo Spree* magazine 31, no. 4 (1997): 79 and *All Occasions* (Notre Dame, IN: University of Notre Dame Press, 2000).]

Old Pilots in the Crowd at Kitty Hawk

The guide says the mannequin with the mustache,
that's Orville. The guide's eyes twinkle
and he points. Orville's hanging head-first
into history, his left fist stiff on the controls.

Inside the visitors' center, the mock-up
never flies, just what scoffers always warned
those quacks from Ohio. Fake props are plastic,
the faces painted gaudy as corpses,

hard to feel for dummies in crash tests.
In grainy pictures, the brothers never smile,
but both look vulnerable and real. Wilbur,
we know, died young. The guide asks pilots

to raise our hands, and all who do
are old. We've all flown fighters, transports,
bombers that could wipe Kitty Hawk off the map,
turn the sandy Outer Banks to glass.

The guide's dramatic, grabs the lower wing
and twists, proving the skills of lift and turn.
We'd rather he step aside, let us roll that crate
out to the tarmac, flip for the right

to go first on our bellies. Goggles down,
cracked leather gloves back on, we'd nod,
face to the wind and history be damned,
full throttle at thirty miles an hour,

a hundred, eight hundred feet down range.
What was Wilbur's record that day, almost a minute?
Never mind the hedge of trees they planted
a hundred feet beyond, watch this.

[Previously published in *Prairie Schooner* 74, no. 2(2000): 163–64 and *All Occasions* (Notre Dame, IN: University of Notre Dame Press, 2000).]

Christmas Bells, Saigon

Buses came late, all drivers sullen, heads shaved
above the ears. At the French country club on base,
we nursed flat drinks while Viet Cong with knives

and fat French planters smoked and ignored us,
easy to blame us for the war. The maitre d' said wait,
he'd find us a place. For hours, we ambled around

outside for tables, four majors killing time
and a half-drunk Colonel. After weeks of rockets,
we needed rest. The youngest major joked

the clerk who promised a table died tonight, his neck slit.
People I'd known for months kept disappearing.
Someone asked what's going on. The Colonel

slowly turned and shrugged. Men I'd seen in 'Nam
for months kept dancing off with girls. I heard a blast
above the band's brassy mix of honky tonk horns

and Beatles. I watched young guards buried in cages
ten feet above us in trees. Five minutes apart
they rattled bells on wires to signal–what?–

"We are alive?" How could any believe in bells
dangling on wires? Sappers could slit the boys' throats

and keep it up, "ring-ring," till all guard stations fell.

l wondered when a bus would come. I needed a ride
back to the hooch to sleep, to dream of home, rumors
of good will toward all. The Colonel left hours ago.

The other majors and I agreed on all things noble,
a little sober on French vermouth and gin, humming
with Beatles and the bells, the bells all through the night.

[Previously published in *After the Noise of Saigon* (Amherst: University of Massachusetts Press, 1988–winner of the 1987 University of Massachusetts Press Juniper Prize).]

When Rockets Fell Like Stars

We prowled the base at midnight, high
on crowbars and rum. We smashed
car lights and ripped the chrome off doors.

Nothing beat being drunk when rockets
fell like stars and bar girls screamed,
one more Cadillac dismantled upside down.

We swore such cars belonged to black-markets
or Vietcong cousins who wanted us dead,
pilots whose war exploded till dawn,

the war of VC rockets and mortars launched
at the base, at us. We roared country songs
with shouts and dirty words put in.

Trying to ignore incoming fire, we swaggered
to the mess hall, daring the wailing sirens
to scare us, swearing we didn't care.

[Previously published in *First Things* 85 (1998): 18 and *All Occasions* (Notre Dame, IN: University of Notre Dame Press, 2000).]

Crashes Real and Imagined

We've seen them crash
on television, the silver
of thin aluminum plummeting,
trailing dark plumes of smoke
we focus on, the dubbed-in sound
inversely shrill.

Unless it's a newsreel,
planes disappear behind cliffs
or convenient forests,
where waiting crews explode smoke bombs.
Few of us watching films fear death
by impact. We believe

they're dead already,
the blood of bitten capsules
streaming from their mouths,
heads slumped like robots shorted out.
The night Ray Bumpass died
in pilot training, straight in

from twenty thousand feet,
we believed his instructor's word
that nothing could force a jet
straight down like that but a coma–
hypoxia, or heart attack.
We knew he risked his own life

trying to save Ray, diving,
screaming on mayday channel "Pull up!
pull up!" For weeks we slept and ate
and kept our take-off times,
and some of us felt our own too solid
flesh impacting in the ground.

[Previously published in *Mid-American Review* 7, no. 2 (1986): 119 and *After the Noise of Saigon* (Amherst: University of Massachusetts Press, 1988–winner of the 1987 University of Massachusetts Press Juniper Prize).]

Grandmother's Thousand Cats

Grandmother majored in French and Latin
and raised cats. She numbered them, digits
in the French tongue lovely, and they purred.

After Granddad's horse tossed him off
and stomped him, she taught college,
the oldest Bachelor of Science

on the faculty. Her students liked her cats,
learned French by riding to the ranch
for practice, counting her cats *deux*,

trois, and grooming mares. My mom
met my father there, branding calves
for his mom. She left him the ranch

she called "Cows and a Thousand Cats."
Mom teased his mother taught him Latin
and French so he'd feed the kittens, more

than a dozen when I was born. He let them
prowl, but never fed milk from cows,
too rich for kittens. When our own grandkids

were toddlers, he lined them up like cats
in the barn, tongues out, squinting and giggling,
my father squeezing quick squirts to them all.

[Previously published in *Ontario Review* (Canada) 55 (2002): 96 and *Climbing the Divide* (Notre Dame, IN: University of Notre Dame Press, 2003).]

Giving Time to the Dirt in Rows

My wife framed a poster decades ago,
"Take time"—picture of a daddy holding a kid.
So I made time for ours at baseball games,
before survival training and Saigon.
Down on both knees, I taught our babies
tickle and horsey rides, caught all three
with the same oiled catcher's mitt

then waved them away on planes. Berries
and beans sustain us, now that the kids have gone—
and okra so slick why bother to chew,
just swallow. There's work in digging our own
potatoes—never mind the worms, dirt
under the nails. It's grace, no matter how high
the water bill, how many bushels we reap.

All that crawling around between rows
takes time, squatting like ducks hunting for bugs,
turning flab into muscles, to tighter skin
and bones. Years ago, each child turned back
and waved, memories we keep of nights
in Montana, blessings of family no one
could earn, like berries, potatoes, and beans.

[Previously published in *First Things* 114 (2001): 11 and *Climbing the Divide* (Notre Dame, IN: University of Notre Dame Press, 2003).]

Taking the Keys Away

Daddy at the wheel is dangerous,
we finally had to admit—Daddy, who drove
tanks for Patton in World War II,
directed fire at steel, at walls
a thousand years old, at trucks

with soldiers. Now, for the fourth time,
he straddled a curb, backed up
almost over a mailman, who leaped
aside in time, with his hands out,
watching his pushcart crushed.

What if tomorrow it's a boy on a bike,
a widow walking her dog, a toddler?
How to tell a white-haired tank
commander, "Please give us the keys."
How to sit down by Father and say,

"You're grounded"? He doesn't lose
the remote control more than once
a program. He calls the dog
the wrong name often, but even the dog
comes gladly, happy for his hand.

[Previously published in *JAMA: The Journal of the American Medical Association* and *Climbing the Divide* (Notre Dame, IN: University of Notre Dame Press, 2003).]

Words I Looked Up in World War II

Migraine takes her away, Grandmother said
when Aunt Marge shuddered and fell,
eyes rolling back like Orphan Annie's.
Until Sunday School, I feared a demon had her.

"Migraine," Grandmother said. Uncle Joe
scoffed "Mammon," "Epilepsy," "Satan," more
big words to learn. I watched my Aunt Marge
writhe, white-faced but sweet. When we hugged,

I laid on hands, hoping to heal her, like the parson.
My brother was ten, with a temper, kicked
her shins once when she won. I dragged him
kicking and scratching behind the barn

and taught him how to lose. Aunt Marge
was tough, a big-boned laughing girl I loved,
always tickling and playing games, pulling dimes
from behind my ears, coins rare as dollars

before Pearl Harbor. Long haired and lovely,
she taught cards and hide-and-seek and horse,
then turned eighteen and enlisted. Aunt Marge
passed the physical easily, handsome

in Marine Corps blues. Her troop ship exploded
and burned off Okinawa. I was fourteen by then,
and big, but enlistment sergeants led me out
to the sidewalk, patting my shoulders, saying,

"Don't worry, Son, it's okay, the war's almost won."
They'd seen so many kids grieving and fierce,
needing to kill to cope—maybe saw my jaw too tight,
my eyes too puffy, the nicks where I tried to shave.

[Previously published in *JAMA: The Journal of the American Medical Association* 287, no. 3 (2002): 287 and *Climbing the Divide* (Notre Dame, IN: University of Notre Dame Press, 2003).]

Marriage Is a Bungee Jump

Marriage is a bungee jump off some box canyon
in Montana, concession manned by a minion
from the fifties high on weed, beard he hadn't brushed
since Vietnam. The cords looked new enough

and he swore he measured them, the fall to the rocks
a lovers' leap eighty stories long.
He made us sign a waiver and pay in cash.
Folding the bills away, he slouched back to the shack

and high-fived a friend who passed the bottle back.
Done it again, like cupid. We heard a match strike,
the sizzle of hemp. We checked the cords, the stiff knots
tied by someone who flunked that lesson in scouts.

We had studied charts, the geology of cliffs
and canyons, but no one knows which fibers split,
which granite ledges crack. On the edge of hope
for nothing we'd ever done, we tugged at the cords,

both cords, blessing the stretch and strain
with our bodies, a long time falling to the pain
and certainly of stop. Hand in hand we stepped up
wavering to the ledge, hearing the rush

of a river we leaped to, a far-off
cawing crow, the primitive breeze of the fall,
and squeezed, clinging to each other's vows
that only death could separate us now.

[Previously published in *Blessings the Body Gave* (Columbus: The Ohio State University Press, 1998—winner of the 1997 Ohio State University Press *The Journal* Award in Poetry).]

Breathless for Twenty Seconds

In the film, she's leaning,
humming to music we can't hear.
Last month, we kneeled by her bed

and barely breathed. Whatever
Mom tried to tell us that last hour,
we'll never know. This movie

of her and Dad before the war
has no sound, so old it's brittle.
Inches of film snap off each time we watch

and the sprockets turn. My God!
she was lovely, our daddy breathless
for twenty seconds, her glossy hair

dark and long, her body marvelous
even after we kids were born. Dad's
not in most rolls, but came back from war

without a scratch, only night sweats,
battles he never shared with us.
He made this film at Christmas–

look how he focused on Mom,
who didn't know he filmed her
stringing mistletoe from the ladder

he named "Mom's Pedestal," while
she lived. Someone probably called,
for laughter turned her around.

Look at that–surprised, delighted.
She mouths our daddy's name,
her long skirt sways, the ladder shaky–

but now, the film is blank spots blinking by,
then only the screen's bright light,
the plastic clicking until I flick the switch.

[Previously published in *Rattle* 8, no. 2 (2001): 60 and *Climbing the Divide* (Notre Dame, IN: University of Notre Dame Press, 2003).]

This Could Be Eden

Contrails slice the sky like diamonds,
the snow-packed mountains so cold
it seems they'd never burn. Hard granite

holds the world together almost as much
as gravity until it cracks and breaks apart.
At dawn, a grizzly attacked a jogger,

deep-gashed her face and chest, her heart
already stopped when they found her.
Who could intuit lava or hate in the heart,

a world of killing fields, boiling volcano
rocks we walk on? On days this calm,
almost balmy, who could imagine wars

or broken hearts, incurable plagues,
a decade without cars, TVs or iPhones?
On this almost perfect day, on the deck

of our mountain cabin, we rock, talk softly
although we haven't heard a door or seen
another soul since dawn. Except for wars

and rumors of wars, even grizzly bears
in some towns around, this could be Eden,
Grandchildren we adore only blocks away.

[Previously published in *The Christian Century* 118, no. 22 (2001): 20 and *Climbing the Divide* (Notre Dame, IN: University of Notre Dame Press, 2003).]

A Little World Made Cunningly

Carl Sagan called Earth a "pale blue dot"
among billions of stars the Hubble telescope
saw, a fabulous fog that dwarfed the Earth,

an atom inside a massively expanding
universe whose size we can't imagine.
What if Hubble's find is only an atom

in another or other universes far more vast?
What a Brobdingnag of galaxies the final
big-bang size would be—unless *final*

limits the infinite too much for words.
I remember pictures of me as a toddler
when my mother and father were the world.

Flip the Hubble, focus on a mote of dust
on anyone's nose, a molecule inside
another universe a billion light years wide.

Think of trillions of molecules in the legs
of each of us, each molecule with a billion . . .
and so on. Imagine a minuscule

Lilliputian kid inside a massive galaxy
inside your own left eye, skipping along
to a candy store with a dime. Drops it,

dusts it off. Each mote of dust ten billion
light years across, each tiny atom a cosmos.
Maybe it doesn't matter. We're on Earth, now.

Maybe we'll never know. Sitting with Mother
for hours between rounds, I had no hunger
for physics, the last thing on my mind

astronomy. When Mother opened her eyes
her last long night, I didn't wonder how many
billions of galactic, giddy girls might be

in tiny high schools inside her, in every atom
of cancer, didn't ponder how many angels
danced on her IV needle. I wanted only

to give comfort, relief, since every second
seemed like time wouldn't end, and every year
with that lady who bore me was too brief.

[Previously published in *Climbing the Divide* (Notre Dame, IN: University of Notre Dame Press, 2003).]

Packing Parachutes in Flight School

We beat each other senseless in football
and boxing, swimming in flight suits
before we soloed. Five resigned

after their first flights, nervous
or breakfast on the canopy. By frost,
most soloed, flew to Florida and back

alone, packed our own parachutes
to feel how it's done, our necks
depending on slender nylon cords.

Weekends, we cruised for Georgia girls
who trained us to love buttered grits
and yams, dancing to Johnny Mathis

who swore we'd be true till the twelfth
of never. One noon, a boy in our class
crash-landed, trailing smoke–Joe,

somebody said–too low to bail out,
smoke billowing, wing clipping
the pine trees and flipping, a fireball

for a thousand yards, some of us
running toward the wreckage
until the captain called us back.

[Previously published in *Poet Lore* and *Climbing the Divide* (Notre Dame, IN: University of Notre Dame Press, 2003).]

After the Mad Songs of Saigon

Squeezing a half-eaten peach,
I rub the other palm
along the saddle horn,

wrap the reins around it twice,
lean back and slide the rifle out.
I tap the stallion's neck

and give the peach. He twists,
nibbles and swallows,
and his whole neck quivers.

He knows the crack
a rifle makes, and waits.
This won't disturb the universe,

a few ounces into the heart
of a big cat sleeping it off.
That lamb would have died

hereafter, but it was mine,
even the cactus by the cave
where the blood-stained cougar died.

[Previously published in *North American Review* 286, no. 5 (2001): 14 and *Climbing the Divide* (Notre Dame, IN: University of Notre Dame Press, 2003).]

Bull-Necked and Square-Jawed After Saigon

I'm a pawn of dawn, of sentimental rhymes
Sinatra sang, even awkward magicians' tricks.
Weep me a Lloyd Webber cello and I'll weep,
glass-jawed and masked like monsters at a concert.
Let choir boys in Vienna hit a high note,

let my grandson's teacher lead him and other
boys in cowboy songs, it doesn't matter,
I'm the bull-necked grandfather I am, reaching
for Kleenex, about to bawl. My cowboy father
fought in Flanders, but after his stroke

he choked back pity at wrestling matches
and game shows on TV, maudlin old man
cracking knuckles of both his massive fists.
Lucky man with allergies, I'm forgiven this nose
I blow, red eyes I wipe as if I'm crying.

Where did this awful heart come from, unless from Dad,
marbled like a slab of prime rib, bloody chunk
plopped on the plate with new potatoes and peas?
I came back from war vulnerable to the Wall
in Washington, a ticking time bomb that explodes

when I'm walking along in Lubbock or London
and come upon someone down on a sidewalk,
chalking a gaudy mauve-and-purple pop art, and I
stumble by like a blind man, blinking as if smog
or sand in my contacts is scratching my eyeballs raw.

[Previously published in *All Occasions* (Notre Dame, IN: University of Notre Dame Press, 2000).]

Caught in a Storm on Hardscrabble

Under an oak, I wait out a hailstorm,
caught in a summer day gone dark,
thunder so loud I can't hear myself

yell to the gelding. I'd rather be
back in the bunkhouse, taking my chances
with poker. Isn't my life worth more

than a gelding so spooked he's stomping?
I grab my Stetson and sling holy water
over the dust. The worst thing to do

is hide under the only tree around,
a lightning rod. I've tried leading this
stubborn fool into rain, but he won't go,

dumber than steers that go on grazing
afraid of nothing but hunger. I should
hobble the horse, wade out and hunker down

in my poncho. Grass floats on the plains
like seaweed. Coyotes and rattlers
slink by two by two, the only shelter.

At last, the gelding lowers his head
and eats, believing my lie that we're safe,
that lightning can't strike us.

[Previously published in *After the Noise of Saigon* (Amherst: University of Massachusetts Press, 1988–winner of the 1987 University of Massachusetts Press Juniper Prize).]

Estacado

Great-grandmother in 1880
raised eight children on plains
she named heaven's tableland.
A Quaker reader from Iowa
with two dead babies
and two that lived, she talked softly

to her husband, a godly farmer,
and called the Quaker town
in Texas their promised land.
They loaded up and left
with nothing but a letter
to lead them. This flat prairie

with waving buffalo grass
reminded her of bread without yeast,
the unleavened body of the Lord.
The only milk flowed from the cow
roped to their wagon,
their only honey, words in a book.

[Previously published in *South Dakota Review* 23, no. 2 (1985): 71 and *After the Noise of Saigon* (Amherst: University of Massachusetts Press, 1988—winner of the 1987 University of Massachusetts Press Juniper Prize).]

Jogging at Sixty-five

Dawn runners call raw wind a bear,
bite it breath by breath until the cold bear roars.
We stumble on ruts frozen stiff as hoes

turned upside down. Sun is a rumor
clouds pass along like gossip,
gossamer strung from the east like webs.

By sixty, nature gives up on bodies
soft as sandcastles after ebb tide.
Puffing, we pump fists doubled on nothing

but lifelines wrinkled when we were born.
Old legs run to get the cold blood
pumping, squeeze, squeeze that blue juice

to our toes, up to skulls of gray hair
sweaty under wool caps flapping our throats.
One old couple could keep this pace all day,

panting around the solid lake to turn
and circle back—shorter to cut across
on ice ten inches thick, but cheating.

Crows hurl themselves from spruce,
cascades of snow we dip through,
not even blinking. Somewhere, a loon

croons its crazy tune, and why not—
our bodies wobble like Apollo 13,
short of oxygen and fuel—makeshift,

but doing what wobbly bodies can do,
the lake a frozen glow that pulls us
like the moon and hurls us home.

[Previously published in *Oxford American* 35 (2000): 112 and *Climbing the Divide* (Notre Dame, IN: University of Notre Dame Press, 2003).]

The Rodeo Fool

We hummed sad country songs all summer,
certain the bulls we shoved were worth it.
Nothing thrills a family crowd more
than a cowboy falling, even the king
of the cowboys, and one or two hurt bad

each night. They know riding bulls is brave
and crazy. They like a good stomping
when rodeo clowns help them die laughing
in the face of danger, a black
two-thousand-pound bull pawing dirt,

goring the cowboy over and over. They scream
so loud they can't hear the screams
of the cowboy. I run out waving my arms
like an angel in makeup and baggy pants,
slam into the bull's broad butt,

grab his tail and twist and twist. The bull
stops goring and lifts his horns.
I'm wiping my hands up and down my pants
hung by suspenders up to my nipples,
like rubber waders Baptist preachers wear.

The bull looks back, stupid on all four
massive legs. The crowd loves it,
safe in the stands, munching beer nuts
and guzzling. I twist the tail till it burns,
drop it and wipe my hands three times

and make a face, then fake a double-take
at the bull's black eyes deciding
by god to kill me. I run,
hoping my aim for the rubber barrel
is better than it was two years ago.

By now, Jay or Billy Ray has dragged
the rider to safety and runs out
baiting the bull. The bull snorts,
swinging his head between us, tail limp.
No one pays to see clowns suffer,

clowns make it fun to watch a grown man
gored and stomped on by a beast. It can't be
bad as it seems if a fool in baggy pants
can shove a bull and crank his tail
and live. Even when we're gored,

bleeding inside our baggy pants,
ribs crushed, unable to breathe,
we pull ourselves up and double over,
bowing. We go on making believe it's fun
all the way from the arena: it's in the rules.

I couldn't say how many crushed ribs,
how many bones Jay and Billy Ray and I have broken
and grown back. They couldn't pay me
enough to do this, if friends didn't grin
and raise a hand when we lift them

into the ambulance. People leaving
laugh at me and wave as if I'm some kind
of saint, a fool holy enough to do what
they'd like to do, nightly to save someone
from death and make believe it's fun.

My stupid moves prove nothing wild
is as dangerous as men. Because of me,
they ride home humming, not troubled
by tons of metal hurtling past their bumpers,
believing death's a black bull mad and charging,

all men are brave and cunning,
that all fall down, get gored and trampled on,
all men can rise with the help of clowns,
able to look death in the eye, to wear
a clown's face, laughing, and walk again.

[Previously published in *After the Noise of Saigon* (Amherst: University of Massachusetts Press, 1988—winner of the 1987 University of Massachusetts Press Juniper Prize).]

Setting the Torch to Stubble

To make fire roll we waited for the wind.
From the east a sluggish low blew in,
time to torch the stalk and burn
dead grain fields clean. Flames jumped

over rows laid east to deep caliche
canyons where the flat world ended.
Skunks and rabbits poured into
box canyons like spillways. Hawks

swooped through black smoke swirling.
We roamed burning rows and clubbed
field rats and rattlers. We believed
in flames and heard snake eggs explode.

Granddaddy grew up believing stubble
had to burn, tight-packed Georgia loam
more than his back could stand.
Each Fall, cane blazed so fierce

Georgia hill stones split. Plains fields
are loose and easy, though, blow-sand
even mules could plow, and we have tractors.
We let grain stubble rot, and plow

mulch rows for planting. Our yields increase
and steel barns overflow. Hawks glide
and sidle over fields without rats,
but rattlers are everywhere.

[Previously published in *New Orleans Review* 13, no. 2 (1986): 21 and *After the Noise of Saigon* (Amherst: University of Massachusetts Press, 1988–winner of the 1987 University of Massachusetts Press Juniper Prize).]

We Called It Entering Heaven

We flew there mainly on a dare,
"Heaven's Gate," two walls of stone
the size of towers, straight up

from the desert. Nothing lives
there but lizards and ants scaling sandstone.
Banked ninety degrees, a jet plane

would fit, we said. Grease it with speed.
Nothing under 500 miles an hour counts.
From twenty thousand feet, split-S,

straight down, and level out at five
and glide head on toward those steep
devil's towers—thirty seconds more,

line up the only approach you dare.
Nudge the throttle to hold 500 knots, roll steep
ninety degrees to the only

earth you've known, face to face
with two tall walls of stone looming fast,
trying to dive through the eye of a needle.

[Previously published in *After the Noise of Saigon* (Amherst: University of Massachusetts Press, 1988—winner of the 1987 University of Massachusetts Press Juniper Prize).]

The Eyes in Jimmy Ray's Shed

Dust in Jimmy Ray's daddy's shed
stunk like the air of innertubes. Something
was there that shouldn't be, still rotting,
molded or alive, hung up by nails on rafters,

or buried in boxes, in jumbles of hames
of horses and buzz saws, the dust-gray heads
of moose and deer and coyotes. Long and low
like a bunkhouse, that shed never had lights.

Jimmy stole a key the summer before it burned
and let us in. He pulled the door almost shut
so no one would notice, and we were alone
in the dark like a grave of our own digging.

Whispering, bumping together, we crept under
wild dead eyes of a lion, the fangs of cougars
snapping at pinpoints of light. Swirls of cobwebs
dusty and old sagged like fishing nets strung up

to dry. They swayed when a breath from the door
passed over, slow as ghosts moaning at midnight.
Nothing else moved, no spiders, no scurry of mice.
Billy Joe wet his pants and lied he always did,

that time of night. In the stink of Jimmy's shed,
better to be called baby than coward. Born poor
in the Texas depression, we were used to dust
and centipedes scuttling on the floor at night.

Whatever was there watched every step
in the shed, heard every breath. Dead eyes
of animals followed wherever we crept. Once,
when I glanced back, they looked away.

[Previously published in *The Windsor Review* (Canada) 25, no. 1 (1987): 84 and *After the Noise of Saigon* (Amherst: University of Massachusetts Press, 1988—winner of the 1987 University of Massachusetts Press Juniper Prize).]

In the Alchemist's Household

Burning coal for gold, my wife
waves our big-eyed children
back from the kiln. Moths
fluttering from joy to joy,

they bob and weave as if she's
a goalie; her studio, a soccer field.
I've seen her spin exquisite vases
from clay, jars of the same sienna sand

we live on. In months, she turned
mere kisses into screams
and tiny fists, squinty infants
who turned her breast milk

into teeth and giggles, into fists
that lifted puppies up and snuggled.
She makes sand paintings
I want to frame and save,

grains of a prairie rainbow
she sweeps at sundown and scatters.
She turns long nights to dawn
by bedsides of the dying,

moans and groaning that hush
when she's beside them in a chair,
stroking their twitching thumbs,
holding their IV hands.

[Previously published in *Southern Poetry Review* 39, no. 2 (1999): 41 and *All Occasions* (Notre Dame, IN: University of Notre Dame Press, 2000).]

The Moves a Body Makes

I like no wasted motion, prefer the blur
in the wings of hummingbirds, the splendor
of dump-truck drivers who know

when to tug the rope, all other jobs
hydraulic, the long bed tilting tons of dirt
then down, the slam and crash of rods

mechanical and tight. I like a riveter's
hard hat, its jaunty cock like Stetsons
on cowboys who ride bulls, no half-hearted

effort for eight seconds or all day.
Even now that I don't fly, I like a pilot's way
with thrust and ailerons, a dentist's

with a root canal, a blaster's fist
shoving dynamite into mountains.
Grandfather took two simple threads

and welded them with spit and fingers,
fishing flies tied for my sister and me.
I like the skillful lift and cleaning

between legs, my wife changing babies
again and again, showing me lift and turn,
skills of aeronautics in the home.

I like instructor pilots teaching the sky,
my wife taking her hands away from toddlers
learning to wobble and walk and drive a car,

then waving farewell till they were gone.
I like slow walks to the park and home,
how long she holds my hand, and lets it go.

[Previously published in *Writers' Forum* 22 (1996): 9 and *Blessings the Body Gave* (Columbus: The Ohio State University Press, 1998—winner of the 1997 Ohio State University Press *The Journal* Award in Poetry).]

To Have and to Hold

> "Didn't they enter that marriage forever,
> didn't they, though? To have and to hold each other
> forever, forsaking all men in tuxedos and elegant
> maidens leaping to catch the bouquet, so clever
> to think it would last."

Some friends seem to say that, sadly or grandly
at parties and ballrooms, always surprised that it lasted
this long. We greet them and offer our toasts
to their brides or new grooms at receptions
with strangers and blooms like bouquets.

Years are like dances with friends changing hands,
new partners for foxtrots or waltzes,
or sitting it out. We're oddly off-guard
when they ask us to dance, odd couple oddly regarded
like wallflowers or parents, quaint chaperones

at mixed-family reunions, monogamous dinosaurs
back from the tar pits, quaint and club-footed—
how charming like sophomores, possessive
or scared, how daring like monks to love only one
or to grow old together thinking it's so. They watch us

for chinks in our armor, flirtations and waves.
"Oh, he's a sly one," they probably say—
"forsaking all others, ha, that'll be the day."
They watch her for bruises, for a drugged,
glassy gaze. Our children have babies

that hurry us dizzy from birthday
to birthday, already almost our age
when we married—"always" now down
to decades or days. We're aging, amazed
and surprised by how swiftly it passes,

no turning back—how awful,
how destined, I see, to leave her alone
with my name behind deadbolts—
or worse, and unbearably so—to lose her
someday, not ever to hold her, not caress

that remarkable face, splotched with age spots.
How could I stand it, to suffer her gone,
not hear her whisper, with gray in her hair,
not ever to rise and build fires for her early
or call her to walk through the garden at dawn?

[Previously published in *Many Mountains Moving* 4, no. 3 (2001): 293 and *Blessings the Body Gave* (Columbus: The Ohio State University Press, 1998—winner of the 1997 Ohio State University Press *The Journal* Award in Poetry).]

Leaving the Scene

Sleet clicking in the trees, and finches flicking
maize and millet from the feeder. This late in spring,
and still the thin smoke whips from chimneys
miles away. We rock and watch the dawn, a ten-watt
bulb beyond the clouds. Is all this sideshow spring

a barker's promise of warmth? Our pears bloomed
weeks ago, awnings of green chiffon. The red oaks bulge,
about to burst. Sleet clicks like thousands of clocks
ticking in our sleep. We take turns leaving the scene
with both mugs to the kitchen for more, draining the urn,

the stiff steam bending as we straighten rugs
and weave back through fifty years of furniture,
drapes opened, sleet beating a mute tattoo, the old oaks
wet and dark out in the pasture, sleet on the steers'
flat backs, bowing to dawn and browsing, always grass

and blocks of salt, the sky nothing they ever watch,
no matter what falls, nothing fat cattle can't endure.
We rock and sip in silence, chairs turned to the porch,
grandchildren far away, knowing whatever force
is coming no one could stop, not even us.

[Previously published in *New Letters* 63, no. 4 (1997): 87 and *Blessings the Body Gave* (Columbus: The Ohio State University Press, 1998–winner of the 1997 Ohio State University Press *The Journal* Award in Poetry).]

Five Fathoms Down Off Hatteras

Can we believe this rubble, these rusted bolts?
Immigrants trusted iron, turned their backs
on Cornish cream and breezes, clambered
up gangplanks for bunks below deck.

Did they guess disaster in the captain's eyes?
Did fields of barley and tobacco seem like gold,
worth risking shoals along the Outer Banks?
Did they imagine drowning near a beach like this?

What did they hope the crew could do?
Grandmother docked in Norfolk the winter
this British ship foundered and beached, broke up
in pounding surf. Boats went out from Hatteras

but found only boxes and a corpse. Now,
in scuba gear, we flip our feet like dolphins
that waver about, escorts, no sharks today,
no sharks. The planks are gone, the portholes

Cornish eyes looked through until sea water
forced them shut. They're down here in the silt.
Zebra fish swim slowly through the hull
like guards with fancy stripes, wide-eyed

as if to say "Don't touch." The bottom shifts, drifts up
and covers bolts we touched. We try to imagine
the last battered hours, each desperate child,
but the surf still hides this massive iron in silt.

[Previously published in *All Occasions* (Notre Dame, IN: University of Notre Dame Press, 2000).]

Look at That, There's Shorty!

How many elk and deer roam down to crop
the leaves we water in drought, to lick salt blocks
we haul from town and scatter? We chart all elk
we see, even bulls with bad reputations, awkward
in collars park rangers strapped around stiff necks,

antlers sawed off. Those go with the herd like wethers,
marked by dollops of paint. Some years, a deer
comes bleeding, ears gnawed off by coyotes
bold as bears that tourists with cameras hunt.
Our children named all babies in the herd. In fall,

bulls learning to bugle bluff their way to rut.
Pictures help us say, "Look at that, there's Shorty–
a rack of antlers taller than his pa's." They strut
downtown, stalling traffic, a glut of elk and offspring.
Not even grain we plant could save them, not rain

nor trees they break by crushing down our fence.
We wouldn't want them pitiful and tame. We clean up
gladly after elk each year, knowing they'll leave,
never nod their racks as if thankful, slow
and clumsy in our garden, graceful on the hills.

[Previously published in *New Letters* 63, no. 4 (1997): 86 and *Blessings the Body Gave* (Columbus: The Ohio State University Press, 1998–winner of the 1997 Ohio State University Press *The Journal* Award in Poetry).]

With Mercy for All

She was a mystery of give and take,
laid open to strangers and neighbors in need,
no thought of lawsuits in those innocent days.
She took abuse from people she helped feed
in the Texas depression, who quarreled
and promised to pay her back, but frowned
and walked away when they saw her

after church. Our mother never doubted
evil was merely need in neighbors.
She carried fables with her to the grave,
although she saw her father pistol-whipped
for giving a man a ride in winter.
A thousand nights she sat with the aged,
the sick and the dying. At thirty-eight,

she ran bare footed to save a child,
jerking him up from the screaming mother,
pumping the marble out. Then collapsed in the briars
coming back, had to be helped home by others.
My sister tweezered sixty stickers from her feet.
Mother moaned how thankful she missed them
going over, though dozens stuck to her feet

when she ran to that baby on adrenaline
and faith. She never fathomed how pluck happened
throughout her life, how fast it left her
lovely and flushed, trembling with a funeral fan
in her hand, a comely woman, mother, nurse,
who believed herself simple, submissive, afraid,
not knowing how able she was, how recklessly brave.

[Previously published in *Buffalo Spree* magazine 32, no. 3 (1998): 55 and *Blessings the Body Gave* (Columbus: The Ohio State University Press, 1998–winner of the 1997 Ohio State University Press *The Journal* Award in Poetry).]

A Glimpse of Silver

I bounced like a ball
on swept wings bending
and bucking. I believed in dials
and gyros, and ignored vertigo
that swore I was falling.

Boots firm on the rudders,
I rode the rotors
through valleys of lightning,
trusting the ratio of stress,
the azimuth of fire.

Slamming through downdrafts,
I broke into sunlight, on course
and almost home. Boys playing ball
may have glanced at a roar
far above, heads back and scanning.

Old men who had seen it all
maybe stared, hands raised,
watching for whatever's there,
stunned by a glimpse of silver
beyond sound.

[Previously published in *All Occasions* (Notre Dame, IN: University of Notre Dame Press, 2000).]

Survival Training

You be a red fox in Rocky Mountain Park,
blackberries by every cave. I'll be the puma
cleaning his claws on a stump. Beware:
black bears roam the tundra. Rottweilers
and Pit Bulls might be allowed, if leashed.

Set free, they'd sniff a frenzy of fox scent
and dash madly from their masters' cars,
whining, brash as blood hounds. Let dogs
bark themselves hoarse alone or in pairs,
let them scramble up rocks, let them come.

Beware mean-hearted bear with cubs.
If slobbering she comes, all fur, foul-breath
and appetite, squeeze through a slit in the cave.
Never trust grizzlies, wolf packs, or wardens
who lock themselves inside at night.

After dark, remember what's here, snakes
dotting the landscape. If whine or yard-dogs'
yapping drifts here while you rest, be ready
to run, be swift. That silence you hear between
barks might be me, crushed by a landslide

or poachers' steel-tipped arrows in my back.
If dogs run silently in packs, you be the fox,
nimble and quick. Be badger, be puma like me
with dagger claws, leap, climb any tree.
If a hawk or eagle dives, you be the wind.

[Previously published in *The Gettysburg Review* 11, no. 3 (1998): 491–92 and *Blessings the Body Gave* (Columbus: The Ohio State University Press, 1998—winner of the 1997 Ohio State University Press *The Journal* Award in Poetry).]

Blocks Grandfather Carved

Hawk or grizzly's head appeared
in Grandfather's oak. Every slice,
every plane of the wood clamped tightly
in the vise might be his last. And so
old knuckles big as walnuts made a fist

that trembled, pain I never understood
till lately, when I bend to pick a grandchild up.
One day I watched him hold the blade
and wait until the tremor stopped, then strop
the sharp steel deep enough in oak to cut a jaw.

I saw the bear's jaw drop, and fangs grew
out of wood, the muzzle dished, a grizzly.
I saw the ears perk up to listen. It sits high
on the mantel now, without eyes, the grain
along the lips rough-cut, unfinished.

I tried to ease Grandfather down, a sack
of bones already gone before I could run
to find my father sipping coffee
on the porch with Mamaw leaning
forward in her rocker when I called.

[Previously published in *JAMA: The Journal of the American Medical Association* 284, no. 19 (2000): 2424 and *Climbing the Divide* (Notre Dame, IN: University of Notre Dame Press, 2003).]

Growing Up by the Brazos

In caves hacked out by tomahawks
we traded knives and arrowheads,
pieces of pottery and bones.
That deep in the country

no teachers prowled, no little brothers
tagging along and crying after dark.
White caliche crumbled when we dug.
We swatted cobwebs, hoping for gold

buried by tribes a thousand years ago,
shovels of nuggets inches away. Now,
nothing tumbles down this canyon
but scorpions and coyotes

starving for the moon. Years
before diggers uncovered skulls
of buffalos and wolves, we believed
this canyon on the plains hid ghosts.

Huddled around fires, spitting
bitter tobacco, we held up bones
and argued what they were, coyote
or human. We told the old lies

faithfully after dark—the one
about the maiden nobody found,
the ghost looking for his bloody arm,
the slaughtered wagon train.

Tatters of cobwebs and ghosts
clung to us all night long,
sockets of dry skulls hollow
and wild tongues strangely close.

[Previously published in *The New Criterion* 8, no. 9 (1990): 44 and *All Occasions* (Notre Dame, IN: University of Notre Dame Press, 2000).]

For All Friends Missing in Action

In cram sessions after midnight at the bar,
we practiced crashing, emergencies we drilled
until we bragged we could fly blindfolded,

stumbling on steps of the barracks. We turned
unnatural acts around in our minds, spins
and loops we would have to fly perfect, alone.

Out of bachelor bunks, out of accident reports
and training films, we swaggered to the flight line,
living on flames in the belly of jets, ten thousand

pounds of thrust. Wings and three good friends
sustained us, men we would die for, table mates
straining to take the instructor pilot's brain

and luck and make them ours, aping his stride,
the cock of his flight cap. No coach ever drove us
like our brash instructor pilot, almost a god,

a man with wings and battle ribbons and touch
on controls we envied. One by one he launched us
solo at night. My turn, I taxied out without his breath

in my headset—exciting silence, the runway
speeding faster and falling away, the full moon
floating up from Savannah, the force in my hand

massive, banking out of traffic with nothing
but my own two fists to guide me, climbing
in baffling darkness into the wonder of stars.

[Previously published in *Connecticut River Review* 19 (1998): 7 and *All Occasions* (Notre Dame, IN: University of Notre Dame Press, 2000.]

Before Flying Off to War

Before war, practice alms. Diplomas, awards
in fancy frames, anything with your name engraved,
give up. Take trophies to kids on the street
too skinny to win. Give away your coat,

both coats. Stock the pantry for your wife,
but haul your tools to a school, slum-side of town,
let them pick crowbars and hammers, drills, your awl,
your favorite cross saw. Donate your second car

to the Salvation Army, the March of Dimes–
it doesn't matter, and give them snow tires
you saved for a dazzling trip to Alaska.
Throw in the pup tent, your Boy Scout badges,

Grandfather's elk heads in the attic.
Give all black Bibles away but one. No,
hold nothing back. Even Saigon has chaplains.
Give up your wife, both children. Silently say goodbye

to Mother, Father far away. Haul out the trunk
and dump whatever's left. Drag it outside.
A truck from the Foundation for the Blind
comes by on Fridays. By Friday, you'll be gone.

[Previously published in *Christianity and Literature* 49, no. 2 (2000): 188 and *Climbing the Divide* (Notre Dame, IN: University of Notre Dame Press, 2003).]

Voices on Jukebox Wax

Pulling our Stetsons low, we whispered songs
to sweethearts who clung so close we danced
in slow motion, musky as steel guitars, vows
we swore with our bones. Their hair was the air
for an hour. We breathed and held them close,
ignoring the war for the night, old voices
on jukebox wax winding around like a rope.
One week we kissed them long and rode off,

swearing we'd bring back souvenirs and silk.
Long after a war no one we cared for survived
without scars, Earl and I are back with wives
as old as country songs and steel guitars,
our children older than all of us were that fall.
Don and Roy and Gary are names on a wall
in Washington. I hear their names sometimes
in talk at class reunions. I haven't heard from Carl.

[Previously published in *The Ohio Review* 56 (1997): 103 and *Blessings the Body Gave* (Columbus: The Ohio State University Press, 1998—winner of the 1997 Ohio State University Press *The Journal* Award in Poetry).]

Spitfire

The first week the prop leaked oil, old engine
grimy no matter how much I scrubbed, down
on my knees or flat on my back, jabbing at cracks
with rags. I flunked basic high school mechanics,
but flew jets all week, then tinkered with the relic,

the Battle of Britain also almost forgotten.
For months I pumped iron, jerking at bolts
frozen by rust, not budging. I inched my wrench
into slits by the magneto, tugging at nuts
that wouldn't budge. They loosened by luck

like seams giving up their gold to only the rude,
the desperate. I'd break my knuckles to make
that Spitfire fly, built the year I was born,
burned out, most canopy rivets cracked.
When my bride took a knife and sliced the cake

with my hand over hers, my nails were swarthy
no matter how much I scrubbed. For months
she came back from town and found me mad
and grimy in the garage, buffing, scrubbing
valves, inserting scarce parts that came by mail.

And then the children, the playpen, boxes
of toys and rocker horses swiftly abandoned,
stacked in the attic. I came back from Saigon
to hold my wife, each child. Nights, I tuned
the engine in the family wagon with the cracked

windshield, drove children to practice, fixed
broken toys and built a picket fence. Old friends
kept dropping by, most back from Vietnam
with medals, testing the Spitfire's metal,
thumping the tires and fondling the prop,

the fuselage. One day, down on my knees
for clues, Carl came with his checkbook
and truck, and when he left, the Spitfire
followed like a colt with front legs bound,
dragged down the winding mountain road.

[Previously published in *The Sewanee Review* 104, no. 1 (1996): 38–39 and *Blessings the Body Gave* (Columbus: The Ohio State University Press, 1998–winner of the 1997 Ohio State University Press *The Journal* Award in Poetry).]

After Thousands of Miles

Can that hummingbird
that slammed against the glass
believe invisible facts?

Does he wobble off
embarrassed and wary,
or dazed? After thousands of miles

on the flyway, through gusts
and over clouds, through rain,
he hit the glass storm door

like flying blind.
If his beak's not bent,
can he ever let it lead him

full speed to nectar,
to yellow gold of blooms?
Is God in the clear, after all,

not beyond, not hidden in clouds
I've stared at, but here
in my heart where I rise

like a blind man leaping
and shouting "Look!"
crying "look, I can see!"

[Previously published in *The Christian Century* 117, no. 1 (2000): 18 and *All Occasions* (Notre Dame, IN: University of Notre Dame Press, 2000.]

I Still Can't Say the Word

Sit still, if you must, and breathe.
Breathe in and let it out. Again. See how
the seconds crawl. Mumble the word you fear.
Or scream, yes, scream, beat wood, dump

the flowers. Break tables if you must. But not
your fist. All right, then, your fist. If it breaks,
it breaks. No one can hold her breath like this
or beat a table like a metronome. Today

is almost dark, tomorrow will be gone.
We'll look back Saturday and call each day
"Tomorrow." Curse cars and alcohol,
damn all drunk drivers, shriek or scream.

I'll never blame, no matter what you do.
Guns can't bring him back. I'd take a gun
and pistol-whip that killer's face to jam,
I'd break his bones and bash his marrow

like siphoning raw gas, and spit the platelets
out, if that would save you pain. I'd skin him
like a deer and stitch it like a shield, if that
would bring back our boy, I'd leap

into the fire myself, if our son could live.
I've said it and meant it, but it's only talk.
The facts are we're in bed, like this
together, grieving, and our son is gone.

[Previously published in *Alaska Quarterly Review* 16, nos. 3, 4 (1998): 236 and *All Occasions* (Notre Dame, IN: University of Notre Dame Press, 2000.]

Uncle Charlie at the Abbey

Uncle Charlie bragged about London smog
dark as the guts of frogs and pond scum,
wherever coal burned. He strolled foggy Oxford
as a Rhodes Scholar, sailed back years later
as a captain in World War Two, England
a troop ship docked at the Channel for D-Day.

Welshmen had dug, had dug, and the green earth
coughed, dark as a smoker's lungs. Now, we choke
on diesel as buses roar and Mercedes swerve,
as if Germany won the war after all. For decades,
workers blasted grime from relics of the coal age,
marble like ex-smokers whose lungs have cleared.

Westminster's clean, even inside where kings rest
under stones and names of soldier-poets are etched.
Uncle Charlie works the ranch in Texas, no nightmares
I know about, both aluminum legs scrubbed daily.
They shift beneath his Levi's like Mercedes gears.
I remember his fists, how he could lean and lift

a bawling calf to his saddle, his jaw muscles grinding,
about to burst. Charlie never married after Aunt Daphne died,
war bride he sent to Texas before his hospital ship
sailed home. London may still be dark and smoggy
in his mind. He keeps his fences tight and rides the range
for strays, tapping the reins to his gelding.

Their ranch was never foggy, not loud like muggy London.
He and Aunt Daphne let me ride on the ranch,
a summer nephew they taught to rope. I rocked on their porch
at dusk, heard them mumble what I knew was love,
far from Piccadilly and the Thames, waiting for night
and coyotes, a thousand miles of stars.

[Previously published in *Dakota House Journal* 4 (Winter 2001/2002).]

The Risk of Having Children

A nurse works here all night,
but I'm up now, hours before dawn,
close to our grandchild, who cries
and tries to turn. Deer on the lawn
graze quietly. Soon, they'll be gone
across the meadow, as if they might

have been only shadows I believed
were deer. At five, another nurse will
come, tuck in the sheet
and stare, and take her pulse.
Our daughter-in-law will stir,
rise to her elbows to see,

lie back and try to sleep.
Our son is home, drained from his watch,
near the phone, falling asleep,
I hope. If only the pain would stop
when she's awake, the cancer stop,
the clocks jump forward

to news some smocked researcher
shouts with joy on the Internet.
Near my elbow, my computer
waits, the blue screen ready,
the cursor blinking, steady
as monitors in intensive care.

In the dark, I start the coffee,
time for my watch at the hospital.
Sipping, I glance out at the red light
steady on the fresh-brewed pot.
My wife wakes, drawn by the hot aroma,
the hope and coffee of another dawn.

[Previously published in *JAMA: The Journal of the American Medical Association* 280, no. 10 (1998): 864 and *All Occasions* (Notre Dame, IN: University of Notre Dame Press, 2000.]

Sympathy

My wife fattened scrapbooks with facts
of somebody's baby or death or wedding
whose parents made West Texas home—

classmates, aunts or daughters of friends.
"She knows them all," I marveled,
watching her read. With blunt steel shears

she snipped obituaries, clippings she sent
in sympathy cards or saved or took with cakes
or casseroles. She scanned the news like rosaries

or puzzles, and sighed or shook her head.
My wife recycled pounds of paper, columns
and dates cut out, the pages dangling. She knew

that puzzles are only puzzles, that wisdom
is different from facts, that even wisdom
can't save us. Our bookshelves sag.

A dozen horses died to make the glue
it took to stick the dead and married in,
a random history of people she met some time

and loved or heard of, all names important to her,
worth keeping track of, even on pulp that yellows
and fades, she knew, even as she clipped.

[Previously published in *JAMA: The Journal of the American Medical Association* 278, no. 21 (1997): 1720 and *Blessings the Body Gave* (Columbus: The Ohio State University Press, 1998—winner of the 1997 Ohio State University Press *The Journal* Award in Poetry).]

Jogging at Sundown

Jogging means time leaps forward
an hour, and dusk begins.
Fast spins the minute hand,

a wheel of chance, and what it brings
nobody knows, or when it stops. God,
who melts the snow without a clock,

whose rocks and boulders
tumble down ravines, have mercy
on grandbabies, on us all,

for we are brief as vapors,
bone built, soap-bubble bodies,
and you are Master mild as snow

but full of force as winter falls,
massive, patient as glaciers,
and Father strong and fond.

[Previously published in *Great Lonely Places of the Texas Plains* (Lubbock: Texas Tech University Press, 2003) and *Faith Is a Radical Master: New and Selected Poems* (Abilene, TX: Abilene Christian University Press, 2005).]

Backpacking the San Juan

On a blue spruce mountain
across a mile of meadow,
a flash of light
in the treeline—field glasses,
or gunfire.

I lift my glasses.
A thousand one,
a thousand two. A deer
darts through a clearing

and sound whines past me
like a bullet. Suddenly
I'm a mile away
crashing through branches,
each bounding leap my last.

Previously published in *After the Noise of Saigon* (Amherst: University of Massachusetts Press, 1988—winner of the 1987 University of Massachusetts Press Juniper Prize) and *Seneca Review* 14, no. 1.

Reading "Ecclesiastes" at Sixty

My great-greats came to Texas plains
maybe on a dare, hair sticking wildly out
of old men's ears and grannies' bonnets,
prairies so wide no one would hear

if they hollered. They hummed gospel songs
anyway, shoring up dugouts to sleep in.
Their horses were lean and hard jawed,
crunching buffalo grass and dreaming.

Too young to marry, my grandmother
fanned her dying brother in a wagon's shade.
I hear the "swish, swish" of the songbook,
hymnal her family packed down from Ohio.

Her daddy believed God was plain as prairies
after Eden. Settlers had lakes to bathe,
to dunk their children, each playa lake
a natural baptistery, a tank for their cattle.

Granddaddy broke mustangs around the town,
broke both his legs, and the hearts of all three
Johnson girls when he courted Cora Graves.
Wolves killed the sheep that winter,

and two babies died. When dust storms howled
in March, families huddled under gusts
for days, choking, cursing when they heard
their windmills and privies flattened.

When the wind stopped, eight families left,
covered wagons tattered, cattle tethered
and scared. Cora Graves's family stayed,
and so Granddaddy stayed.

[Previously published in *All Occasions* (Notre Dame, IN: University of Notre Dame Press, 2000).]

Watching Parades in the Game Room

We didn't know we'd find them in the cemetery,
hobbling arm in arm to the bus stop. We almost call,
although we saw them at noon, watching parades
on TV in the game room. Caretakers have dredged

the last grave of the day, ridden back to the barn
and gone home. By now, they've washed their arms
and brows, sat down to beans and cornbread,
or maybe steak. Soon, my wife's Mom and Dad

will enter the hall of the rest home. She'll help remove
his overcoat, gently, and lead him slowly to his room.
She'll hang his hat and ease him into bed. He'll frown,
as if trying to decide "who is that woman, how long

till supper?" She'll smooth his thin, white wisps of hair
into place, part them with fingertips and kiss him.
After supper, after hours of TV, she'll wave goodnight
and hug her coat and scarf down the hall to her room,
close enough to hear him, if he calls.

[Previously published in *Image* 14 (1996): 41 and *All Occasions* (Notre Dame, IN: University of Notre Dame Press, 2000).]

Living on Buried Water

This chalk dirt yields sweet onions,
beans, red peppers that make us weep.
Two times a year it rains, run-off
that tumbles stones down arroyos.

Witching with sycamore twigs,
we stalk dry acres for springs
to soak caliche. It never works,
though we've heard rumors.

Flat as a desert, studded with cactus,
hardscrabble farms never need fencing.
Cliffs slough off each year
down canyons. We plant curved rows

and call it home. Our pets are coyotes
that sleep in the sun. The only snakes
are rattlers. Horned owls patrol the night
and stare with dark eyes over us.

We hear the mice they kill. Hawks
glide on thermals that shimmer like lakes
in another state. Each time a hawk
dives and scoops a rabbit, we take

two sticks and jog there, witching.
Sometimes a twig drags down to water
and we risk digging. We haven't found it,
but we believe it's here.

[Previously published in *Southwest Review* 72.2 (1987): 237 and *After the Noise of Saigon* (Amherst: University of Massachusetts Press, 1988—winner of the 1987 University of Massachusetts Press Juniper Prize).]

Flood Fishing

Upriver, hens keep tumbling in like lemmings.
Fences flooded by spring rain set them free
to peck worms slithering to the river, luring hens
to banks that crumble. At night, white hens
float by like chunks of ice. All night we could cast

and cast and never get a bite. Flood brings
what fish want, no luck dangling our lines
along the bottom. Crappie and bass are feasting
deep on the runoff of worms. Night fog coils,
searching across for strays. The woods are still

on haunted nights, but alligator gars thick as arms
reach up and strike, the white hens splashing,
sinking before our eyes, the gars' broad tails
slapping, the hens flap-flapping, dark trees
on both banks listening, the thick fog moving on.

[Previously published in *Southern Poetry Review* 23, no. 2 (1983) and *After the Noise of Saigon* (Amherst: University of Massachusetts Press, 1988—winner of the 1987 University of Massachusetts Press Juniper Prize).]

Old Men Fishing at Brownwood

Spitting tobacco juice on hooks,
we skewer silver minnows that writhe
in the light of the moon, lining our boat

with big bass fighting for the line
in the shallows, the home of moccasins,
deep mud of the turtles. Our flat jon boat

wallows, bumps over stumps, and stalls.
Slowly, slapping mosquitoes, we pole it
off and glide in moonlight like scarecrows.

What we desire winnows the dark under logs
flooded for decades, in tunnels of reeds,
deep pools in the shallows. We believe

we'll hook what we need when we find it,
though it often takes weeks on still waters.
We're too old to turn back, to settle

for perch in the daylight, willing to risk
pneumonia or stroke for a catch any night,
even the hiss of fangs for a strike.

[Previously published in *The Missouri Review* 9, no. 3 (1986): 226 and *After the Noise of Saigon* (Amherst: University of Massachusetts Press, 1988–winner of the 1987 University of Massachusetts Press Juniper Prize).]

Night Missions

Tonight will be like any other.
At two or three the phone will ring
soon as I've drawn the first good hand.

I'll spread the cards face-up,
knowing solitaire won't peek. Pecos,
Abilene, it could be anywhere

south of Denver, someone burned
or skull crushed in a fall,
needing a surgeon in the west

who could put him together again.
I fire up the engine, propeller
spinning so smooth

the Cessna shudders. In the red glow
of the cockpit, I run the checklist
and find all gauges in the green, flip on

collision lights and release the brakes
and taxi out. Turning onto the runway,
I firewall the throttle and line up

on the roll. Airborne, I clip moonlight,
tuned blades humming like mercy,
wings climbing for somebody's child.

[Previously published in *After the Noise of Saigon* (Amherst: University of Massachusetts Press, 1988—winner of the 1987 University of Massachusetts Press Juniper Prize).]

Nothing to Do but Start Over

Bury the milk, and let the trucks be idle.
Even heating vats can't cure this virus
killing all we own. We feed doomed cows
their last crushed grain and lead them faithful
to slaughter, tossing their Holstein heads,

eyes wide and asking Why, it's almost dark
and all of us came home, as always. It's sleep,
not dogs, sick cattle need, not knowing
they're condemned. The health inspector
is home, not watching this. He knows

we'll lead a parade past the last still water
in the tank, out to the pasture grazed down
and dying. We go, four sober men
on horses behind them, silent as the dogs
nipping their hoofs, but not barking,

knowing something's wrong. All day,
a Caterpillar tractor dug and snorted,
heaping a mountain we hired, odd
on dry plains flat enough to last forever,
never enough rain for runoff. It's parked,

now, yellow and square, the concave blade
dull gray. Soil scooped from that deep down
is white caliche, silver in moonlight.
We couldn't do this at noon. The excavated
ditch is wide, a coliseum, and slopes

so gently the cows believe it's safe,
and enter, wearing their bells, tolling
step by heavy step, muffled, going down.
We count them, easy to count, they stand
so still down there in fresh-dug dirt

of a silo, as if waiting to be milked.
White eyes and gentle faces give them away,
but something's almost crazed about them,
the way they wait without appeal
under a quarter moon. Only the labored breath

and trembling of one sick cow
keeps ringing her bell, no closer to death
than the others. There's nothing, nothing to do
but dismount, rifles already in our hands,
take in our breaths and let them out, and aim.

[Previously published in *The Windsor Review* (Canada) 20, no. 1 (1987): 83 and *After the Noise of Saigon* (Amherst: University of Massachusetts Press, 1988—winner of the 1987 University of Massachusetts Press Juniper Prize).]

A Fed Bear Is a Dead Bear

Bears waddle off, glancing back
at tourists who ignore signs posted
on every road—"Don't feed the bears."
"If bears come by, stay in your cars."
Feed bears today, park rangers warn,
we'll have to kill them, tomorrow,

spoiled by the easy treats of tourists,
and hungry. Any hour, let sightseers
glimpse a bear in bushes by the road—
holding his toes and swaying on his butt
to beg, or munching huckleberries—
there's gridlock, cars for a hundred yards

stopped at all angles on the asphalt,
drivers with cameras and snacks hopping out,
flagging down on-coming cars, *Look,*
look. Sometimes, though, a grizzly turns,
stares down hard at scraps and biscuits
pitched, and bows her massive back.

[Previously published in *Appalachia* 54, no. 3 (2003): 45 and *Climbing the Divide* (Notre Dame, IN: University of Notre Dame Press, 2003).]

Fog on the Outer Banks

Fog rocks us almost to sleep,
waves roll and wash the beach at dawn.
Holding hot coffee on the deck, we rock
and watch our breath make smoke that drifts

and disappears in mist so dense
we listen for foghorns in the harbor.
My wife drags her moccasins
to stop us, leans out and listens

to the hissing beach. No one seems up
but us, and we're too numb to stroll.
Let snails and starfish crawl,
let jellyfish float up in foam,

conchs and shark pods beached
for the picking. Today at the beach
there's nothing to see but fog-shifting
shapes, so we don't focus,

mystery enough to rock and watch it
turning our eyelids clammy as cobwebs,
damp enough to shiver, coffee
already cool although our full cups slosh.

[Previously published in *Trouvère: A Literary Review* 1 (2001): 102 and *Climbing the Divide* (Notre Dame, IN: University of Notre Dame Press, 2003).]

Twins and Oral History

> "If you think ground squirrels are fun,
> wait till you see a coyote."

I'd never say that to grandsons, but even coyotes
have to eat. So what do I say at their taped
school project tomorrow? What dreamy teacher
makes historians of kids in the second grade?

With a flourish of her tongue and Xeroxed lists
of questions, she'll flick me back to Saigon
or Da Nang, memories static as paper weights,
saying, "What did you do in the war, Grandpa?"

Shake me with cassette tapes and watch snow flurries swirl.
What do I say about native kids their age?
They were hungry but cute, slit eyes and tangled hair.
"Did they play?" Yes, they played "Hide and Seek,"

and ran a lot. No, they didn't have Santa Claus,
but Halloween was all year long. The tarmac track
at Saigon where I jogged was hot. Yes, I sunburned,
and others, most younger in jogging shorts or boots

and tennis shoes. No, I killed nobody at the track.
Yes, some jogged in the jungle with back packs
and rifles. No, boys, I never saw tigers eat people
on the battlefield, but if your teacher's daddy says so,

I guess they did. No, I don't have guns to show you,
no enemy's teeth or dried ears in my duffle bag.
Have I been back to Vietnam? Do I have nightmares, still?
[What's next on this teacher's list? "Have you stopped

beating Grandma?"] It was long ago, and kids,
you know what happens when you sleep.
We never know what might trot by inside our minds—
a friend from school who moved away you thought

you'd never see again, a horse in a Disney show,
a dog gnawing a bone. But that's enough. Come, hug
me, both of you, then race me to the swing set
before your mother calls us to wash up.

[Previously published in *The Missouri Review* 20, no. 3 (1997): 52 and *Blessings the Body Gave* (Columbus: The Ohio State University Press, 1998—winner of the 1997 Ohio State University Press *The Journal* Award in Poetry).]

How It's Done

Lazy deer bend down black snouts
to grass. Dawn was hours ago, and now,
like dominoes, the does fold
knobby toothpick legs to lie on slopes

we would tumble down. Snow flickers past,
no sounds, not even birds. From the back,
we watch the deer a hundred yards uphill,
and sip. Before the coffee's chilled,

one by one the does sprout legs
and rise. They arch their backs and stretch.
White tails flag rapidly twice—no danger,
yet, no scent they can't ignore, no hunger

they can't take with them as they twist
and wander off, nibbling this blade, this,
and that one, bowing to bare
slopes farther on, whatever's there.

[Previously published in *The Formalist* 8, no. 2 (1997): 81 and *Blessings the Body Gave* (Columbus: The Ohio State University Press, 1998—winner of the 1997 Ohio State University Press *The Journal* Award in Poetry).]

Anniversary: One Fine Day

Who would sit through a plot as preposterous as ours,
married after months apart? Chance meetings happen
early in stories, but at operas, darling, in Texas?

A bachelor pilot, I fled Laredo for the weekend,
stopping at the opera from boredom, songs I least expected.
Of all the zoos and honky-tonks south of Dallas,

who would believe I would find you there on the stairs,
Madame Butterfly about to start? When you said "no"
a year before, I lost all hope of dying happy,

dogfighting my way through pilot training, reckless,
in terror only when I saw the man beside you.
I had pictured him rich and splendid in my mind

a thousand times, thinking you married with babies
somewhere in Tahiti, Spain, the south of France.
When I saw the lucky devil I hated—only your date,

but I didn't know—he stopped gloating, watching you wave,
turned old and bitter like the crone in *Shangri La*.
They say fate happens only in plays and cheap movies,

but decades later, still on my finger is your ring,
and I hear songs from another room of our home,
and when I rise amazed and follow, you are here.

[Previously published in *The American Scholar* (Phi Beta Kappa magazine) 65, no. 3 (1996): 416 and *Blessings the Body Gave* (Columbus: The Ohio State University Press, 1998—winner of the 1997 Ohio State University Press *The Journal* Award in Poetry).]

The Fox All Winter Long

How cautiously it's done,
crouch with one paw tucked,
and pounce. The fox
eats the field mouse

with its teeth bared,
fast little bites
as if it's bitter,
the mouse tail stiff,

flicking like a toothpick.
Swallows, looks around
like a schoolboy finding a dime,
trots on, hoping

to find more coins,
a hole in some boy's pocket.
The fox all winter listens
with one ear to the wind, hops

on the slightest sound,
burrows down toward fast
tiny feet, cold grass
no match for a fox

that survives mountain lions,
sometimes even eagles
that can hear fox paws
pounce and pounce.

[Previously published in *Pembroke Magazine* 30 (1998): 221 and *Blessings the Body Gave* (Columbus: The Ohio State University Press, 1998–winner of the 1997 Ohio State University Press *The Journal* Award in Poetry).]

Grandfather's Pocket Watch

Sequoias can't tell time until they're dead.
Cut down, they tell their age, confessions at the stake
before they burn. Counting rings, we marvel,
knocking on hardwood. We stack fresh cords
of oak against the barn, but find logs dark

next fall, the slow inferno of decay. I thought
this hardwood deck Grandfather built would last.
I handed nails across, watched his big arm
pound the hammer down. Nothing stops the rot,
not even caulk. New planks I've fitted in

are flat, mismatched, patchwork of boards
that splinter, have to be ripped for firewood or trash.
Grandfather got this watch for forty years' hard work–
a handshake from his boss, a watch fob, and a plaque.
Retired, he took it out sometimes and stared at it

and rocked. It dangles by a chain above my desk,
the monotony of "tock-tick-tock" hypnotic.
I miss his big-boned callused fists,
the way he wound the stem till it was tight,
the way he held it to our children's ears.

[Previously published in *College English* 57, no. 7 (1995): 840 and *Blessings the Body Gave* (Columbus: The Ohio State University Press, 1998–winner of the 1997 Ohio State University Press *The Journal* Award in Poetry).]

Catching My Grandson

"Oh, look," old Galileo whispered, "look, we move."
And burning, burning in the sky, the sun stood still.
Earth turned and spun and whirled about the ball,
but no one else believed. Not then. "Take time,"

my father called, watching our first adopted toddler fall,
push up and waddle to my lap. "It goes so fast."
Yeah, yeah, I thought, patting my daughter's goldilocks,
thumbing her tears away. I loved that chubby cherub

with the grape-juice grin, took turns changing Pampers,
scrubbing that kid in bubble baths, giving time
and horsey rides, a thousand tasks each day
before I slept. I confess, I doubted my old man.

What passes fast, I thought, was time enough to do
what must be done—another flight, reports overdue,
the grass I had to cut. The earth does turn,
no, spins. I crouch now, catching my grandson

firing the ball, the red seams spinning. He's older
than his mother was that night my father called,
when my knees could duckwalk a mile, my shoulders
and biceps bulged. "Ouch," I mutter, now,

a pain each time I lob the baseball back,
my right aim stiff, old shoulder bony,
the slow ball wobbly, plopping in his glove.
Look how he burns it back, curve ball inside

I have to dive for, falling again for physics
faster than reflex, and I'm laughing on the ground,
my grandson laughing, pounding the ball
in his glove and staggering off the mound.

[Previously published in *First Things* 77 (1997): 31 and *Blessings the Body Gave* (Columbus: The Ohio State University Press, 1998—winner of the 1997 Ohio State University Press *The Journal* Award in Poetry).]

Alone in the Tundra

Marmots flop in the sun and scratch, face-down
on lichen plastered to rocks. Tundra is a jungle
of blooms and vines thin as an eyelash.

Here, the heart skips, mountain air too cold
for snakes. These tiny flowers sprouted
before Bunker Hill, in topsoil thin as skin.

Tundra grows under snow, releasing oxygen
one molecule a month. Spring is pastel
and bees—not bumblebees with heavy chests

in meadows miles below, but bees the size
of gnats that float and fumble the tundra's pollen,
bantam blossoms changing into seeds.

Buck-toothed marmots look up, no lack of flowers
to feed on. Now we're alone, out of breath
in the tundra, even giddy, and kneel like Gulliver

to watch exotic worlds, mauve and olive forests
no taller than our thumbs. We breathe
this aroma of ferns, fighting an impulse

to pick tiny vines intertwined like Velcro,
to taste the buds, these dots of blooms
so small we need a microscope to see.

[Previously published in *The Cresset* 61, no. 4 (1998): 17 and *Blessings the Body Gave* (Columbus: The Ohio State University Press, 1998—winner of the 1997 Ohio State University Press *The Journal* Award in Poetry).]

PTSD, or For Friends Who Never Left the Battle

They're back, the mad, back-scratching bullies.
I turn, shove up and sit. They vanish in chinks
and fissures of walls with almost audible noise.
Rockets no longer fall, no sweet gunpowder stink.
Saigon is gone, no longer its name. Our boys
asleep, no shouts or cartoons on TV.

And there, out there is the street we live on.
This is the floor my own feet touch, our phone
beside our bed. The joists are snug, the walls
and rafters. Our porch is pocked with holes,
the yard around the house. Men came with awls
and probed the wood and dirt, drilled holes

in the porch, trenched down into the grass
but found no signs of termites. They shot the gas
and sealed the plugs with hard epoxy,
like armor I put on. My demons find all cracks,
but wood is a roof for our children's dreams.
Some nights I close my eyes, and if they're back,

they're tame, wart-faced, snarling hardly at all,
watching me twisted on my side, slack-jawed
and mild, if that's how I look without dreams.
Those nights, it's up to sirens and trucks
to shove me out to the harbor, under the screams
of wheeling gulls, the clatter of barges

and stink of scows, love boats taking on wine
and diesel, peaceable kingdom of nighttime
without bats. Count on it, though, they need me
to stay awake, someone to torment with crimes
of flattery–swearing I deserve to see
unspeakable acts past corners of my mind,

to smell the bile and belly in their breath
puffed into the dark, to feel their bone-hooks
stretching my eyelids wide to watch them die,
to see what I did overseas, the fire I gave
and took–my demons damned on the mountain,
the holy bush still burning, and me, about to look.

[Previously published in *Blessings the Body Gave* (Columbus: The Ohio State University Press, 1998–winner of the 1997 Ohio State University Press *The Journal* Award in Poetry).]

Losing It Again in Bozeman

Once, in Bozeman, we saw trucks coming,
an Army convoy, a block of cars stopped
at the green light, state motorcycle cops

in boots and helmets looking back, revving,
ready to roar away. Then a flash of white
in the inside lane, old couple with faces cocked

so they could see. If they saw the cops,
they didn't believe, rolling past toward the light
at the legal speed. Ten thousand times

they'd stopped on red, but gone on through on green—
but not then, a blast of shattered glass and screams.
The truck hit like a boulder crashing through ice,

crushing the car like a beer can kicked,
tumbling and spinning. I saw steam, but did they die?
Maybe they weren't even rushed, taking their time

passing the last stalled car, hearing the click
of seams in the concrete, all of it orderly,
careful, believing in signs. I can't recall driving on,

not another block. What makes the mind go numb,
stumbling about in the dark? Files I want to retrieve
are locked, password denied. Trying to tap a nerve,

I think of Fred decades ago, flat on his face on the floor,
Montana hardwood holding him like a Tilt-a-Whirl,
the barkeep wiping his rag as if he'd served

a thousand drunks. Why Bozeman? College boys
from Texas, hoping for summer work in Yellowstone.
I see a campus near the town, I smell cologne

but can't see faces, just names, "Fauncine" and "Joy."
I don't know which I kissed, which one kneeled over
Fred, or left. I think that's how it happened, sudden

as a truck roaring with the right-of-way, or a drunk
in any town. I think I drove us back to Yellowstone,
but someone was lucky behind the wheel.

The jaws of life couldn't pry apart my mind,
that summer and that wreck. I think they died,
the flatbed loaded with tanks, the speed of steel

like a freight train. I remember a hubcap rolling
around and around like a roulette wheel,
like a hound whining, sniffing the street,

circling a turtle shut tight, the hubcap rolling
wire, wire wirewirewirewire like a wheel,
the last sound at the wreck, except steam.

[Previously published in *The American Scholar* (Phi Beta Kappa magazine) 67, no. 4 (1998): 62–63 and *Blessings the Body Gave* (Columbus: The Ohio State University Press, 1998–winner of the 1997 Ohio State University Press *The Journal* Award in Poetry).]

As Natural as Lions

A neighbor's cat ambles by, wetting our sand
casually, as natural as lions in the Kalahari
marking their range. That cat killed
a squirrel, sniffing to be sure it died.

We saw her drop it near the porch
in a heap of leaves, not really eating.
Later, I hauled it off, the dumpster loaded
with leaves, dust in the air, spring cleaning,

people sneezing when we jog to the park
and back, squirrels and cats everywhere,
the leash law only for dogs. Noon, the drowsy cat
saunters across the road toward home, yawns,

and leaps to the porch like a Baobab tree's
wide bough, lolls like a lion, eyes closed
with one paw dropped, tail flopping,

dreaming of the hunt, of a screaming
panting impala as jaws snatched the throat
for a better hold and squeezed.

[Previously published in *First Things* 82 (1998): 27 and *All Occasions* (Notre Dame, IN: University of Notre Dame Press, 2000.]

My Father Light as a Boy

Still shaves himself, electric, flat on his back,
chin up to tighten skin on bone. Done,
he holds the shaver on the bed, palm out

like an offering, silver and black and gold.
Decades ago, my dad could lift a man-thick log
and heave it over a fence, neck muscles bulging.

Now eighty-nine, he's Mother's size, but bald.
He lifts the razor like a crane, underpowered
for such a weight, thin fingers trembling

toward the tray. I shove up from the chair,
too late. He turns his palm to dump the razor.
And since I'm that close now, he cuts his eyes

at me, a sign he'd like to turn. I lift his bony
shoulders and begin to twist, reach down
and move the gaunt hips bruised from shots,

the knobby knees. He doesn't groan, won't say
a word, biting hard to swallow. I smooth
his parchment scalp and rub, I won't let go.

He's staring at the door, but no one's there.
I hear his stomach noise, his breath, his breath.
His eyelids blink, so sticky dry they pop.

[Previously published in *JAMA: The Journal of the American Medical Association* 286, no. 4 (2001): 390 and *Climbing the Divide* (Notre Dame, IN: University of Notre Dame Press, 2003).]

Old Men Are Dreamers

Old men are dreamers, plotting escape all day.
Nights, we're surrounded, millions of stars
that fall. We rise in the dark and feel our way
to chairs. At dawn after coffee, the strong
take walks in malls, or slowly past wives in parks,
and toddlers, past girls and boys on bikes, and dogs.

Walking, we argue, cases we seldom lose.
Hackles up like hawks, if we stumble, we refuse
all strangers' hands that lift us anyhow.
A hawk alone knows nothing it couldn't do,
gliding, soaring among thunderclouds,
scrawling its brief, bold name against the blue.

[Previously published in *JAMA: The Journal of the American Medical Association* 284, no. 13 (2000): 1625 and *Climbing the Divide* (Notre Dame, IN: University of Notre Dame Press, 2003).]

The Summer Uncle Carl's Herd Was Sold

Knuckles battered by bulls,
Uncle Carl locked the paddock
and leaped back, dusting his pants

with both gloves. Buzzards kissed
his calves goodbye when he rode off,
keeping watch on cattle in drought,

stray calves in valleys of coyotes.
My brother and I loved that bearded
old man, bow-legged and bald.

When we rode his colts
and stayed on, his growl was the praise
we worked for. When we fell,

his cigar bobbing smoke told us both
"No worry." One month,
when his gelding tumbled, only buzzards

soared to his rescue. We were in school,
a mile from that canyon. Calves
bawled and wandered off

from his broken back, no one to hear
Uncle Carl groan, or the rifle
he kept firing after his gelding died.

[Previously published in *Connecticut Review* 23, no. 2 (2001): 49 and *Climbing the Divide* (Notre Dame, IN: University of Notre Dame Press, 2003).]

Facing It

I suppose you turn on the horizon
expecting me, both of you on tiptoe,
others bumping past like pilgrims.
That time when I was five at the Royal Gorge
comes back to haunt me, wandering off
across that swaying bridge a thousand feet
over the fast, white-water Arkansas.

While my father checked the oil and water
and Mother spread sandwiches in the shade
and made my brothers help, I leaned
and spat at that deep drop-off,
watched the white foam arc and wobble
until gone. Cars chugged behind me, old cars
that would have to last four years more

during World War II. "Don't fall,"
some mother called, and I heard my mother
also calling "Walt, don't fall!"
from back on the canyon rim, helpless
as if afraid her weight might snap the cables
with me precarious and trapped.
Two decades later, I banked an Air Force jet

at 20,000′ and snapped the camera at that bridge
an inch long at arm's length, to show you
it was nothing. I held the wingtips vertical,
spiraled down to 500′ above the crowd,
nudged the throttle and climbed until the bridge
was an inch, a quarter inch. I hummed
and held 10,000 pounds of power

in my fist. I flew to Saigon a decade later
and came back to the scramble of surviving,
to children running and tumbling
over dangerous bridges I'd never crossed,
and to my aging father and mother almost gone,
the drawbridge rising while I stood helpless
and waving a hundred yards away.

[Previously published in *JAMA: The Journal of the American Medical Association* 282, no. 21: (1990): 396 and *All Occasions* (Notre Dame, IN: University of Notre Dame Press, 2000.]

Clouds Whip by in the Valley

Come feel sleet in your face,
see clouds whip by in the valley.
Crows beat wings and stagger for trees,
pines flapping like flagpoles.
Watch this elk calf bite a stiff

plastic blue tarp and flip it
from the sand pile. Watch her chomp
and toss it. Always it settles
like a flabby ghost. She thinks
it's covering weeds, green leaves,

forbidden grass. She bucks like a colt
and kicks, nipping the tarp. Fiercely
she shakes and flings, but it flutters
and falls around her hoofs.
Watch her twirl and quake, a tantrum,

and lower her hornless skull to jerk it
billowing again, spoiled teenager
tossing a bedspread, one corner tucked
at the footboard. Elk cows with winter fur
know grass from plastic, grazing stubble

like luck, aware of calves they carry
kicking, a pack of wolves upwind
a hundred yards uphill at dawn,
and somewhere higher up, watching,
a puma lying quietly behind rocks.

[Previously published in *Envoi* (UK) (1996), *English in Texas* 31, no. 1 (2001): 53, and *Climbing the Divide* (Notre Dame, IN: University of Notre Dame Press, 2003).]

Finding Great-Grandfather's Hands

My wife keeps hearth and kitchen clean, bills tallied,
and guests invited back. What's a great-grandfather for—
fists scarred and knuckles stiff, steers in our pastures

fat and horses saddled, but no sons home? We raised
four kids who married and moved away, and now
as a daddy I'm broke, no easy advice like cash

to wave around. I taught them to ride and rope, toss
loops and take sick cattle down, to brand and release
wild calves. The ranch made money in spite of drought

and hours without us, ball games and camping trips,
car wrecks and teenage rage, the highs and lows
of seasons that taught us to let go. Now, more toddlers

crawl from cars and waddle to our arms, in-laws
and grandchildren with babies they bring. I spend time
giving horsey rides, learning by crawling what to do,

any games they want to play, "Pawpaw" gladly
down on my knees and knuckles, great-grandbabies
giggling and hugging, what great-grandfathers are for.

[Previously published in *JAMA: The Journal of the American Medical Association* 285, no. 2 (2001): 142 and *Climbing the Divide* (Notre Dame, IN: University of Notre Dame Press, 2003).]

The First Months Home, PTSD

Not even twelve, but up, beside her in the bed,
watching shadows, the same moon haunted
by the hour. They're out there tonight like sappers.

By now, they've killed the horse. So much at night
is Vietnam. I can't keep it out, drapes drawn,
storm shutters tight. Our children sleep, well-fed

and glad their daddy's back. It's midnight in the bones.
They're out there, somewhere, flogging the horse
gone lame. They've come floating on skiffs

of eyelids they've ripped and stitched.
The kitchen floor blinks step by step. Door opened,
the light stays on. I take a bottle and softly

close the door. Closed, the fridge is dark. The clean,
sweet, bitter taste of hops makes time all right for now,
cold bottle sweaty to the touch. I count the hours

till daylight. Too much to do tomorrow not to sleep,
too much. I pour the beer in the sink and listen,
the sizzle of foam. By now, they've found the gate.

The motor whirs to keep the next beer cold.
Listen: is that the twang of barbed wires
in the yard, the creak of footsteps on the porch?

[Previously published in *Nightsun* 16 (1996): 17–18 and *Blessings the Body Gave* (Columbus: The Ohio State University Press, 1998—winner of the 1997 Ohio State University Press *The Journal* Award in Poetry).]

My Cousin and the VA Nurse

It isn't easy swinging dead legs,
but Roger does it, flinging that walker along,
clop clop, then shifting both stumps, a gallop
on aluminum sticks with rubber boots. Before
the war, he never walked when he could ride horses

or hike mountains, my cousin from Montana
who went Airborne before eighteen. Corporals
taught him to stalk and crawl through jungles
and kill, how to pause or play dead for hours,
then wiggle off like a moccasin through swamps.

Months later, nurses taught him to call
for help from a bed, to squeeze the toggle switch
and swing a wheelchair down the corridor
without landmines, to open doors, where Roger
slipped and fell one day down a ramp, and tumbled,

the battery dead, beating the floor until his knuckles bled
until one young nurse came rushing in a starched
white dress, dashing to him in a stunning, sun-lit garden,
white cap, even her shoes and stockings white, running
with arms out wide and calling his name, his name.

[Previously published in *Blessings the Body Gave* (Columbus: The Ohio State University Press, 1998–winner of the 1997 Ohio State University Press *The Journal* Award in Poetry).]

Grandchildren in the Maritime Museum

In a hall of coastal birds airborne on wires
in seaside, diorama skies,
our granddaughter watched them all,
believing those stuffed owls would wink,
their cartoon eyes soon blink.
Hands on her knees, she stared at possums

that held their breath, and natty,
stiff raccoons with bandit eyes.
Leaning, she waved at eagles and hawks
with rubber snakes clutched tight,
and painted pelicans that never dived.
At a roped-off marsh of splendid, pink flamingos,

our grandchild slowly raised one foot,
like one of the birds. She pursed her lips
to make a flamingo beak, balanced
like part of the flock on the edge of wonder.
This child of flat horizons on the plains
gazed at displays of mammals and birds

like Oz and Disneyworld, believing it all,
the backdrop spotlights bouncing gold
and rosy on her face, making her pink cheeks shine.
She heard a squeal of joy down the hall
and ran to the main aquarium,
tall panels where girls and boys

watched sea bass wide enough for saddles,
dolphins with silver-dollar eyes.
Schools of tuna glided past under tons
of aquarium ocean, even nurse sharks
harmless as dachshunds. Turtles
big as golf carts paddled by—

thousands of rays and reef fish
drifting, waving wide fins
at children giddy to see them all,
dashing from panel to panel,
shouting in whispers, "Look! Look!"
pressing their hands and noses to the glass.

[Previously published in *Climbing the Divide* (Notre Dame, IN: University of Notre Dame Press, 2003).]

Between Two Shores of Toledo

Swimming Toledo Bend one summer, we were afraid
of nothing but boats with drunk drivers. A mile from shore,
we felt like hitchhikers, motorboats like Porches stopping
to offer rides. Waving, treading water, we watched them

glance at each other and roar away, the wake of their motors
bobbing, swamping us in troughs between two shores
of Toledo. At last, far out on the lake, we rolled and rested.
The sun was white fire, bluffed between blinks squeezed

to see. I remember kisses at eye level, and fingers
nibbling my own like fish. We floated between shores
thousands of miles from our children at the ocean.
We heard the beach in our ears, the roar, that lovely roar.

Without a word, with a nudge a wave might have made,
we rolled and went on swimming, knowing we'd passed
the point of no return on a lake swarming with skiers.
Lifeguards shouted alligators keep to themselves

on shore, easy for them to say, atop platforms
twenty feet high. Tiring, we kept reaching through waves
that always looked the same, as if we were going
nowhere. We fought the urge to thumb down a boat

and let them drag us aboard. Giddy, glimpsing
each other gulping air, we kept crawling through water
for a shore we believed was worth it, and dozens of friends
splashed by, skiing with one hand and laughing.

[Previously published in *After the Noise of Saigon* (Amherst: University of Massachusetts Press, 1988–winner of the 1987 University of Massachusetts Press Juniper Prize).]

Flicking Its Tongue at the Sun

This far out in the country
pronghorns the size of fawns
tremble and stare,

dip down and graze
as they have done forever.
This range grows nothing but pale

yellow yucca and cactus and grass
like dried moss, almost green.
Hawks living on thermals glide

in summer skies so blank
they wheel without cover of clouds
for hours, waiting for mice

or rabbits to dart into sunlight. Lower,
slower, another is slithering,
flicking his tongue at the sun,

testing the prairie wind,
the wind like a god,
the wind always delivering.

[Previously published as "Balance" in *Southern Poetry Review* 27, no. 1 (1987): 10 and *After the Noise of Saigon* (Amherst: University of Massachusetts Press, 1988–winner of the 1987 University of Massachusetts Press Juniper Prize).]

Watching Rose Embers Wink

Now it begins, the soft ripple of sparks.
The final campfire flames are gone,
unless we breathe on embers. Shadows
of piñons flare and fall away. You whisper,
Will these coals live? Nothing that breathes
risks even this much light in a forest.

Today, we gave ourselves to simple tasks,
unfolding, the clang of steel-on-steel stakes
for the tent, finding sticks to build a fire
for water that boils without getting hot.
This high in mountains, air is scarce as friends.
Close in folding chairs, we watch rose embers

wink like mountain lions. Sparks fling
themselves and fade in the only air there is.
All those years to keep a roof for children,
grown now and gone faster than sparks. Now
we're back to one campfire at a time, deep
in the mountains. This heady air and stars

are our comfort, and a breeze that hovers over us
all night. We lie on eiderdown and hold each other.
Later, I wake and listen to sounds of eagle's wings
or owl's. Quick cry of a coyote rises nearby.
Nothing else for minutes, only your steady breathing,
asleep, believing nothing's out there that shouldn't be.

[Previously published in *The Ohio Journal* 11, no. 1 (1987): 10 and as "The Middle Years" in *After the Noise of Saigon* (Amherst: University of Massachusetts Press, 1988–winner of the 1987 University of Massachusetts Press Juniper Prize).]

After the Lost War

I buy my wife expensive vows that always start
"I promise." I've promised to stop grumbling
about the past, neglecting her like bets I wad
and toss away. She's borrowed enough

to bail me out a thousand times, in hock
to a mob of apologies with flat noses
and pin-striped suits with guns. She locks
my fists with hers and kisses my eyelids open

so I can see. I pledged to take a vow
of poverty of rage, be baptized in faith
that all drivers aren't dying to drag race,
that I don't have to stomp the gas and frown

to keep pickups with gun racks from passing.
I swore I'll stop planting fields of wormwood,
all bitter herbs I've grown, I'll sell the tractor
and talk about war no more. I promised.

[Previously published in *The Formalist* 7, no. 2 (1996): 16 and *Blessings the Body Gave* (Columbus: The Ohio State University Press, 1998—winner of the 1997 Ohio State University Press *The Journal* Award in Poetry).]

For God in My Sorrows

Now on the highway, the dwindling traffic,
a leaky faucet of lights after midnight.
I try to believe, the stars a billion witnesses
that I give myself to beyond, not even gravity

holding me back. Not stars always on fire, not fire,
that power that scattered them, that power.
I've seen a world on fire, from bunkers, each man
alone, hunkered down at night to survive the rockets.

Not fire, not the world that burns and bloodies us
in wars or car wrecks, hurtling out there even now
behind headlights, or on foot at noon, distracted,
crossing the road and crushed, like roadkill.

Night has answers I don't want, but when stars
collapse, after all that mass snuffs out like a match,
how much remains? Does dawn have answers
after all, night vision blinded by the light

that guided wise men? No, that's over, servant
of the source I yearn for. Astronomers call it
no star at all, scoffing. I believe as I know
my hand is inches away from my face in the dark,

my eyelids wide, hands cunningly made to grope
along a wall for a light switch. Magically, it's here.
This, this is what I need without city lights or stars,
not knowing, but simply believing I'm known.

[Previously published in *North Dakota Quarterly* 62, no. 4 (1994–1995): 95–96 and *Blessings the Body Gave* (Columbus: The Ohio State University Press, 1998—winner of the 1997 Ohio State University Press *The Journal* Award in Poetry).]

The Tongues of Sparrows

Under the threat of summer, trees
bring forth their fruit, here in a zone

so dry no trees grow native. The last
late killing frost was years ago.

We're overdue. Thousands of robins
dip down and believe it's spring,

listening to the tongues of sparrows
which seem to sing, bland little birds

that never go anywhere all winter,
and somehow survive.

[Previously published in *Images* 11, no. 3 (1986): 7 and *After the Noise of Saigon* (Amherst: University of Massachusetts Press, 1988—winner of the 1987 University of Massachusetts Press Juniper Prize).]

Traveling in Packs

A splash, and sharp teeth drag the wildebeest
down, off balance, thrashing in slippery mud,
jerked to the churning foam of its own blood feast,
into a rushing river swollen by the flood,

kicked by the hoofs of wild-eyed others leaping
and splashing, the beast still kicking for breath
but feebly, crippled by fear and the death grip,
one crocodile thrashing to snap its neck,

tail flip and fangs sunk deeply in the throat
going under, dragging it into the darkest water
this wildebeest ever crossed, legs limp, as if floating,
coughing its goat-like bark under water,

the hungry herd scrambling up to the plains,
traveling in packs in the food chain,
a thunder of splashing hoofs and groans
over the swirl of bodies already bloated,

the bubble eyes of beasts like uninvited guests
with scales and appetites and tails, slowly
nosing upstream, without hurry,
choosing which one, which one is next.

[Previously published in *New Texas* (1998): 229 and *Blessings the Body Gave* (Columbus: The Ohio State University Press, 1998–winner of the 1997 Ohio State University Press *The Journal* Award in Poetry).]

With Our Son's Bow at Dusk

I call, and hear thistles flick by.
Our son comes running with his bow,
empty quiver flouncing on his back.

Whatever he shot at in the arbor
he missed, maybe pears too green
to pick. The full moon bulges,

and next day's lessons wait.
Tomorrow we'll hunt the arrows,
and I'll say again don't shoot

unless you follow the feathers.
Tousle haired and eight, he hands me
the bow and skips away

and the back door slams. I almost call,
but I'm eight again myself
and lift the bow and aim, string taut

and tingling in my tips. I pretend
the arbor's dark, one shadow darker
and gobbling, one fat turkey I can't miss.

[Previously published in *Prairie Schooner* 75, no. 3 (2001, 75th anniversary issue): 81, and *Climbing the Divide* (Notre Dame, IN: University of Notre Dame Press, 2003).]

After Fires in Montana

Uncle Carl invited all, after fire
blackened every house for miles
but his own brick lodge in Montana.
Dozens of friends and strangers came

for beds and sleeping bags and food.
Carl's daughters thought it a party,
but not his girl-shy boys. They'd rather fish
and watch grizzlies. They watched the clock,

the swinging gong Uncle Carl shipped home
from the war. Every hour, he sent them out
to sniff the smoke, to wield the garden hose,
just in case. TV warned the winds might shift,

most trees still smoking, all roads still blocked.
Cougars and bears were out there, the ones
not burned. Uncle Carl's voice boomed
"Next twelve!" and neighbors checked

their numbers, leaned back or wedged
their way to the dining hall, past friends
who nodded, others in the lobby counting
their children again, or cupping palms

to their ears to hear, a dozen cell phones
but relay towers down, stranded another night,
no danger of starving with Carl's basement
of kegs and smokehouse. After the waiters ate

and tourists put away their phones
and shrugged, bald Uncle Carl climbed up
on the counter, singing, waving his Smokey
Bear hat and harmonica, calling us all to song.

[Previously published in *Open Spaces* 4, no. 2 (2001): 29 and *Climbing the Divide* (Notre Dame, IN: University of Notre Dame Press, 2003).]

Island Hopping with MacArthur

My father loved MacArthur, and why not?
my brother Bobby a prisoner on Luzon
if he survived the death march from Bataan.
Often our father stared at the globe
and the pin he called Australia,

the General's pin, inches from one he kept
for Bobby. I tried to spin the globe
but he caught my wrist in his fist
as if I'd whirl my brother off the world.
I was six, and ran to friends and baseball,

forgot my brother and the nightly news.
At meals, my father prayed "MacArthur,"
and my mother nodded. Then I was nine
with a Babe Ruth bat, when the radio shouted
"MacArthur's back with a thousand ships

to liberate '*his boys*.'" When he waded
ashore—striding head-high with his pipe,
captured by a cameraman—my father wept.
"People of the Philippines," the far-off voice
came scratchy on the radio—"I have returned."

Later, I heard when the General set survivors
free, when he took my starving brother
by both shoulders, my brother could hardly
whisper, "You came back"—and MacArthur
nodded like a God, like Father.

[Previously published in *Literature and Belief* 20, no. 1 (2001): 152 and *Climbing the Divide* (Notre Dame, IN: University of Notre Dame Press, 2003).]

Song for One-Armed Cowboys

—for Jimmy

Take the reins in your teeth,
twirl rope with your only fist.
Let go and trust the coil. See it flick
quick as a snake's tongue
tasting the wind for a feast.

When your horse jerks the calf
flat on its back with a thump,
spit out the reins and dismount,
bounding off balance to the calf
kicking to get up. Only your fist

can beat the calf and the doc
who sawed off your roping hand
after the pickup crashed. Feel
the flank of the calf, grab a leg
with the nub of your other wrist

and twist. Wrap once, twice
and leap back, stroll to the stands
with your hat off. Don't bother
about time or the trophy. Tonight
you ride for the brand.

[Previously published in *Bellowing Ark* 13, no. 4 (1997): 28 and *Blessings the Body Gave* (The Ohio State University Press, 1998—winner of the 1997 Ohio State University Press *The Journal* Award in Poetry).]

Stones Grandfathers Carved

So this is where great uncles yowled their vowels
and raised cathedrals coal smoke turned to tar
but bombs did not dislodge. Windows leaded tight
still fit, and gargoyles scowling at my Texas drawl
leer down and wink. St. Andrews bulges with tourists

faithful to stone walls and golf. The Thames flows
slowly and the buses roar. No one is timid
in these left-hand lanes. Hard to believe
plague stalked these streets. Here they killed a king
and laughed at slobbering Swift in Bedlam.

Is London burning? Do natives over sixty
still hear buzz bombs in their sleep? Is the blitz
handed down like titles, like the Tower
and chopping block? They still ride after foxes,
open castles to tourists who swat at aphids

trapped in tapestries. Last night, a woman in a flat
leaned out, dreaming of fame in this realm
of masonry, gauze curtains flapping in the heat.
Last week at Gatwick, a man with nose rings
and magenta hair strutted the terminal

banging a drum, no longer novel in a city
sober as its name, thousands of actors writing plays
near a tower announcing London time. Back home,
I'll lift a glass to masons I never knew, but love,
eroded names and dates I found on English stones.

[Previously published in *Southwest Review* 81, no. 1 (1996): 45 and *Blessings the Body Gave* (Columbus: The Ohio State University Press, 1998–winner of the 1997 Ohio State University Press *The Journal* Award in Poetry).]

Weeding Strawberry Gardens

Flashes of light and thunder, then sprinkles,
splashes of rain, then rain loud as faith
if faith has sound. That's hope and prayer
in the garden, chopping crust with steel prongs
delicate as lace, pulling up weeds like needles,

strawberries still sour. Another week, they'll all
be ripe, if sassy crows stay away. A patched
scarecrow savant called Sherlock looks down
with prune eyes plastered in clay, scowling
even at me. Hung there to dry day and night,

he holds out broomstick arms like a child,
this wide—tall witch's hat like a lightning rod.
If rain stays, let the steep slope flood, let it hail.
I merely plant and hoe so earth can breathe.
Let storms soak neighbors' trees and just enough

for berry roots. All year we'll share with neighbors,
not hoarding strawberries, for we have more
than we could eat from last year's crop, preserved,
pressure-cooked, pressed down, running over,
this plot of earth still fertile, the lightning almost here.

[Previously published in *Hubbub* 13 (1996–1997): 9 and *Blessings the Body Gave* (Columbus: The Ohio State University Press, 1998—winner of the 1997 Ohio State University Press *The Journal* Award in Poetry).]

All I Know to Do

I rattle the porch as I walk, closing the screen door softly,
guided by the coffee pot's red light. Quietly,
I fill the china cup, a gift from my wife, still sleeping.
Four, no, five a.m., the clock's red digits say. Pace if I must,
but on the porch, far enough away from the bedroom

so I won't wake her, if I don't knock the cup off,
hunched at the screen still blue, waiting like me
for words that shoved me out of bed at three. Outside,
I hear crickets as if there's not a screen between us.
Cicadas have been quiet for hours, no barking dogs,

no trucks on the highway miles away, or I can't hear them.
I haven't heard a coyote since midnight, no owls,
nothing but crickets and the computer's hum, and the porch
that creaks and rattles when I pace, thinking of something
to write our son overseas, soldier at risk in hills

of Bosnia. In Desert Storm, he was out of touch for weeks,
when nothing, not even a phone call or a FAX,
could reach him. My father fought in Flanders so his sons
would never fight, far off on Saipan and Guam,
island hopping with MacArthur. Where I went

is a footnote in history books, stacks of facts we compiled
about a war already lost, stored in a vault in Saigon unless
someone shredded and burned them before pulling out.
I see blurred silhouettes of trees in the east.
I write about those trees, the crickets. I make up jets

overhead, letting down from Dallas. I lie about coyotes,
claiming they're back, howling the way our son heard them
in these fields a thousand nights. I say his mother's up,
here on the porch, sipping her second cup. I say
she sends her love, which is no lie. I say she'll write

tomorrow. I ask "How are you," but scratch that,
add reports about the crops, the herd bull's shoulder
he hurt butting the barn. I go back inside for a cup,
and pace the porch until the sun is up. I close
with "Love," and sign it "Dad," all I know to do.

[Previously published in *Prairie Schooner* 71, no. 3 (1997): 100 and *Blessings the Body Gave* (Columbus: The Ohio State University Press, 1998–winner of the 1997 Ohio State University Press *The Journal* Award in Poetry).]

That Clatter in the Attic

They're back, pattering along the walls
and gnawing, almost chewing through,
beavers of pine and foam board.

God, let the rodents rest. Frenzied,
they nibble. We picture needle teeth
dripping with microbes or rabies.

Daily, we check the crackers, the loaf
of bread. Last year, when we closed
this mountain cabin, did they move in?

Do they think they own these walls?
What do they think of us down here,
our creaking oven door and fireplace

popping at dawn? Nights, do rocking chairs
keep them awake? Do beady eyes bulge wide,
mouse whiskers tense, afraid to twitch?

[Previously published in *The Seattle Review* 23, no. 2 (2001): 143 and *Climbing the Divide* (Notre Dame, IN: University of Notre Dame Press, 2003).]

Bless Weeds That Bloom in Fall

If lips I've kissed since seventeen are boredom,
give me decades more–her weathered skin,
squeeze of her knuckles wearing the same old rings.
Give us Deer Mountain always above us, boulders

balanced ten thousand years. We abandoned
celibate lives like shedding skin, "I do, I do,"
the stretch and tensile strength of marriage
and bungee cords. We drive to the cabin now

past the same mad traffic, gamblers on snow tires
turning off at Black Hawk, casino parking lots packed.
Above 8,000', we rock on the porch at dawn
and watch the same spring silver showers

and snow that flurries and burns away by noon.
We gamble on marriage the old way, playing the hands
we know by heart, lips familiar as clouds that puff
and bump the Rockies and keep coming back.

Bless weeds that bloom in fall for elk and mule deer
nibbling the same steep slopes, ignoring bears
and slit-eyed cougars lolling in the rocks, flicking
dark-tipped tails, picking which one, which one's next.

[Previously published in *Witness* 13, no. 2 (1999): 149 and *Climbing the Divide* (Notre Dame, IN: University of Notre Dame Press, 2003).]

The Year Biology Made Sense

When blue-eyed Trudy moved to town,
we boys in fifth grade saw
what biology was for. We'd heard,

but sullen girls were nothing yet
but skinny kids who rolled their eyes
and made good grades. They whispered a lot

and wept and never played our games.
Then sleepy-eyed Trudy came in March
near the end of school, and all she taught

we learned. To watch her cross the room
was college. Trudy was curves and honey,
the show and tell for well-thumbed magazines

big brothers bought, and cars we saw at night
abandoned at the park. That year, theology
and math made sense, the puzzling parables

of puppy love and Oz. Each class,
when Trudy touched her curving hips
to sit down at her desk, we spoke in tongues.

[Previously published in *The Listening Eye* (2000): 44 and *Climbing the Divide* (Notre Dame, IN: University of Notre Dame Press, 2003).]

Blizzards When I Was Ten

Cattle would freeze before dawn,
so Father rode off in the dark.
In deep snow by the porch, his boots
sunk a foot, but maybe that was drifts.

Drifts stacked deeper by the fence
where steers wandered and stopped,
mashed against barbed wire, too dumb
and cold to shove, to break it down.

Down at the neighbor's gate, how many
more snow-covered lumps would have died,
how many wires he'd have to cut
when he found the herd. I came back

back-weary and sleepy, most steers downwind
by the grove. Father lost a toe and forty steers
in that blizzard, while I slept downstairs by the fire.
Oh, I tried saying awake all night while he rode,

rode somehow in the saddle covered in ice,
to be a man like him, but slept in Daddy's chair
under quilts Grandmother spread–a boy,
after all, who couldn't stay awake one hour.

[Previously published in *The Adirondack Review* (Summer 2002) and *Climbing the Divide* (Notre Dame, IN: University of Notre Dame Press, 2003).]

Aunt Linda and the Pink Bikini

Her tongue was spice and lightning
even at nineteen. She caught her husband
playing doctor with a nurse and cursed him,
calling all doctors frauds. She kept his name

for herself, the cars and house for their children
but sold most stocks for a wardrobe. In time,
Cadillacs came by, Mercedes, pickups with gun racks–
I couldn't count the cowboy boots that strutted

to her door. Men liked her summer laugh,
pink thongs and terry cloth. I remember Aunt Linda
in bikinis at picnics, divorced in-law, but family.
I was bold with mustard for her burgers,

the perfect nephew. Linda always had a sticky kiss
for me, and whispered six-packs of advice, "Shave close
and take no prisoners." She clipped me on the chin
and left sweet lipstick on my cheek. One year,

I listened hard and heard Aunt Linda whisper vows
in a veil Uncle Cal lifted–she made me call
the tall cowboy that–and he kissed her
glistening lips, and all the family sighed.

[Previously published in *Visions International* 55 (1997) and *Blessings the Body Gave* (Columbus: The Ohio State University Press, 1998–winner of the 1997 Ohio State University Press *The Journal* Award in Poetry).]

The Midas Touch in Texas

I never needed much, a Midas touch,
a mile-wide ranch of Angus, a sky of geese
and rain, a lovely woman who nibbles my ear
and then says “Please, hubby, love me.”
I’ve flown to Saigon and back, shot thousands of geese
on the flyway with cameras and prayed for rain,

hardscrabble dirt like rocks. We sank all we own
in orphans, named them and blessed them
as each left home. They gave back grandbabies we adore,
who gave us names, Mamaw and Pop. Nights,
we rock on the back porch, watching stars.
I’m stunned that a woman can be this lovely

at sixty. I thought old women and men
were only old. I see her eyes, the shadows
of her face, thin flecks of silver in her hair.
It hasn’t rained in months, but I’m healed
wholly by her touch, amazed each time
she lifts my gnarled, stiff knuckles to her lips.

[Previously published in *Windhover* 4 (1999): 113 and *All Occasions* (Notre Dame, IN: University of Notre Dame Press, 2000).]

The Women Under Rubens' Thumb

All Rubens loved, they scoffed, was fat flesh
he pinched pink. Under his thumb, burnt umber
smudged ear lobes and buttocks. If models
blushed, he loved them, indecencies of brush.

They claim he never corrected, so arrogant
he touched a flip of a brush to an eyelash or lip
and hurried on, keeping flushed models hungry
and hot by windows he kept locked, shouting

"No breeze, no eating until I'm done!"
Count on it, when the rich went to heaven
on canvas, some saucy goddess exposed herself,
eyes bored and hands behind her neck.

They claim he made a mockery of myths,
a shamble of classics. Patrons bad-tempered
and vain begged him to paint them. He made
legends swiftly to mock them, big-loined

and blonde, lips so wet they glistened.
He made fat flesh magnificent, no way
to save it, nothing to do but capture it in oils.
Named after Peter and Paul, the main apostles,

Rubens knew what men growing old
wanted most, the same as him. When he died
in his sixties, his wife was carrying a tenth child.
Deeply he loved and painted Jesus and thought

all art led to the cross—and who would make the cross
be lifted more than once? His life was practice
for painting his Lord just once. Watch the Madonna,
reluctant to suckle her child, to watch him grow,

knowing the blood and pain of his fate. Rubens
loved her son and her. Consider his canvas
of Christ on the cross in Antwerp, the agony enough
without saying, "Wait! Let's do that again."

[Previously published in *Climbing the Divide* (Notre Dame, IN: University of Notre Dame Press, 2003).]

Jogging with Oscar

When I take my dachshund jogging, boys and widows gawk
and stop tossing balls or lopping limbs off shrubs. They call
and point at long, pot-bellied Oscar trotting like a rocker horse,
tongue wagging, dragging on grass when he hops over skateboards,

long muzzle wide as if laughing, eager, sniffing the breeze.
All Oscar needs is a tree like a mailbox, postcards from dogs
he barks at, at night, and odd whiffs he can't place. When he stops
and squats, up runs a neighbor's collie tall as a horse,

stalking like a swan meeting an eel, muzzle to muzzle in dog talk,
collie tail like a feather fan. Wherever we go, we're not alone
for an hour, devoted hobblers on the block, the odd couple–
long-legged bony man jogging along, obeying the leash law,

the black, retractable nylon sagging back to Oscar, who never balks
or sasses when I give the dangling leash a shake, but trots to me
desperate for affection, panting like a dog off to see Santa,
willing to jog any block for a voice, a scratch on the back.

I've seen that hunger in other dogs. I watched my wife
for thirty years brush dogs that didn't need the love he does.
When my children visit, my oldest grandsons trot with him
to the park, that glossy, auburn sausage tugging and barking,

showing off. The toddlers squat and pat him on his back.
They touch his nose and laugh, and make him lick them on the lips.
Good Oscar never growls, not even if they fall atop him.
He was a gift from them, last Christmas, a dog their pop

could take for walks and talk to. Oscar would have loved my wife,
who spoiled and petted our old dogs for decades, coaxing them up
for tidbits on the couch beside her, offering all the bliss
a dog could wish for, a hand to lick, a lap to lay their heads.

Oh, he's already spoiled, barks at blue jays on his bowl,
fat and lonely unless I'm home. But how groomed and frisky
he could be if she were here, how calm to see us both
by the fire, rocking, talking, turning out the lights.

[Previously published in *The Southern Review* 32, no. 4 (1996): 637–38 and *Blessings the Body Gave* (Columbus: The Ohio State University Press, 1998–winner of the 1997 Ohio State University Press *The Journal* Award in Poetry).]

Part 2

Mesas I Never Took the Time to Climb

I nudge this sweating gelding with my knees.
Old leather creaks as I lean between mesquite
and cactus. Our crops are rattlers and starry skies
we pretend are diamonds. My wife must know I'm coming,
lights bright in the kitchen. We live in a bowl of sand,

ten miles to any mesa. Coyotes prowl at night,
thinking we're fools to roam boldly in daylight.
Dawn, I shove old boots through stirrups and ride away,
content in a saddle, that perfect slap of leather chaps.
Torn gloves I've worn to brand castrated calves

still fit, no way I'd throw away a glove
because it's ugly. Hawks see no farther
than I could see from a mesa. The view is there,
if I want it. Today I found a buzzard in the field,
too weak to flap away. Panting, it hobbled

as if on stilts, others above us
wheeling a slow blessing on flesh. Will it miss
the soaring, the glide toward wide horizons?
Someday soon, I'll cut the fences down and let the bulls
run wild. I'll ride my gelding straight toward a mesa

I never took the time to climb. I'll dismount
and slap the sorrel to send him back to the corral.
I'll look at these flat fields from far above,
the same parched sand and cactus after sundown,
night shining not with diamonds, but real stars.

[Previously published in *Southern Poetry Review* 32, no. 1 (1991): 49 and *Counting Survivors* (Pittsburgh: University of Pittsburgh Press, 1995).]

Marriage

The neighbors' dogs have howled
at the last siren and gone back to sleep.

The lights of the park switched off
at midnight, a dark garden of swings

and fountains. I hear jet-roar
far away like a waterfall.

This late at night she returns
with slow breaths, bearing vines

of the darkest grapes,
pomegranates which open soft as lips.

She knows my eyes are open
and kisses them shut so I can see.

Her fingers know the dark
corners of my mind,

her mouth repeats the mysteries,
her flesh becomes flesh.

Animals trot by outside our window
for the blessing of names.

[Previously published in *Tar River Poetry* 22, no. 2 (1983): 22–23 and *Night Landings* (New York: Harper & Row, 1989).]

Summer Nights

Evenings, when our parents had put away the food,
they'd bring chairs out on St. Augustine grass
under the shade of Grandmother's magnolia tree,

where we climbed through half the jungle scenes we knew,
the sun not ready to settle down any more than us.
For them, we leaped from higher and higher branches,

hitting the lawn and rolling, flinging ourselves
like all the stunt men we had seen, the world turning dark
like a circus, the gasps and laughter of our elders

proof we were the center ring. Peacocks screamed
in a neighbor's field and someone whispered
"Dracula!" From then on, scissortails and sparrows

seemed like bats. West Texas echoed screams
between us and peacocks. Without a moon, our eyes
turned into radar. We saw stars fall between branches,

fireflies too high to reach, the glow of uncles' pipes,
red eyes of things that were not there. And breathing hard,
sneezing, itching from the grass, one by one

we fell before our elders and heard amazing stories
of murders before our time, great-uncles who fought
in wars, houses we never dreamed had ghosts.

We listened hard and heard far in the distance
the evening train to Houston wailing long after
any human hand could have pulled the cord.

[Previously published in *The Windsor Review* (Canada) 18, no. 1 (1984): 27 and *Great Lonely Places of the Texas Plains* (Lubbock: Texas Tech University Press, 2003).]

Oranges for My Sister When She Was Nine

I'd squeeze and squeeze until the strainer clogged,
orange pulp and seeds that filled a cup,
all for one orange juice apiece.

My sister always chose the glass
with more bubbles, foam like Daddy's beer.
Hot summer brought out her best, even in bed

with an IV dripping in her arm, her favorite scarf
knotted at her throat, loose over her bald scalp.
Always, she made me sip mine first and sigh

and wipe my lips with my wrist. She licked
the rim of her glass and tipped her tongue
to the foam, leaned back and closed her eyes.

She was nine, and spoiled me, a boy of five
she claimed was her nephew, not a bratty brother
like boys her friends whined about.

I never knew why. She was my favorite sister,
who died while I was in school one noon,
chewing peanut butter and bread,

sipping canned juice through a straw
until it was gone, when a teacher leaned down
and whispered I was needed at home.

[Previously published in *JAMA: The Journal of the American Medical Association* 285, no. 22 (2001): 2828 and *A Thousand Miles of Stars* (Lubbock: Texas Tech University Press, 2004).]

Digging in a Footlocker

Crouched before dismantled guns,
we found war souvenirs
our uncle padlocked in the attic,
a brittle latch easily pried off.

Stiff uniforms on top, snapshots
of soldiers young as our cousins,
a velvet box of medals
as if he fought all battles

in World War II. Bayonets, machetes,
a folded flag, two hand grenades
with missing pins. We picked up teeth
like pennies, loose, as if tossed in,

a piece of something dark and waxy
like a fig, curved like a question mark,
a human ear. We touched dried pieces
of cloth stuck to curved bones

and held them up to the light,
turning them over and over, wondering
how did uncles learn to kill,
what would happen when we grew up.

[Previously published in *The New York Review of Books* 36, no. 15 (1989): 19 and *Counting Survivors* (Pittsburgh: University of Pittsburgh Press, 1995).]

Buzzing in a Biplane

Rocking the wings like drunks in a rowboat,
we give them something to think about
down there, dodging,
grabbing their heads on the midway,

the roar of our radial engine
drowning the lies of the barkers,
freaks at the sideshows
halting their acts and gawking.

Pulling up, we climb for the dark
like a roller coaster
loose from its tracks,
twisting a tear-drop turn

back at them, our blades
flashing fast in the night sky,
aiming at girls on the Ferris wheel
watching us dive

and screaming, wheel stalled
above the wings of our Waco.
Banked between girls
and high wires, we hope

all the gang is down there
choking on hot dogs,
holding their girls' hands wet
and trembling. We give them thrills

no carnival ever dared,
no sideshow this shocking,
two of their own in an open cockpit.
They won't forget us,

all of them screaming and pointing,
streaming like sheep in a stock pen,
the pony ride stampeding, ticket lines
swaying intact like a conga.

If we had the power
we would buzz them all night,
climb toward the dawn sun
blazing so bright we'd blind them.

[Previously published in *Poetry* 146, no. 5 (1985): 275 and *The Flying Dutchman* (Columbus: The Ohio State University Press, 1987—winner of the 1987 George Elliston Poetry Prize).]

The Songs We Fought For

We drank while half the stars came out,
Willie and Waylon, Loretta and Patsy,
ours in the glow of the jukebox.

Over the laughter and smoke
of local couples groping for our lives,
they sob-sang all we hoped to know

of lonesome love. Nothing like
honky-tonk songs could break a heart
with the draft and war in Vietnam

drawing us closer daily. We slumped
under our Stetsons, squinting
in blue smoke layered like gunfire

and bought pitchers of beer for women
we never hoped to marry. Each time
I took Sweet Darlin's hand and led her

onto the dance floor, I felt the world
should end like that, slow dancing
close as we'd ever be to another in clothes,

lost in a sad, sweet fiddle-rhythm,
sliding on polished boots
and humming softly to ourselves.

[Previously published in *Poetry* 143, no. 2 (1988): 100 and *Night Landings* (New York: Harper & Row, 1989).]

Night Solo, Georgia

We practiced late into the night,
trying to keep the nose up
in the turn, back pressure,

back pressure to hold it
while the wings bent back around
through darkness and rolled out

touching pale blue taxi lights
a thousand feet below. Down there
the Georgia pines spread for miles

in all directions, down there
the Okefenokee Swamp sprawled
with all the snakes and gators

in the world. Yet there we were,
new as bait trolled on propellers
in a dark, starless Georgia night,

trying to land our first time
solo, turning final,
gear-down and falling.

[Previously published in *Sundog: The Southeast Review* 6, no. 2 (1985): 86 and *The Flying Dutchman* (Columbus: The Ohio State University Press, 1987—winner of the 1987 George Elliston Poetry Prize).]

Flying a Perfect Loop

It doesn't feel like falling when you do it right,
five hard G's jamming your spine. Check wingtips
equal between horizons sliding like a visor

over your eyes. Vertical, don't stop, back pressure
to keep it coming, breathe from your knees, squeeze
to stop blood rushing from your brain. Sunlight

flashes rainbows on the canopy. Swing your eyes
like incense on a chain, there's gold at the end of all
good loops. When the world opens downward

like a grave, don't worry, the sky won't disappear
forever. Hold the controls steady in your fists,
toes on the rudders upside down. The earth

that fills your staring eyes is home. Dive down
through skies sliding from your grasp. Don't grab,
steady pressure will save you. Nose coming up,

"thump," you enter your own invisible prop-wash
where you began this loop in thin unstable air
over fields of the earth, this other world you love.

[Previously published in *Night Landings* (New York: Harper & Row, 1989).]

Night Landings

In easy orbits we learned to land night fighters
by the numbers. Line up the propeller cone
a thousand feet above the lighted runway, pitch
sixty degrees and hold it, back pressure,
back pressure, a nudge on the rudder to hold

the nose up. Roll out, trusting the darkness,
drop the landing gear and count one thousand one,
one thousand two, and turn back to base, airspeed
falling, nose falling in the turn to final approach,
lights of the runway pulling you home

like a magnetic compass, wings rolling level
as the nose lifts, the tire-streaked runway dim
between the skimming lights, at last the shudder
of wheels rolling on concrete. All by the numbers,
easy. The night I soloed, red lights rolled flashing

toward the woods, searching for Pennington, his first
night solo, a nice kid eager for wings. What happened
in those seconds approaching the base we only guessed.
The tower controller reported granting clearance
to land, watching the T-28 approach and pitch out

steep as it should, but keep on rolling in the turn until
upside down, and begin to dive. The controller called
"Pull up!" and Pennington, inverted, the lighted runway
gone forever, pulled up, he thought, pulled hard
toward the voice in his headset, his eyes frantic

for stars, darkness this wooded night in Georgia
on the face of the deep, the voice in his ears pleading
"PULL UP!" and Pennington obeyed with all his might,
his right hand holding the control stick to his groin,
the throttled engine popping fire out the manifold,

the lit wings arching a tight Split-S like a pilot's
inverted hand going down, down, the canopy
suddenly plain as glass over acres of dark-green
Georgia pine, each needle and branch vivid
in the light of Pennington's eyes bursting in flames.

[Previously published in *Mississippi Valley Review* 15, no. 1 (1985–1986): 55–56; title poem of *Night Landings* (New York: Harper & Row, 1989).]

Hazards of Flight

We see them fold
like schools of fish
in blue waters, starlings
and cranes, pheasants

intent on mating, ignoring
risks of engines. Nothing
drives them away for long,
not shotguns or nets, the size

of massive jets ahead.
They crash in rotors
of giants designed to fly
faster than sound.

[Previously published in *San Jose Studies* 15, no. 1 (1989): 88 and *Night Landings* (New York: Harper & Row, 1989).]

First Solo in Thunder

So this is the way plain men can fly,
lashed to a cannon-ejected seat in a jet
high over Denver. A harness holds me
close like a lover, keeping helmet

and head from banging the canopy,
bounced like a ball in a thunderstorm
at night. Not even controllers and radar
can stop the noise, on trial by lightning

blinding, in thunder exploding, the buck
and crash of downdrafts more than my spars
are stressed for. Wings in wind tunnels
rip apart, and forests hide wreckage

of planes missing in action. Better jets
than mine have crashed in thunderstorms.
Flying by dials, feet firm on the rudders,
I kept the stick and throttle steady by faith.

What can flesh do but go on knowing
storms like our lives have to end,
that wings never level enough can
hold me, that only a turbine is burning.

[Previously published in *Memphis State Review* 7, no. 1 (1986): 32 and *Night Landings* (New York: Harper & Row, 1989).]

For Dawes, on Takeoff

I could have died
winding down the caprock road at night
driving hard to reach my father's bedside.
Canyon shoulders like the best vows
cave in, caliche ruts that crunch
soft as quail bones.

I drive black roads for bread, now,
tar roads soft all summer.
They whine on tires that spin me asleep.
I might die asleep, the calm habit we have
of saying of uncles, he slipped away quietly.
I could have died like Dawes,

suddenly inverted
two hundred feet on takeoff,
ailerons hooked up so both went up,
or down. He must have taken off
by faith. And rolled,

in spite of everything he tried,
inverted. Head down, yawing,
jerking the stick,
he must have squeezed the last controls
still working, ejecting downward like a dart,

and why not, about to crash anyway.
We found his head
stuck to his helmet.
In trees downrange, we found his arms
flung out from the body as if asking why.

[Previously published in *Poetry* 144, no. 6 (1984) and *The Flying Dutchman* (Columbus: The Ohio State University Press, 1987—winner of the 1987 George Elliston Poetry Prize).]

The Children of Saigon

Always at night I found them climbing
the piles of junk burning on the base.
Around a track I ran for miles, tight muscles
jogging past bleachers where French soldiers,

in parades for years, passed out in the sun.
Children climbed those bulldozed heaps
for food, for clothes, for trash piled up to burn.
I saw them crawling the last flare of the sun

spangled on garbage, the dump blazing
in the sweat and blink of my eyes, children
and old men ragged and golden, clawing
through flames long after sundown, no matter

how many nights I went without supper, how many
leftovers I begged and carried in darkness
out past the tarmac and bleachers, passing it all
to children who grabbed it and backed away.

[Previously published in *The Dalhousie Review* (Canada) 66, no. 4 (1986–87): 529 and *Night Landings* (New York: Harper & Row, 1989).]

For Friends Missing in Action

Near the coast in snow,
we marched to the flight line,
swinging our arms in formation.
Old pilots huddled in hangers,

watching us shiver in flight suits.
Four hours of cockpit time a day,
staring at dials and switches,
hoping to solo soon. We sat in jets

we would know before long
blindfolded, cleared to take off
even in weather like that,
climbing through clouds to the sun.

We studied gauges and codes
like prayer beads, believing
nothing that big could kill us,
those wings would hold us up.

[Previously published in *Mississippi Valley Review* 21, nos. 1 & 2 (1992): 88 and *Counting Survivors* (Pittsburgh: University of Pittsburgh Press, 1995).]

The Gleam of Silver Wings

After Darren's jet fell spinning
out of an Asian sky,
we learned the myth of perfect flight,

all of us Icarus, birds of a feather,
accident-prone blue yonders
riding throttled fire.

We'd all seen jets in movies,
tumbling and spouting flames
and smoke from under,

but not like real flesh, like Darren,
the first I knew overseas
who vanished

out of clear skies far from home,
no parachute open,
ten thousand pounds of thrust

and one of us reduced
to this, a silver matchstick
tossed indifferently away.

[Previously published in *Shenandoah* 40, no. 3 (1990): 21 and *Counting Survivors* (Pittsburgh: University of Pittsburgh Press, 1995).]

Bargaining with God

I switch from praying hands to fists.
It's the itch of a trigger finger
without a gun, digging out from rubble
of the Tower of Babel, grunting,
yearning to speak in tongues.

I'm long past rage, most days,
Bearing the DNA of Cain
even at this age. I don't dread the Bomb
or tornadoes. Lying awake, I beg Take me
instead of my darlings. Take the ranch

and bank accounts, the mountain cabin,
but save our granddaughter now.
Let me be Job in rags, Jeremiah in tears,
but please, heal this little child now.
I prophesy how many test tubes it takes,

how many angels dancing on highways
could stop a drunk from swerving
into the doctor who might find
a cure–if not today, tomorrow,
good God, soon.

[Previously published in *New Texas* (2002) and *Faith Is a Radical Master: New and Selected Poems* (Abilene, TX: Abilene Christian University Press, 2005).]

Wherever Puff Goes

I am bones and veins, a slab of meat
shrink wrapped. Even rawhide withers,
plump bacon dries, and home-smoked
venison, taped tight, evaporates.

So skin wrinkles, sags under jowls
and eyes, throats pucker like meat
in the freezer. Old age should bulge
with wisdom firm as bones,

but I am tallow soft as English sausage,
the gristle butchers slice
before plopping a pound of sirloin
on the scales. I'll never be granite,

but sand, the sift on plastic
after coffee beans are ground,
grit in an hourglass, the sticky stuff
on a spoon. Lord of more than a pound

of brain and a voice box, I'm breath
under pressure, a coffee can
pierced by a blade that spins
until the lid pops loose.

I don't know where or when,
but wherever puff goes, leaving dregs
when the last cup's gone,
I'll follow, wherever You are.

[Previously published in *JAMA: The Journal of the American Medical Association* 289, no. 7 (2003): 811 and *Great Lonely Places of the Texas Plains* (Lubbock: Texas Tech University Press, 2003).]

Rembrandt and the Art of Mercy

They say the luster of gold addicted him
to fat, round guilders' purses.
They claim his florid nose exposed
a painter's lust, that even the scent of stiff,
splayed bristles glazed with oils aroused him,

and skin like honey on the tongue
provoked him, made him pose models sweating
till they wept. They claim he painted haunted faces,
that nothing glistens but their hats and helmets.
No, what he loved and pitied most was flesh

that's caught but never saved by canvas. Consider
his florid elders astounded by Susanna bathing,
his naked Danae with her god of gold. Behold
the fragile, eggshell flesh of sad Bathsheba,
her toes and thighs scrubbed slowly

for a king. If only he could capture those
in ocher, rub her troubled eyes so they could see.
Notice the gold, pig-bristle swirls that touched
his dying Saskia's neck, her honey lobes,
the sweaty radiance of her breasts.

[Previously published in *New England Review* 16, no. 3 (1994): 68 and *Counting Survivors* (Pittsburgh: University of Pittsburgh Press, 1995).]

First Solo

I see her thumbs-up sign
go down to take the throttle.
She turns away, chin up
and urgent, flesh I have held
in these two hands. Until now,
I could have saved her.

Rolling, the Cessna gathers
faster down the runway, leans back nose-up
and lifts. Light shimmers between her
and the earth. The wings bounce
through bumpy air. I feel my spine like hers
slam down into the seat.

Was it enough, what I gave her,
the dual hours, the time in bed
rehearsing with our hands,
emergency steps we drilled together?
If something happens to me,
I said, be able to land,

then worry about a doctor.
And she was willing,
bouncing her first dual landing,
ballooning to fifty feet and stalling
before she eased it down.
She banks, now, gear down,

falling in a turn
toward final. Nothing I can do
on this hot day but beg the pheasants
nesting in fields north of the runway
and pray they have grain enough
to stay clear of traffic.

Bring the nose down, down,
don't reach, believe the glide
will hold you, the nose rise in the flare—
There! her wheels touch, lovely!
and faster and faster, she's up again
into the blue, the dazzling sky.

[Previously published in *Hiram Poetry Review* 41, no. 35. (1986–1987) and *Night Landings* (New York: Harper & Row, 1989).]

Nights on the Porch Swing

I see from my wife's green eyes
we're not alone. Our stock tank
shimmers in moonlight. Whatever warns her

makes her squeeze my neck—a whiff of fear,
a riffle of feathers. Owls own the night,
round eyes thrust downward. I've seen her

rescue five baby ducks a day, a night-light on
for ducks waddling spoiled in the washroom.
Rocking, I talk of hunger,

the natural curve of talons. "Hush,"
she warns me. Her body knows the rhythms
of the moon, expects owls most nights

and ignores them. But tonight, her fingers
strum the short hairs of my neck.
We hear a scream squeezed out by talons.

I shove the porch swing higher with my boots,
but her moccasins stop us,
dragging the swing off balance. "Hush,"

she says, her nails in my flesh.
She tugs my beard and squeezes,
her fingers stroking, stroking my neck.

[Previously published in *Carolina Quarterly* 44, no. 3 (1992): 31 and *Counting Survivors* (Pittsburgh: University of Pittsburgh Press, 1995).]

Nothing Should Be Alone for Long

I've seen her lift a calf
half-starved, lost in a thicket,
carry it twisting between mesquites
from cow to cow until one
full-uddered and lazy
would take it. She believes

nothing should be alone for long.
Every drought, we find buzzards
stacked in spiraling cylinders,
bald heads and fanned black wings,
tip feathers pronged like knives,
coasting, waiting for something

to lie down under a circling mobile
and close its eyes. Grass stubble
clings to caliche, crackles when anything
tries to run silently away—lizards
with slit mouths, lost dogs, fawns
with rapidly beating hearts.

[Previously published in *The Flying Dutchman* (Columbus: The Ohio State University Press, 1987—winner of the 1987 George Elliston Poetry Prize).]

A Woman Acquainted with the Night

My wife is not afraid of dark.
She uses lights like handholds,
climbing down caverns she accepts as found.
She's as comfortable as blossoms

when the sun goes down.
Forests we've camped in at night
are forests, for her, clear-eyed,
seeing no visions she cannot

blink away. In sudden dark,
she goes on mending clothes by feel
while I sweat and rage
to make the spare fuse fit.

When she was six, a fat man
digging a storm cellar
shut her and a friend inside,
stood on the black steel door

and stomped like thunder.
Frozen, too frightened to reach
for Becky screaming in her ears,
she felt nothing could ever

be that dark again. In time
the door clanged open and light
baptized her with perhaps
too deep a trust in saviors.

She lies down now in darkness
with no human hand but mine
to cling to, nothing but faith
in the moment to let her sleep.

When storms short out
the relay stations, she knows
how far to reach to touch me,
to make romance of failure,

knows how many steps to the candles
so if our children wake
and cry for light,
there will be light.

[Previously published in *Poetry Canada Review* 7, no. 3 (1986): 17 and *The Flying Dutchman* (Columbus: The Ohio State University Press, 1987—winner of the 1987 George Elliston Poetry Prize).]

Opening the Cabin in April

Above the red asbestos roof
a blue spruce disappears
through aspens.

The stream frozen all winter
rushes over stones
and trout feeding on runoff.

Pine needles sponge under us.
We circle the cabin
and find red bark sloughed off

slabs of the west wall,
the hummingbird feeder empty,
one porch-step smashed,

everything else suspiciously
the same. How many nights
in carpeted rooms on the plains

have we begged to be here
half-buried in snow,
the iron stove

crackling all night,
even if something's outside
smashing the top step.

[Previously published in *Three Rivers Poetry Journal* 27/28 (1986): 50 and *The Flying Dutchman* (Columbus: The Ohio State University Press, 1987—winner of the 1987 George Elliston Poetry Prize).]

Casting at Vallecito

Each season, because we snag
fingerlings first,
gulping for anything,

we learn there's a limit
to water. Trout
try to starve.

They believe
the eye is quicker
than the wrist,

and live by choosing.
In August, hoisting a fat
brown trout to the creel,

we say it's skill
but know it's hunger
and blind luck.

[Previously published in *Poetry* 146, no. 5 (1985): 276 and *The Flying Dutchman* (Columbus: The Ohio State University Press, 1987—winner of the 1987 George Elliston Poetry Prize).]

Heirlooms

"They will beat their swords into ploughshares, and their spears into pruning hooks."
—Isaiah 2:4

We're down to an anvil and conch,
seashell and useless steel,
not much from four hard years
of war. Mother's grandmother

blew this shell like a horn,
one steady roar to warn
of soldiers scouring Alabama pines,
two blasts to bring him back.

Feel the smooth, curved shell,
taste the dust of the mouth hole.
Touch the knobs like knuckles,
the wavy edges chipped

before we were born. Rub the nicked,
smooth steel of the anvil.
Grandfather felt the smithy's blast,
watched his father pound red iron

until the muscles bulged,
about to burst. Grandfather touched
those fists, the massive biceps.
Feel the pink bowl of the shell,

slide your hand through the spiral
back to the days of Lincoln,
imagine owning ten burned acres
and a leg a Minie ball took off.

Sniff the Alabama pine,
a thousand miles of powder.
Hold it close and hear an ocean
roll near Mobile, blow it long,

now rapid puffs like a hoot owl—
listen to the ringing steel
on the anvil, the clang of hammers
pounding iron to plows.

[Previously published in *The Atlantic Monthly* 270, no. 5 (1992): 118, *Counting Survivors* (Pittsburgh: University of Pittsburgh Press, 1995), *Great Lonely Places of the Texas Plains* (Lubbock: Texas Tech University Press, 2003), and *Faith Is a Radical Master: New and Selected Poems* (Abilene, TX: Abilene Christian University Press, 2005).]

Wind and Hardscrabble

It's wind, not rain, dry cattle need.
Vanes of windmills spinning all day
turn lead pipes into water.
Wind makes metal couplings sough
like lullabies. As long as there is wind,
calm steers keep grazing, believing

there is always water. On still days
steers are nervous,
lashing their tails at horseflies
always out of reach. They stomp
flat hooves and tremble, bleeding,
and thrust their dehorned heads

between barbed wires. When it blows,
steers don't need heaven.
Wind is mystery enough.
They lick dry tongues across salt blocks,
eyes closed, and wind brings
odors of grain fields miles away.

Even in drought they feast,
the curled grass crisp as winter stubble.
Parched, they wade still pastures
shimmering in heat waves
and muzzle deep in stock tanks
filled and overflowing.

[Previously published in *The Atlantic Monthly* 256, no. 1 (1985): 46, *The Flying Dutchman* (Columbus: The Ohio State University Press, 1987—winner of the 1987 George Elliston Poetry Prize), and *All That Matters: The Texas Plains in Photographs and Poems* (Lubbock: Texas Tech University Press, 1992—winner of the 1993 Western Heritage Award ("The Wrangler") for best book of poetry, National Cowboy Hall of Fame).]

Magical Hammocks at Bedtime

Ever the weaver, my wife taught my arms
to hold babies like yarn while she treadled
and bedded them down after bottles and baths.

Dressed them and blessed them, my lady
who raised them in sickness and health,
in a cradle shaped like a loom. She taught them

to waddle to swings after playpens, pulled them
each autumn in wagons, then on sleds across lakes
frozen hard, where trucks drove loaded with stones.

On their bed, she told of a star and three kings
and cold shepherds, and a boy with sweet songs
and slingshots and harps, then kissed them,

weaving magical hammocks at bedtime.
They're grown, now, and "poof!" they're gone,
and our home is a loom. I'm stiff-thumbed, clumsy,

our garden a jungle, our oak trees ripe for cracking
in winter storms and ice. She's white-haired and smiling,
folding shawls and granddaughters' doll clothes.

She twinkles, twenty in every way but age, rubbing
my shoulders and neck when I'm weary, together
at night by the fireplace, watching old embers glow.

[Previously published in *Perspectives* 17, no. 6 (2002): 16 and *Faith Is a Radical Master: New and Selected Poems* (Abilene, TX: Abilene Christian University Press, 2005).]

Nights without Rockets

Goats keep us fed, bless them for butting.
They jab sharp horns between barbed wires
and climb our plows like ladders.
They leap the fence into acres of oats

like locusts, dancing on sheds like circus dogs,
hopping on shaggy legs to nibble pears,
afraid of nothing. The peach tree bark is gone,
all leaves they can reach. Grandfather

worked these plains for steers, alert for rustlers.
Last night I heard an old board crack,
too loud for prowlers. My flashlight
nailed a billy stalking the barn. I watched him

bluff the stuttering owls, butting the door.
I swore I'd sow these fields and let crops grow,
but I lie here counting nights without rockets,
even though goats patrol the fence line.

I'm thankful for only odor, no mortars,
no madness anywhere they strut.
Goats cough, hoping for trouble. They stomp,
their bold beards vainly impatient.

They've never gone to war or killed,
drag no load of guilt into nightmares.
I've watched them roam for hours in moonlight,
jabbing their horns like sabers at the barn.

[Previously published in *The Georgia Review* 47, no. 3 (1993): 562 and *Counting Survivors* (Pittsburgh: University of Pittsburgh Press, 1995).]

Crows at Dawn in Montana

Two crows make a mockery
of sonnets. I close the book,
stop rocking on the deck, and watch.
They dive, then flap straight up
with peanuts, and the branches bob.

Beaks rip and flip the flimsy shells
and gulp raw peanuts down like pearls.
Our neighbor tossed the nuts at dawn,
but his car's gone, and he won't mind us
watching the gobbling act.

This mountain chalet's quiet
except my wife inside, humming,
strumming a comb through silver hair.
If Carol finds more gray, she'll go on
humming, knowing it's okay,

our children five hundred miles away
but fine, when they called last night.
She comes outside with coffee,
closing the door so softly
even the crows don't stop.

[Previously published in *The Midwest Quarterly* 44, no. 2 (2003): 170 and *A Thousand Miles of Stars* (Lubbock: Texas Tech University Press, 2004).]

Whatever It Takes

In Pakistan, three elephants go around
and around a hill, crushing an avalanche of limestone,
men ten feet below seining for gold.
Three shirtless men go up and down the necks
of elephants all day, their ribs like xylophones.

In Spain, couples crouch through vineyards that go up
and down over the stones of mountains.
They gather grapes like amethysts, like emeralds.
Later, they crush them under their feet.

In Arkansas, people pay two dollars each
to stalk the public land head-down,
hoping for diamonds, for opals,
whatever the earth delivers.

In Carlsbad Caverns, bats upside down
in the dark of day build hills of guano.
By night, men wired with headlamps
scoop tons of nitrogen like pearls.

Outside Bandera, a man dismounts, drops the reins
and his horse stands grazing. Defying snakes,
he stoops by a cactus, lifts and carries two stones
to the barbed wires, drops them

by a tilted fencepost, jerks it straight,
shoves one stone then the other
to prop it, stomps down around this post
to wedge it tight between two perfect stones.

[Previously published in *The American Poetry Review* 14, no. 5 (1989): 22 and *The Flying Dutchman* (Columbus: The Ohio State University Press, 1987—winner of the 1987 George Elliston Poetry Prize).]

Seining for Bass

Carp keep coming back, no matter how many times
we seine the lake, that pond no bigger than a bathtub,
we joke with friends over for the weekend.

Trying to fish away our cares, we cast our bread
on the water for bluegills or bass, but hooks
get bent by carp jaws tough as bones and wires

and not worth eating–ugly, scaly heirs of goldfish
our daughters dumped last summer. Laying down
our rods and lures, we scuba dive, searching the bottom

of this hardpan tank clear as a lagoon and cool.
Later, resting near the warped pine pier, burgers
sizzling, we dream of hooking largemouth bass,

bones easy to lift, the taste like a breeze in aspens.
The last thing we need this year is carp. Where carp hide
must be in fissures of stone or shadows of our heels

as we swim by. Trying again, we unfold the seine
weighted with sinkers, bite down on oxygen like hooks,
and let the long net reel us along the bottom. Down here,

the shadows are clear as dawn, too light to hide more
than frogs and minnows. Feeling along like warlocks,
we scrape the bottom for newts and owl eyes, anything

to cancel the gloom over us all month, dragging the seine,
waving our flippers at carp with time on their side,
watching us go by like minute hands. The first one up

kicks off his flippers, digs in and pulls us in like climbers
dangling down the sheer face of the cliff we struggled up.
Then one by one we surface and tug the net to shore

like a barge, heavier this time, like all the fish in the sea,
the net flouncing, nothing but hundreds of minnows,
twigs dark as water moccasins, some snarling catfish

the size of thumbs, and carp, one carp not even flipping.
We could have saved the time, dead carp not fit for cats.
We flounce the net to rinse and fold it, feeling the months

close over us, wishing for someone to come walking
on waters of our lives and tell us, though we have fished
all night and taken nothing, to let down there, down there

where the waters are still, where baskets of bass and blue gill
school, easy to seine and haul to shore, to share the feast
with friends and strangers who could be angels unaware.

[Previously published in *Chariton Review* 9, no. 2 (1983): 52–53, *The Flying Dutchman* (Columbus: The Ohio State University Press, 1987—winner of the 1987 George Elliston Poetry Prize), and *Faith Is a Radical Master: New and Selected Poems* (Abilene, TX: Abilene Christian University Press, 2005)].

Living on Open Plains

We thought we knew these flat,
flat miles by heart, mileage counters
inside us like circadian clocks.

Born to the plains, we learned stars
like hollows of each other's flesh.
We gauged the wind by how deep

sand could drift, the drought
by how many coyotes howled.
In time, our children drove away.

This one took the stars,
this one, the moon. They moved
to cities without flat horizons.

How does the sun set there?
Where are the coyotes, now?
Where is the sand flying to?

[Previously published in *Kansas Quarterly* 19, no. 3 (1987): 155 and *Night Landings* (New York: Harper & Row, 1989).]

Loading the Steers

They are coming from the winter wheat,
eyes bloated, heads down and floating,
bellies drooping, swaying like balloons.
Without horns, they resemble cows.
As calves, they jerked their necks
and bellowed, they slavered when the saws

rasped fast and deep, their skulls
shuddered. If they remember loss,
frost muzzles them. Now, they trudge,
chewing their cud, hooves crunching
the frozen crust. The only flowers
are winter weeds they know are bitter.

In the corral, always a feast of grain
is set, and so they come obediently
past the last still water
through the wide gate, the loading
chutes open, trucks from the slaughterhouse
backed tight against the ramps.

[Previously published in *Seneca Review* 14, no. 1 (1984): 64 and *The Flying Dutchman* (Columbus: The Ohio State University Press, 1987—winner of the 1987 George Elliston Poetry Prize).]

Finding My Father's Hands in Midlife

What enters my hand is stiff
and cold, like old leather,
rough like the hide of a bull.

So this is the fist
of my father, the fist
he fed me with, the claw

my hand turns into. Even the nails
are his, brittle and thick, beveled
when I hold them under light.

Broad fingers, puffed at the joints,
knuckles of both fists buckled,
crisscrossed with lines like scars.

I see his blood in veins here
and here, like dry Texas streams
that flow and disappear in limestone.

When I make a fist, I see his
half-moon thumb fold over four
tight fingers, a picture of family,

that big thigh-muscle shank
of his thumb something we closed on,
muscle we loved.

[Previously published in *College English* 49, no. 7 (1987): 774 and *Night Landings* (New York: Harper & Row, 1989).]

Grandmother's House at Kitty Hawk

Even the old stroll by. Wind blows
and tides roll wide across the dunes.
Miles of condos dare the hurricanes,
homes that tumble down like sand.
Couples holding hands hike past,
widows, families with dogs. Puff clouds

miles away could be gunfire, and were
when U-Boats sank freighters in 1942.
As a boy in World War II, I skipped flat rocks
on ponds, nothing else for boys to do,
big brothers shipping out, mothers
biting their lips, our fathers looking off

and coughing. Out past the Outer Banks,
four centuries of ships went down, hundreds
of masts and hulls reduced to scuba brochures.
And still they sink, trawlers hull-deep
in troughs, freighters from Singapore
and Spain, ignoring the lighthouse and sonar.

Grandfather fished for flounder, croaker, drum,
his beachfront shop no bigger than the shack
the Wright boys hung hammocks in at Kitty Hawk.
Grandmother heard a clatter of pistons, but guessed
it was only their glider crashing again,
and didn't watch. She huddled at night in the cold,

winter winds so loud she said the devil's at the door,
ripping the roof. Storms made her fear flying
forever. She grieved for me in pilot training,
hanging a Gold Star already in her heart.
She believed I'd crash, cursed wild Ohio boys
who tinkered with wings and rudders,

nothing safe at Kill Devil Hills, not even the water
Grandfather fished, his rod bent double with mullet,
supper for children forever hungry. All year,
he brought home oysters and sea trout, conchs
and starfish as toys, until the sudden December storm
when his trawler and a dozen other boats went down.

[Previously published in *New Letters* 66, no. 3 (2000): 102–3 and *A Thousand Miles of Stars* (Lubbock: Texas Tech University Press, 2004).]

Bulldozing the Outer Banks

Surf pounds the Outer Banks
and syphons tons of sand most nights,
eroding maps they drew
of what the east coast means.

No landmark stays the same,
even silhouettes on maps
of animals we fancy—Nag's Head,
Fetlock, Parrot's Beak.

We stack fat concrete slabs
like building blocks, pile-drive
steel piers for houses and hotels,
but water knocks them down,

floods docks and beach-front condos,
inlets, even Kitty Hawk.
The tide shifts sand like assets
in Swiss banks, and sand

ends up in Georgia, Scotland,
who knows where. Like kids, we haul
and stabilize the sand, and drag
lighthouses back from beaches

that ebb like playtime days
we wished would last forever,
when one by one at dusk
our mothers called us home.

[Previously published in *Michigan Quarterly Review* 40, no. 1 (2001): 17 (Special Issue: "Reimagining Place") and *A Thousand Miles of Stars* (Lubbock: Texas Tech University Press, 2004).]

What the Wind Delivers

Living on wind, hawks ride out the drought.
Rodents with round eyes and rapidly beating hearts
stay in at night, ball up in burrows and dream of seeds.

A terrapin, dragging on bent legs hard as stones
his armor ridged like bones, sometimes seems
the only moving thing on earth too dry for plows,

a miner lost in the desert, bearing his claim
on his back, slow as rain clouds wind may bring.
Lower, slower over the stones, another is slithering,

drinking the dust, the dry ground perfect
for shedding skin, diamonds emerging on its back
bright as its eyes, which know the way to live

is hard and ancient as stones, simply to go on
searching, rattle tip-up and silent, the wind knowing
where, the wind always delivering.

[Previously published in *Poetry Northwest* 24, no. 2 (1983): 13 and *The Flying Dutchman* (Columbus: The Ohio State University Press, 1987—winner of the 1987 George Elliston Poetry Prize).]

Settling the Plains

For here and for the afterlife
they worked and sang, kept time
with hymn books in both hands,
old songs of God's good grace

in a land so dry they planted
cottonseeds to prove they believed
in miracles. They buried their dead
on plains with no native stones,

deep in the earth to save them
from sandstorms that pounded
daily from the west. They prayed
for rain, the sun so dry for months

they couldn't curse. Rain fell
in floods like manna twice a year.
Like Moses, they walked across
dry land and called on God

to bless them all for doubting.
They believed whatever they put
in the dirt would live, if it was
God's will and soft rains came.

[Previously published in *The Sewanee Review* 97, no. 1 (1989): 29 and *Night Landings* (New York: Harper & Row, 1989).]

Wind in the Rockies

Because a million trees absorb it,
the wind seems tame. Back home
a wind this fierce is called a blizzard

or summer scorcher. Prairie people go mad
without such wind. Now, pine smoke
from campfires a mile north whips treetops.

We swing on the screened porch, blinking.
Those children throwing frisbees
could be ours in a different time.

Our own have moved away.
We shake our heads–grandparents.
We look at our hands, our parents' hands.

Outside, the red disks whirl. Those children
catch and flip them. Sometimes, a stray disk
wobbles, rises into the wind,

and flies off like a hawk riding a thermal.
The children chase it with the wind,
precarious, flapping their arms downhill.

[Previously published in *The Windsor Review* (Canada) 19, no. 2 (1986): 57 and *The Flying Dutchman* (Columbus: The Ohio State University Press, 1987–winner of the 1987 George Elliston Poetry Prize).]

Praying for Rain on the Plains

If it comes, let tractors stall hub-deep.
Pull off your boots and walk without socks,
squeeze globs of what we are. Feel mud

like Vaseline, the crushed and processed ferns
and dinosaurs. In centuries, we'll ooze from vaults
and metal caskets, back in the dust where we belong.

Even West Texas soil grows beans and cotton,
hot peppers that make us weep. Let rain come
by the bucket, let prices soar after floods,

let it hail. Pastors throughout the plains
have prayed, have prayed. Sun-burned farmers
who sulk at home and tinker with plows

while their wives drive pickups to church,
even gambling, skin-cancer farmers stare
at flat horizons without a cloud, and blink.

[Previously published in *The Gettysburg Review* 10, no. 2 (1997): 278 and *Faith Is a Radical Master: New and Selected Poems* (Abilene, TX: Abilene Christian University Press, 2005).]

Living Near Oak Creek Dam

Out here no one but losers stop, too late
to lease the better range for deer. I swing
the barbed-wire gate and sign them in.
I point where not to shoot, up there
and where the widow lives, cross canyon.

Already drunk, they dig out, spinning
caliche, and unload at the bunk house.
All weekend I hear them banging away,
the bald mesa five miles east bouncing
the shots' wild echoes. I'm here on a lease,

nothing to do but write and take deer hunters'
cash, count sheep and keep the windmills
turning. No one would live out here this way
except for time. Last week, I saw our daughters
picking mesquite leaves, playing, waiting

for the school bus. "He loves me," one said,
"he loves me not." I climbed a windmill
and watched drunk hunters through binoculars,
only a hundred sheep, and I don't want
ninety-nine. Last night, I read until both

sweet daughters fell asleep in my arms,
the way they used to. Windows wide, all night
I listened to my wife's slow breaths. I saw
billions of stars, the dark skies distant.
Wind slapped our roof's loose boards.

I heard rifles and knew where, then thunder.
I lay awake for hours and wondered
how many shots to a rifle, how many angels
dance on a shingle, how many times
a gate slams shut before breaking.

[Previously published in *Mississippi Arts & Letters* 2, no. 3 (1985): 23 and *The Flying Dutchman* (Columbus: The Ohio State University Press, 1987—winner of the 1987 George Elliston Poetry Prize).]

The Mind Is a Hawk

The mind is a hawk, trying to survive
on hardscrabble. Hunting, you wheel
sometimes for hours on thermals

rising from sand so dry no trees
grow native. Some days, you circle
only bones and snakeskin, the same old

cactus and mesquite. The secret
is not to give up on shadows, but glide
until nothing expects it, staring

to make a desert give up dead-still
ideas like rabbits with round eyes
and rapidly beating hearts.

[Previously published in *The Florida Review* 15, no. 2 (1987): 33 and *Night Landings* (New York: Harper & Row, 1989).]

Retrievers in Winter

Dogs paddle back one by one,
white fangs around green
and blue mallards, noses

held high like butlers,
or as if the ducks smell bad.
They trot to our boots

and deliver, and shake,
a shudder that grasps them
like a fit and ends

in the hind legs, quivering.
Well shot, all ducks on the ground
shine. Limp-necked,

they could be sleeping. The big
dogs pant, done with the ducks.
They turn their black,

wet heads and drool, their pink
tongues flick. Their eyes
never leave our guns for long.

[Previously published in *The Kenyon Review* 8, no. 4 (1986): 83 and *The Flying Dutchman* (Columbus: The Ohio State University Press, 1987—winner of the 1987 George Elliston Poetry Prize).]

Blue Jays in Summer

Jays are insane in summer.
They raid each other's nests,
swooping and screeching
madly away, blue flames

rising on elevators of air.
Pecans are safe in top branches,
too high for people to harvest,
an orchard of saved provisions.

Jays are like angels, swirling
and diving for dropped pecans
they wedge between pickets,
tilt back their razor beaks

"tap-tap," and glower, jerking
blue heads with helmets. Jays
scream as if in pain, and fight
each other for each pecan,

swirling like crepe-paper
streamers tossed in a whirlwind,
dropping cracked shells for sparrows
hopping quietly on the grass.

[Previously published in *The Literary Review* 31, no. 1 (1987): 63 and *Night Landings* (New York: Harper & Row, 1989).]

Perpetual Motion

Grandfather swore it would work
and worried that dream to oblivion.
After his stroke, after he had to slump
in that rolling chair forever, turning

with one angry hand a wheel
within a wheel, around and around
in a circle, he finally let my mother
bring him home. She gave him

the garage for his continual tinkering
with machines, with broken lamps
and toys he wired back together.
All year, Grandfather took gadgets apart

and put them back, all the physics he owned–
levers and gears, ball bearings, books
with cracked bindings about inventions,
and cans, a dozen cans of lubricants.

He never accepted news our mom
kept telling him over and over,
that he was already there, the perfect
father. At ninety, flat on his back

except when we turned him,
he breathed in slow motion, his eyes
wide with pain, the timing
between groans almost perfect.

[Previously published in *Rubicon* (Canada) 9 (1987): 56 and *Night Landings* (New York: Harper & Row, 1989).]

The Golden Years

Oh the night beasties that slither
and grope under our window,
all that quick plopping and sucking,
like bare feet wading mud.
We are curious, even aroused,
but not enough to roll over. Later,
they slink off under the stars.

We like the dark boring hours before dawn
when nothing is happening,
the long weekends we can slave
all day in the sun, if we want to,
the years since marriage became
a blunt coupling of boxcars
far off in Nebraska, on a siding.

[Previously published in *Poetry* 146, no. 5 (1985): 277 and *The Flying Dutchman* (Columbus: The Ohio State University Press, 1987—winner of the 1987 George Elliston Poetry Prize).]

All That Aches and Blesses

All that aches and blesses lives in the skin,
the thinnest organ, that turtle shell we scrub
and rub the wrong way daily, like lamps
no genies rise from to save our bones and ashes.

We wade uncovered into guilt like ice and curse
our towels that leave the same thick hide
as always. We envy snakes that shed their skins,
chameleons that hide in exotic costumes.

More than the heart, we give ourselves
away in skin, the touch all lovers love.
We feel the deepest loss of fathers
not in our bones, but skin they'll never touch.

[Previously published in *New Southern Literary Messenger* 2, no. 6 (1994): 26 and *Night Landings* (New York: Harper & Row, 1989).]

Geldings on Mountain Ranches

Horses in barns survive the cold on oats
trucked up from town, vacation from tourists
who pay to kick their ribs in spring
and jerk them nervously on trails.

Switchbacks a thousand feet straight down
are nothing to geldings lifting bristled tails.
They pass stale gas like code to each other,
clopping iron shoes single-file up mountains

one hoof at a time. Climbing is all they do
under tight-fisted people they'll never save again.
They take two extra steps before turning, the gasps
and squeezing knees well worth the jolt of bits

twisting them back from the edge, uphill.
They know how close to the ledge they can go,
how many times before the wrangler scolds them.
If they remember loping green pastures,

the bucking days before castration, hay muzzles them
after a day of trails, stroking their tongues over oats.
They never nod for strangers patting their rumps,
"Nice horse," or smooth their necks and whisper

"Sweetheart," or dig in tight Levi's for sugar cubes
crushed to powder—strangers thankful to be alive
after cliffs where they would have died
but for these steeds, these massive, muscled thighs.

[Previously published in *Kansas Quarterly* 24, nos. 2 & 3 (1992): 160 and *Counting Survivors* (Pittsburgh: University of Pittsburgh Press, 1995).]

Tornado Chasing

At night the CB Radio crackles
and I back out. Hail pounds the pickup
like a hammer. I chase blurred lightning
for hours on highways and gravel roads.
I can find it, if it's here. In twenty years

I've seen a thousand twisters. Most nights,
I'm the fool they think I am, risking my all
for nothing—but they listen like prayer
for my eyewitness news from the dark,
and they believe. Bouncing down dirt roads,

I call "tornado sighted" and chase the devil
until the road dead-ends or the lightning dies.
They know the force I follow, the vacuum
of black funnels in flashes. They gasp like me
and breathe the name of God.

[Previously published in *Concho River Review* 2, no. 2 (1988): 101 and *Faith Is a Radical Master: New and Selected Poems* (Abilene, TX: Abilene Christian University Press, 2005).]

Stalls in All Weather

Deep inside silos,
layers of spoilage ripen
vinegar-sweet, stubble of sticky maize
fermenting wine for cows. They love
the sour stalks, the half-digested
casserole of sap.

They loll those foot-long toothpicks
in their lips, grind them like grain
and swallow. Cows stare at snow fields
white as cream. If they remember calves,
the shudder of bulls at breeding,
they find relief in maize.

They lower heads like gourds
and scoop dark silage like manna,
turning mulch to milk, full udders
bulging, grasped in the pre-dawn cold,
the clang of gates and tug of suction
all they need for now.

[Previously published in *Descant* (Canada) 25, no. 1 (1994): 9 and *Counting Survivors* (Pittsburgh: University of Pittsburgh Press, 1995).]

Ranching at Glacier

Whatever elk sniff, they ignore
for a few more bites of grass,
then twist indignant heads like camels
and waddle off, wagging silver rumps.
Soon they'll climb to summer range

near timberline, except the old
and orphans cougars catch.
We'll drive our cattle out to graze
and turn the chickens loose to feast
on ticks the elk herds shed,

pecking, until coyotes slink back
from town, drawn by our bawling calves,
the cluck and scent of feathers,
wary of our guns but cagey,
coyote pups to raise before the cold.

[Previously published in *The Gettysburg Review* 14, no. 3 (2001): 497 and *A Thousand Miles of Stars* (Lubbock: Texas Tech University Press, 2004).]

Signs of Prairie Rattlers

The days of rattlesnakes are back,
fat rattlers on every trail. All day
in the saddle I see jackrabbits hopping
to wide horizons. We shove sticks down

to make mad rattlers strike, snare them
with wires and cage them. Not one
more rattle can save them from the fire.
Preachers quoted Moses, serpents impaled

on poles. Watch warnings—coyotes
trying to mate with your dogs at noon,
a mirage at dawn, lost owls without a barn.
I've found rattlers mangled at dawn, eyeless

in Gaza. I've seen coyotes lame in the hip
and starving, at risk from rattlers in daylight.
My wife believes home remedies are best,
hot cornbread and beans, red-eyed chile,

kindness, hard work, and homemade love.
I've sawed windows in the walls to save
barn owls from cats. The rafters are an ark
for owls, but that won't keep the rattlers out.

[Previously published in *The Missouri Review* 14, no. 3 (1991): 132 and *Counting Survivors* (Pittsburgh: University of Pittsburgh Press, 1995).]

Sleeping with Strangers

Bare boards listen to our steps like owls
and creak. We pause, mounting stairs
of distant relatives. Two globed lights

glare from chains, double looped,
three doors closed like a hotel's,
one door open to a commode

and blue shower curtain drawn
as if an aunt waits, too shy to meet us.
All day we drove, too late to see cousins,

but those with no reason to know us
wrapped us in their arms like their own
returning home. Names we've always known

bloomed into faces at the funeral home,
a family album, and strangers consoled us
as if we were the most bereaved.

At last, here in some cousin's room
we lie between starched sheets and springs,
the double bed a flat sack of feathers.

Springs sag each time we touch,
boards groan. Trees we've never known
stare in through windowpanes all night.

[Previously published in *The Sewanee Review* 97, no. 1 (1989): 27 and *Night Landings* (New York: Harper & Row, 1989).]

Big Dogs after War

Back from war, Uncle Bob had faith in dogs,
the only folks he trusted. I worked his ranch
in summers, learned how to cuss when anything

went wrong, heard nightmares that waked me
down thc hall, shouts only Aunt Kay could stand.
Often, I found him in the barn at dawn with coffee,
alone with a pre-war pickup he polished like a toy.
Decades of dogs jumped over his tailgate to sniff
the news from pickups around the ranch and down
state roads. Balanced, unbalanced in turns and stops,

they watched my uncle inside the cab, doing magic
with wind flapping their lips. Troll was the first dog
after World War Two, a fluffy St. Bernard that leaned
and made that pickup rock. Years swift as crops
slid by, a long, fast litany of dogs big as horses, Attila,
Goat Boy, Little Caesar learned that amazing trick
to please him, big legs shoving gravity away
and soaring over the tailgate, the whole world swaying,
drooled on, pounded with massive, wagging tails.

[Previously published in *Great Lonely Places of the Texas Plains* (Lubbock: Texas Tech University Press, 2003).]

Where the Train Slows Down

Slumgullion and bread fed bums
on Aunt Pearl's ranch near the railroad
in the Great Depression, Uncle Elmer dead.
Within months, she lost cows and riders,

barbed wires cut down, old cars abandoned
in her pasture, trails trampled past her ranch
by migrants. Windmills and a foreman
old as her daddy saved the herd.

The bank failed before it foreclosed,
and calves brought enough by fall. Hobos
spread the word for miles by signs I never saw—
"Look for the house 10 miles ahead,

around the bend where the train slows down.
That widow will feed you." Two at a time
they came, making a trail from the tracks
to her back porch. Hats in hands,

they would ask, but she already had bowls
and spoons, tin mugs for water at the well.
They sat on the porch to eat
or out on the grass under oaks,

then rinsed them clean and stacked them,
found the axe in the stump and chopped
a few thick logs, or raked the yard
the hundredth time that month.

[Previously published in *Great Lonely Places of the Texas Plains* (Lubbock: Texas Tech University Press, 2003).]

Fences

This is the rage for order on the plains,
barbed wire cinched tight from post to post.
Acres of land each year go back to sand

and disappear. Nothing not tied down
stays home. Canadian geese fly over us
each fall, each spring, and never land.

Our steers two times a year trudge up
ramps of trucks from the slaughterhouse.
Even our children rise up like owls

and fly away. Nights, you turn for me
to hold you. We pretend we go away
by writing French love notes

in dust on the headboard. At dawn,
you smooth old cloths over all we wrote
the night before. By dusk, the film is back,

the earth we live on, the dust our fingers
string new fences on, holding each other
one more night with loving words.

[Previously published in *The Antigonish Review* (Canada) 66–67 (1986): 217, *Night Landings* (New York: Harper & Row, 1989), and *Whatever the Wind Delivers: Celebrating West Texas and the Near Southwest* (Lubbock: Texas Tech University Press, 1999—winner of the 2000 Western Heritage Award ("The Wrangler") for best book of poetry, National Cowboy Hall of Fame).]

Praying for Rain in the Rockies

These shacks are screamish. Believe me,
even birds have ears. They flutter
low enough to let us know they're brave.
Fires have burned up every stick

not ten miles east. Pine smoke
settles down like winter. As dry here
as the plains, and all this timber.
Except indoors, fires are forbidden.

The old man here since prohibition
sells all he has and bars the door.
At night, his still bangs empty in the wind.
Our first week here, no clouds in sight.

Whoever leased here last
split pine enough for years,
unless the forest burns. We might as well
go home, dust off the lawn chairs

and dream our elms are aspens.
Nothing to do but pray for thunder.
Living on dry land, we know
even with silver iodide and prayer

it rains only when it rains, and we're never
sure we caused it. Nights on the roof
and screen doors we hear tapping and scratching
like two of everything trying to get in.

[Previously published in *College English* 48, no. 4 (1986): 355 and *The Flying Dutchman* (Columbus: The Ohio State University Press, 1987—winner of the 1987 George Elliston Poetry Prize).]

Cattle in Rain

Cows know what to do in rain.
Grackles dive for the trees,
and chickens flap for the barn,
squeezing their wings and waddling.

Caught in the fields, cows
shove their muzzles down
and graze. Something in the sky
is falling. Their round eyes glaze,

and everywhere they stare
is green. They never blink,
they drop their dished heads
down and grind off all grass

they can reach. They believe
when it is time to lie down
in the pasture, they will go on
chewing this green haze forever.

[Previously published in *Country Journal* 14, no. 1 (1987): 54 and *The Flying Dutchman* (Columbus: The Ohio State University Press, 1987–winner of the 1987 George Elliston Poetry Prize).]

The Tap of Angry Reins

Last day of the month, and I can't make
friends meet. Sullen, they'd rather quarrel.
Bury the pride and let debates go begging.
We buy back nothing we give away with the tongue,

the quickest organ, that tap of angry reins
on a mule. Miles from the nearest road,
we sit in a jeep surrounded by derricks of oil,
the bones of quarrels like dinosaurs.

Even with carbon dating we can't name them,
feuds the way to graveyards of old friends.
Sometimes it's thunder, voices so loud
the dog shakes, wetting himself, eyes begging.

After a lashing, the tongue is bleached
like cow bones. Ears believe whatever they're told.
Even deep wells dry up, plains where
discouraging words come easier than drought.

Quarrels are mesquite trees ranchers bulldoze
and burn for pastures. In spite of tractors
and chain saws, still the old roots grow back,
massive, tangled with roots of bindweed.

If little words led goats to market,
we'd all be rich. They turn up decades later
when our own best schemes are ribs and skulls.
Bulls gorge all night in the mind's silo.

Bloated at dawn, they blow their red-eyed breath
across the room and lower pointed horns,
snorting, pawing the dust. Bury the dead
and let good fences save us, if they can.

[Previously published in *Michigan Quarterly Review* 31, no. 2 (1992): 226–27 and *Counting Survivors* (Pittsburgh: University of Pittsburgh Press, 1995).]

The Flying Dutchman

Someone I flew with
has gone to the moon and back.
I haven't touched a rudder in decades,
my only cockpit the family wagon
with a cracked windshield. Still,
I'm up there in famous make-believe,

dreaming of Stuart,
straight-in from 20,000', Dave
who scooped a sand crane in the engine
but steered away from Waco
where he crashed, Keith
vaporized when a bomb
exploded in midair near Hanoi.

I might have died like Karnes
in Georgia, his first night landing.
He pitched too steep,
and the wings kept rolling.
When the controller called, "Pull up"

Karnes jerked the stick back
tight to his groins, trying to obey
at two hundred knots, a thousand feet,
wings level by now, but inverted,
nose coming down, diving,
someone screaming, "Pull up!"
in his headset.

Bold instructors taught us to fly—
chandelles and loops, snap rolls,
tight Immelmanns with a twist on top—
each turn was to get behind
somebody else, a touch,
a touch on the button
to bring him down. The last trick
they taught was the victory roll.

Sometimes, squirting a thin jet
to water Texas grass trying to survive
another drought, I feel flames
in my fingertips and squeeze
to strafe begonias like a practice run.
At dawn, driving to work,
I keep feeling a tingling in my hands
and the weight on my backbone in a turn.

[Previously published in *TriQuarterly* 64 (1985): 112 and *The Flying Dutchman* (Columbus: The Ohio State University Press, 1987—winner of the 1987 George Elliston Poetry Prize).]

The Art of Growing Old

It happens when you're rolling oats
around your tongue, like brunch
after your first baby teeth fell out
or that Daddy pulled, years before you learned
that horses love oats, too. It happens

when you're thinking about retirement
and throw away the daily paper and keep
the classifieds. Or drop the toilet-tissue bar
in the trash and try to shove a new roll
over the empty cardboard, the magazine

we read stuck with glue from horses' hoofs.
All survivors are naturals in this game.
As long as we breathe, we're practicing,
each year a black belt, easy as licking ice cream
in July, or banging our first jalopy fast

down the town's main street, hoping the gang
could see you now—or later in your old,
familiar rocker, or suddenly in a rest home,
wishing anyone would come—you've mastered it,
here's the expert sitting in his chair.

[Previously published in *Concho River Review* 16, no. 2 (2002): 96 and *Great Lonely Places of the Texas Plains* (Lubbock: Texas Tech University Press, 2003).]

A Round Horizon without a Town

The prairie on any day is endless,
too much to take it in between blinks.
My wife and I aren't Atlas
toting the world. We carry the cosmos,
not a globe but stars and rocks

in a billion different directions,
if we could track them, like canoeing
the Brazos River after a rain,
ripples and flow forever changing.
Horizon is fragile on the plains.

Grazing cattle shift, and buzzards glide,
vast details that don't match. Boots
and horse hoofs turn the globe,
and skyline scrolls. We raised four babies
on the plains. They toddled off and fell,

shoved up, and now they're gone.
Explorers learned the signs,
established trails highways bypass.
Step any direction and pastures change,
a herd of antelopes galloping

by the time binoculars change hands,
strap quickly off and my wife
lifts them with a twist to fit
her eyes, counting four pronghorns
or five, not the ten I claimed I saw.

[Previously published in *Great Lonely Places of the Texas Plains* (Lubbock: Texas Tech University Press, 2003).]

Dogs in the World They Own

This is the rage for order on the ranch,
dogs barking at cars and pickups on the road.
Any post inside the fence, they own,
wetting the weeds, the shadows of clouds.

Skunks waddle by and die in their own
dark smell sprayed on mad dogs
ripping them apart. Coyotes know
which fields have dogs, and lope for miles.

Sometimes a prowling cat hears snarling
too close to outrun and climbs the only
light pole in the yard. Dogs bark for hours.
The hot sun melts their tongues.

Even when dogs lie down, the cat stays there
all night, stares at the woman
who comes at dawn coaxing with water,
or a saucer of milk. The cat stares,

cramped like a skull on a post. And then
one day it's gone, the dogs patrolling
their dirt, the black wings wheeling by,
all gates and grazing cows in place.

[Previously published in *Grand Street* 37 (1990): 35 and *Counting Survivors* (Pittsburgh: University of Pittsburgh Press, 1995).]

Letting Go

Raised on the plains, we believed
in bald horizons where the sun burned
every crop. We clung to the myth

the world is flat under skies so dry
weeds wilt. Buzzards glided
always in sight, and rattlers coiled

in our yard. Born in the Rockies,
our babies climbed before they could walk,
their eyes brimming with trees.

The steepest roofs were dwarfed,
and snakes hid above us on boulders.
The spoor of cougars tempted

our children to climb, to wander off.
They scaled the Rockies,
thin air they evolved to, believing

wilderness was the world, and bears
owned no more of the woods
than our children prowling

miles from the hearth
where we lived stoking embers,
sweeping, oiling the locks.

[Previously published in *Prairie Schooner* 68, no. 2 (1994): 67 and *Counting Survivors* (Pittsburgh: University of Pittsburgh Press, 1995).]

Time for the Traction of Docks

I've stopped wading for trout in Montana.
Time for the traction of docks thrust boldly
onto lakes, like bridges going nowhere.
Now let them come to dinner, granddaddy catfish
cruising the bottom, crappie forever hungry.

This rig my grandkids gave is all crossbeams
and swivels, a mobile of silver hooks. I'll take
whatever bites. Who needs the battle of bass
in the shallows? Fish eager to believe in bait
confess their faith in trinkets. I reel them in,

doffing my cap to grandkids screaming and laughing.
They hug me as if I'm feeding thousands,
blessing their gift with magic. I let them touch
the quivering crappies, the mica scales.
If it's a catfish, I grit my teeth and reel,

bowing my back to raise a rod bent double. They gasp,
their wide eyes shine. Keeping the sharp barbs
covered, I let them touch the slippery tail,
the rubber lips. If the fish swallowed it all,
even needle-nose pliers can't tease out a hook

without ripping. Holding the squirming fish
out of sight, I point at hovering gulls or a speedboat
splashing by, while I tug or cut the line, some other
summer time enough to show how much
a catfish suffers, how rough old men must be.

[Previously published in *New Texas* (1992): 208–9 and *Counting Survivors* (Pittsburgh: University of Pittsburgh Press, 1995).]

Leaving Sixty

Riding flat, hardscrabble plains,
we hold the reins of geldings
with fingers stiff in leather gloves.
The sun burns mirages blue as oceans:

Shanghaied, we're trapped in a fleet
of boats, these creaky bones.
Charming Columbus, his scrolls
rolled into a globe, his tales of gold

and spice enticing. Look ahoy,
they're dropping off the horizon,
old friends once young as Columbus.
The world is flat. Isabella's fool

proved that by dying, leaving a skull,
the only gold of a dunce.
Columbus found the edge of the earth
years later, and no charts

or spinning globe could save him.
Only his nurse saw the old man vanish.
Far from port, my wife and I
wave semaphores of love

like *Santa Maria* scrolls:
We're headed west, loaded with gold
and spice, stiff riggings locked,
no way to shift the sails.

[Previously published in *College English* 57, no. 1 (1995): 83 and *Counting Survivors* (Pittsburgh: University of Pittsburgh Press, 1995).]

Reaching Sixty

Now the cycle starts, reviving trees
before the last late killing freeze.
Grandfather fought this battle for gold

in the garden. He'd fold his fists
and "flick-of-the-wrist" snatch carrots
for us to nibble, each crunchy bite,

and strawberries he picked and rinsed.
My sister moaned, munching
the pulp, juice sticky on her chin.

Our pears have budded early again,
peaches and purple plums in bloom,
chill in the air as we mulch,

clutching sweaters in the breeze.
It may not freeze again this month.
This may not be the cruelest season.

There may be time enough to spray,
to save the plums, to teach grandchildren
games, to kiss them many times.

[Previously published in *Presbyterian Record* (Canada) 121, no. 4 (1997): 19 and *Faith Is a Radical Master: New and Selected Poems* (Abilene, TX: Abilene Christian University Press, 2005).]

Losing a Boat on the Brazos

Downriver rocks were rapids. Believe me,
even fish have ears. Sweating, we coasted
too far out on a river we've fished
for forty years. I swear it's never
been this low, but two old cousins
can't keep the Brazos full forever.

Sharp rocks are death to aluminum boats
harder to split than wood. We're safe,
spitting out mud and minnows, but alive
after months of drought and a soaking.
Bury the boat and forget it.
We could have drowned any wet year

under tons of the Brazos flooding
downhill to the dam. We could be food
for alligator gar and catfish.
That rip in the boat is wider than the lies
we'll tell for months—the size of bass
that got away, the granddaddy cat

we finally caught that flipped
and disappeared through the hole
of the boat, going down. Let's sit
on the bank and laugh at why we let
a thousand dollars of rods and tackle
sink and saved a boat shell worth less

than beer cans we crush for salvage
every day, two old fools splashing ashore,
dragging a gashed boat out
as if dry land could save it,
like old bones mired in mud we've proved
can rise and walk again.

[Previously published in *Poetry* 149, no. 5 (1987): 281 and *Night Landings* (New York: Harper & Row, 1989).]

Saying the Blessing

I can't say anything new to children
on their own. They need my blessing
as I wanted my own old father's love,
but nothing more—no roof

or weekly allowance, no easy advice.
I'd say it all again, abridged
and edited, if they'd let me,
convinced the old songs are the best—

the thunder of prairie rain,
the sober mourning of doves,
the joy of work in the wings
of hummingbirds, the holy Psalms.

[Previously published in *Clockwatch Review* 6, no. 2 (1990): 57 and *Counting Survivors* (Pittsburgh: University of Pittsburgh Press, 1995).]

Turning Sixty-five on Hardscrabble

"More!" the body roars, the heart begs "more,"
the only demands worth saving. Muscles sag
no matter how many hours a week I jog.

We hike rock canyons to see what's west,
but fingers fumble turning the calendar, "Do this
and this today, and what's for tomorrow?"

Our home's a clutter of clocks and bowls,
craft and carpentry hobbies. I'm thumbnails
cracked and brittle, smashed black by hammers.

Drought hangs on all summer and pastures burn.
If readiness is all, my old bones boast,
"I'm here." Trees wilt, and wildflowers limp along.

"All life is grass," our hot steers snort,
chewing their endless cud. Pull Bermuda grass
from flower beds, lay plastic down,

but still the sprouts grow back,
a tangle of tough albino roots, like fish
in caverns underground, eyeless but alive.

[Previously published in *The American Scholar* (Phi Beta Kappa magazine) 73, no. 3 (Summer 2004): 78 and *A Thousand Miles of Stars* (Lubbock: Texas Tech University Press, 2004).]

Honky-Tonk Blues

Shoving another quarter home to make jukebox stars
keep wailing all night in Texas, Uncle Paul's job
was chopping wood, heaving his bad back to it, in town

again for a weekend. Chips flew from his axe like curses.
Puffing, he hummed the same old country tunes
that kept him fed and human, half the honky-tonks

in Texas more like his home than Plano. Aunt Myrtie
lived alone five months out of six, pedaling a Singer
sewing machine to stay faithful, trying to spin gold

from cotton threads and telegrams he wired her
twice a week. Whatever she sewed sold fast at auction,
in the mall and county fair. Now Paul lives alone

in a trailer park in Austin, bait for tornadoes, his stove
a butane heater he seldom lights. He sits outside
as late as neighbors let him, strumming, humming

old songs like scabs he keeps picking at over
and over, no new tunes written for ballads about a cruel
good-hearted woman who let down her spun
silk rope one night and slid out of his arms forever.

[Previously published in *Outerbridge* 6/17 (1985–1986): 5 and *Night Landings* (New York: Harper & Row, 1989).]

The Price They Paid for Range

Bone-white caliche undercuts our dust.
Most trees dry up, stunted on starving roots.
To save imported ferns, we ditch the fields
with peat imported from swamps,

tamp bone meal into dirt for roses.
Cactus rode here as burrs with soldiers,
their Spanish ponies stumbling
under the sun, dumping knobs of seeds

from weed fields miles away.
Wind taught our fathers how to survive
so far from forests: build low and far apart
and ration water. Let stallions and cattle

be enough, rough bunks and windmills
the way to pray, cow chips for fire, cactus
and rattlers the price they paid for range
and a thousand miles of stars.

[Previously published in *Manoa* 4, no. 2 (1992): 152 and *Counting Survivors* (Pittsburgh: University of Pittsburgh Press, 1995).]

On the Gunnison

Whatever lives and dies
under the brows of pine banks,
pools, the backs of boulders,
believes the eye is quicker

than the hand, that anything
offered free means trouble,
that seeing is believing.
To bring them up, we go down

where the sky is a dome
and all are moving targets
and the way to win is to starve.
We kneel on the bank, far back,

showing nothing but flies
we've tweezered and stitched
all winter, staying out of the eyes
of trout, the arc of refracted light

trout believe like creeds
and will die for. Back on a bank
beyond eyes, we flick, flick
the dry flies softly onto rapids

where nothing nibbles, our hooks
bearing gifts like the scheme
of the river bobbing toward bellies
of fish, the river bringing all

they will need, gills fanning
the river like wings often blessing,
blessing the bounty they believe
they're about to receive.

[Previously published in *Willow Springs* 16 (1985): 18 and *The Flying Dutchman* (Columbus: The Ohio State University Press, 1987—winner of the 1987 George Elliston Poetry Prize).]

Uncles on Sunday Battlegrounds

Old boys, gone off alone down range,
I miss your sweaty arrogance and bluff
about Pearl Harbor when most of you
weren't twenty. Stiff necked and grumpy,
you would have died for all of us at Midway,

Normandy, islands I wouldn't have heard of
except from you, who fought and came back
gaunt and giddy or weary, bitter and lame
as years went by, nothing ahead but scandals
and politics in a country gone to the dogs,

parking lots crammed with foreign-made cars,
Okinawa where buddies died given back to Japan.
Sunday afternoons were uncles who argued
and smoked cigars, a rut of politics in fall,
old bulls butting each other with sarcasm

they called logic. They were always my heroes,
and never off balance for long. Loud out-shouted
whoever talked. After potluck tables that sagged
like belted bellies, after seconds of cakes or cobblers,
the battles raged, smirks and sneers but never fists.

Pachyderm or mule, it didn't matter—all snorted
or brayed cousins and bureaucrats to scorn.
Old soldiers shook gray heads and lowered cigars
like horns and scoffed, flicked inch-long
sagging ashes and watched them fall.

[Previously published in *Ontario Review* (Canada) 59 (2003): 116 and *A Thousand Miles of Stars* (Lubbock: Texas Tech University Press, 2004).]

Wishing for Easter All Year Long

Spring, and a blizzard howls. A blue,
bug-hungry jay attacks the walls—
"hop, hop"—hits the planks like a toddler
and pecks the wood worm out.
My wife may think I'm playing darts.

I hope she rolls, goes back to sleep,
for all's quiet, now. The jay flies up
to the feeder, gobble gobble, swallow.
We've come five hundred miles
to climb steep slopes and stare,

far from grandchildren and friends.
Like a monk at dawn, I say the names
I know on the wall in Washington.
I wish for Easter all year long.
I don't hear rockets or gunfire, now,

but glass rattles behind me, jet bombers
taking off at the base. This week, let
blizzards glide, let peaks turn gold or white.
let elk climb higher slopes for grass,
let cougars come, whatever we can't stop.

[Previously published in *The Florida Review* 28, no. 1 (2003): 107 and *A Thousand Miles of Stars* (Lubbock: Texas Tech University Press, 2004).]

Tracking on Hardscrabble

I squat with a rifle jammed after the only shot
since noon. Mesquite twigs silk-screen shade on caliche.
Riding hardscrabble, a man keeps his rifle handy.
You don't get many shots out here. Sometimes five,
six days before someone rides out with orders.
I go where they send me, northwest with pliers
along the barbed-wire border, or down through arroyos

searching for strays. I slide another bullet home
and lock it, gather the reins and climb up slowly
in the saddle, old leather cracking, the filly snorting
and sidling, wary of blood. One lone cougar
long in the tooth, calf-hungry, can stampede a herd
worse than thunder. I've seen a hundred cows run off
a cliff, broken boned and bawling, good for nothing

but slaughter. I've hauled as much meat home
as my horse could carry, calves looped together
so they won't choke behind the mustang staggering
under their mother's meat. Rifle high, I find the track
and aim, a cougar careless and dying, more mercy
to the cat than to the herd, which always go on
grazing whether one or a dozen calves are missing.

[Previously published in *The Kenyon Review* 8, no. 4 (1986): 22 and *The Flying Dutchman* (Columbus: The Ohio State University Press, 1987—winner of the 1987 George Elliston Poetry Prize).]

A Little Night Music

If Mozart watched willows in storms,
he saw concerto chords–not trunks and leaves
but songs, sheet music in the air, the highest C

and frenzy of violin lightning, then calm adagio
after gusts, branches like French horns relaxed.
If bats flew by, he saw allegros of wings

zigzagging after gnats. Squalls were sonatas,
vivid and finished, easy to transcribe, overtones
already there, like the clash of bat snouts

sniffing fizzing mosquitoes, the elegant
glissando of owls diving after mice.
Why bother jotting that down? Who in Vienna

could tell a genius from a copy boy? Who else
detected melodies from bats, heard wings
in that dimension, harmonics odd but clear

as bird songs in his ears? Others would take
the easy way someday and scribble the obvious,
pretend raw dissonance is modern, and some

rich emperor, tone deaf, would call that chaos
opera. Most of us could hear staccato
in wings of hummingbirds, discern irregular

cadence, eighth notes of bouncing butterflies.
"But musical bats?" they'd say and sniff
their snuff, "My God, Mozart, you're mad!"

[Previously published in *The Sewanee Review* 113, no. 1 (Winter 2005): 53 and *A Thousand Miles of Stars* (Lubbock: Texas Tech University Press, 2004).]

Opening the Cabin in March

Out past the deck, light dazzles the pines,
the wet bark frozen dark. Montana sun turns ice
to oil and crashes in spangles. Up high,
cubs bump and nuzzle slumbering mothers.
Dam bears have heard ice crack before

and pinch back winter a few more hours.
They're half October's size. They'll be hungry
and blink at the sun like us, although we're old
and bundled in coats. We might not see that bear
but marmots will, and picas, maybe too late,

caught in the jaws, their squeals gone hollow,
swallowed or tossed to cubs learning the taste
of blood, the crack of ice shattering above on steep,
slippery slopes, and delicious comfort of milk
when nursing bears roll clumsy on their backs.

[Previously published in *Connecticut Review* 26, no. 1 (Spring 2004): 145 and *A Thousand Miles of Stars* (Lubbock: Texas Tech University Press, 2004).]

Dawn on the Outer Banks

Someday, if grandchildren
flip through family albums and find
these brittle photos of the coast,
the week they ran to us
and giggled in the surf,
will they remember?

Hoard, work fingers to the bone,
give heart and dollars
to all good causes that knock,
it doesn't matter. This conch
washed up and hollow as a heart
is ours, for now.

If all our heart strings snap,
flapping in the gale-force sugar
of good deeds, and we're old,
picking up pennies spilled
from a thousand alms,
it doesn't matter. Give,

if we wish, just do.
The tomb takes care of time.
On a peaceful beach one year,
grandchildren danced and called us
Mamaw and Pop all salty summer,
sweet as homemade ice cream.

[Previously published in *Westview* 21, no. 2 (2002): 10 and *A Thousand Miles of Stars* (Lubbock: Texas Tech University Press, 2004).]

How Much Time We're Promised

Suppose a truck backs over you
in your alley, its warning horn
not working as you lift the lid

of a Dumpster to toss a trash bag in.
That's how my neighbor Bobby said
the heart attack hit Fred. Built like a bulldog,

Fred was a plumber five doors down,
a check-up only last month. Big Fred
won Golden Gloves in high school,

nose broken twice, five kids and a wife.
I heard the siren at dawn like a gong
under water. Out of the shower,

dried off, I saw nothing by the curb
through the curtains, sat down for coffee
and heard a knock, and it was Bobby–

for Fred was gone, maybe dead
before his face hit the floor
and his dropped coffee splashed.

[Previously published in *The Gettysburg Review* 16, no. 2 (Summer 2002): 332 and *A Thousand Miles of Stars* (Lubbock: Texas Tech University Press, 2004).]

Father's Field of Pheasants

Daddy came back bored, too many pheasants
in the fields, the sheen of green and bronze
in every row of stubble. When he was a kid,
the nearest pheasants nested four counties east.

He shot the first in our fields when I was ten
and made me clean it. Feathers clung to my skin
like static, intestines ruptured by buckshot.
I carried the stench for days. For Christmas

he gave me a twenty gauge, taught me to draw
an oiled cloth slowly through the barrel.
When pheasants settled in his fields,
he called lost cousins to bring their guns.

For years they came, stalking wild cocks
in ranks, rows of uncles reaping our fields
each Fall, the boom and flash like muskets
along a half-mile front. Then Uncle Ernest

died of cancer, Uncle Claude in a car wreck.
One season, my brother and I took to the fields
like rear guards, bagging our limit
in stiff wind whipping from the north,

in sight of the porch where Dad rested,
rocking, whittling some duck decoy,
the nearest duck lake ninety miles away.
Noon, we found him hunched on the porch

without a hat, twisting the wood
augur-eyed, rubbing his thumb with the grain
as if feeling for clues to the future,
his white hair whipping in the wind.

[Previously published in *Hampden-Sydney Poetry Review* (Winter 1991): 47 and *Counting Survivors* (Pittsburgh: University of Pittsburgh Press, 1995).]

On a Saturday Afternoon

Not once in the canyon west of here
had we ever killed a thing. And so
the afternoon we saw buzzards
swirling like a whirlwind, we knew
they'd found what they needed

without us. We sat on the screened-in porch
picking them off with our fingers,
eyes squinted against the sun
they soared across, dull black against
the light, the blackest we'd ever seen,

and on a day when nothing
was happening to us, rocking,
one of us thinking of something
to say to break the silence,
shelling our black-eyed peas for supper,

when down in the canyon something
came into our minds, something quiet
and final, teeth bared and grinning,
something that made it that far
up the canyon, this time.

[Previously published in *New Orleans Review* 10, no. 4 (1983): 16 and *Great Lonely Places of the Texas Plains* (Lubbock: Texas Tech University Press, 2003).]

Grace and the Blood of Goats

Ghosts of old prospectors pick up their beds
and walk, but even here we're home.
I hear you swear your faith in mountains,
snow reflecting nothing we have at home.

We need what prairie eyes don't hope for,
that isn't ours to feed. Owls wear feathered chaps
like prairie hawks, night-riders over sage
and cactus. Come back to bed and ignore them.

The moon is silver beaten thin. Together
we'll tease away trick knees that lock,
bifocal eyes that open early. We salvage nothing
we gave away in rage, wasted in overtime,

trying to make the dust we are yield more
than rushed fumbling after a shower, then back
to cactus and goats spraying a trail of pellets.
A man I flew with went to the moon and home,

a hero riding a rocket aimed at no one.
That was years ago, after I flew back from Saigon.
Crossing a log today, we stared at water tumbling fast.
Don't look, I said, as if blind faith could save us.

We confess everything takes luck, even a friend's
jaunty steps on a moon we're staring at. Tonight,
even if we call to it, "Peace, be still," the moon
keeps changing before our eyes. We depend

on grace in a world in chaos, where the blood of goats
can't save us. The babies we raised were worth it,
but now we're alone in a snow field at night
in mountains. Tonight, we swear we'll worship love

and grace with more patient ears, but never again
mere goats grazing plains where nothing changes
but names chiseled on marble. We know
we won't change much, but anyway we swear.

[Previously published in *College English* 54, no. 7 (1992): 826 and *Counting Survivors* (Pittsburgh: University of Pittsburgh Press, 1995).]

Rowing in Eden

—Romans 8:19–22

Lovers in tents make forests
come alive, the campgrounds

roamed by twos, by twos,
sniffing the air for food,

for rain, for the way in,
the call gone out

of people up to something.
They circle the tents,

sniffing, they slink away,
they look up, startled,

the tents too small
to save them.

[Previously published in *The Malahat Review* (Canada) 71 (1983): 82 and *The Flying Dutchman* (Columbus: The Ohio State University Press, 1987—winner of the 1987 George Elliston Poetry Prize).]

Bones in a San Juan Mine, 11,000′

Anything this rare is worth it, he must have thought,
alone in this tunnel hidden near timberline, 1880
carved over the door. All aspen timbers have rotted,

tin roof propped by snapped rafters. Here are his axe
and rifle as he left them, the basin where he sometimes
scrubbed himself. Inside the jumbled, caved-in tunnel,

what did he scream when the crossbeam broke
and the mountain collapsed? When he squirmed,
unable to move one stone, what did he curse,

what did he promise? To give it up, climb down
to St. Louis and marry, and shave on Sunday?
If he could shove just one boulder from his legs,

he would go, even though so near the mother lode
he could smell it, even his burro smelled it, braying
the last few times he dragged it kicking into the dark.

[Previously published in *The Flying Dutchman* (Columbus: The Ohio State University Press, 1987—winner of the 1987 George Elliston Poetry Prize).]

Someday

Horse thief or lover,
or merely innocent squatter?
What posse knotted the noose
and tossed it over?

Why shouldn't it be this tree,
grooves in the bark like rope burns?
Imagine a cocked neck bowed,
the hanged man's boots on tip-toe,

fists tied behind him.
Imagine a thousand thieves
swinging the same ballet.
Hear the twist of ropes under tension.

Why shouldn't it be this posse
galloping out of a canyon,
black hats and puffs of pistol shots?
Even from here I know their mounts

are mustangs, able to run
till sundown. They're in no hurry
but coming, five, no, six of them
twirling new ropes and shouting.

[Previously published in *The New Criterion* 9, no. 10 (1991): 37 and *Counting Survivors* (Pittsburgh: University of Pittsburgh Press, 1995).]

Farms at Auction

Bidders from out of state drop by and stare.
They kick our neighbor's clods
and wade mirages like walking on water.
My barn a mile away appears to burn.

My neighbor's barbed wires shimmer,
his cattle blur, about to disappear.
Three years hailed out, he's quitting,
enough debt to break his children,

enough silage in his silo to feed one winter cow.
The auctioneer calls "gimme," "gimme,"
all our neighbor owns gone twice and sold,
even the dirt, the oaks his father planted.

I remember summer clouds miles away,
downpour a dozen churches prayed for.
I envied his rain, the runoff I needed,
nothing but thunder for our parched stalks.

I didn't see the rain, too busy cursing hail
to count my blessings. Sheared off,
his stubble rots. His beds are gone,
his trunks and keepsakes, hauled off to town

in a trailer returned to the farm for auction.
The man with wide suspenders kisses a bullhorn,
a sideshow barker. Loaded with luck
we gather close and watch some bidder

poke our neighbor's plows and tractor,
his wife's best nightgowns
like touching her slips and dresses
to satisfy himself they're silk.

[Previously published in *The Missouri Review* 17, no. 1 (1994): 73 and *Counting Survivors* (Pittsburgh: University of Pittsburgh Press, 1995).]

Rodeo Bulls

The danger more than horns
is hooves in the belly, a black
two-thousand-pound bull intent
on stomping. Nothing beats

being lucky, hard to stay on
a twisting tornado snapping
your spine like a whip, hard
to keep your fingers crossed

for luck, fist cramped, on fire
on the hump of his shoulders.
A mad bull moves more ways
than one, no guessing when

he'll coil or lunge, anything
to fling the rag-doll body off
his back, and fires of metal spurs
raking his belly. Half whale, half

killer shark, he leaps and fishtails
in the dust and blood of the rodeo,
wild-eyed, foaming at the mouth,
dying for someone to crush.

[Previously published in *Berkeley Poetry Review* 23/24 (1990): 125 and *Counting Survivors* (Pittsburgh: University of Pittsburgh Press, 1995).]

Coyotes and Dogs

Uncle Carl kept a St. Bernard in his tavern
before the county banned it, the patron dog
of his dance hall. My knuckles knew his rubber lips,
his purple tongue, thick double chins stuffed with fur.
He clung like a python when I scratched him,

digging my fists in his ribs. Cowboys taught him
to howl sad tunes with the jukebox. Girls tossed
beef jerky, the only dog on the dance floor,
trotting past couples locked in each other's arms.
Lapping draft beer, he lay down by blondes

and cowboys who tugged off leather gloves
and let him lick stiff knuckles busted in rodeos.
Fists that shot wild dogs and coyotes
burrowed deep into folds of fur and made his
massive tail keep time thumping the floor.

I remember how he howled and tugged
toward the door after the sheriff left, the moon
no jukebox, a dozen pickups, but not one fist
to pet him, sniffing packs of coyotes miles away,
dragging the stiff chain tight.

[Previously published in *Poet & Critic* 25, no. 3 (1994): 13 and *Counting Survivors* (Pittsburgh: University of Pittsburgh Press, 1995).]

Neighbors Miles Away

Blistering heat shimmers our fields
like lakes. It seldom rains.
Surveyors rode here in 1880
hung over, swearing they'd mapped
these miles before, cursing sextants
and starving overseas investors

who dumped these desert plains
on settlers. Coronado's army
crossed four hundred years ago,
coughing, praying for clouds,
crossing themselves and grumbling,
tugging their stumbling

Spanish mares, rumors of gold
in their eyes, hundreds of miles
from leaky galleons anchored
in the Gulf. Our wells flood the dung
and hoof prints of their route.
We pump the purest water

four hundred feet up to grain
they never dreamed could grow.
This sky is what they saw,
these level fields. We're not alone.
When we drive flat roads to town,
neighbors miles away look up and wave.

[Previously published in *Connecticut Poetry Review* 1, no. 1 (1992): 5 and *Counting Survivors* (Pittsburgh: University of Pittsburgh Press, 1995).]

Uncle Jerry and the Velvet Dog

Uncle Jerry lost a fortune and won it back
a thousand times, hunched on his elbows,
knuckles and blunt nails taunting, tapping the bait.
Men rob each other blind with their eyes,
bluffing their way to money. Storm doors he promised
had to wait till Labor Day after the rains.
Aunt Martha's wrath hung like a sword above him.

By Halloween, he brought home bathroom tiles
and had the roof ripped off, installed plush carpet
for her corns, a velvet dog in the corner
with silver dollar eyes, big as a bear,
something stuffed she could pet which didn't bark
when Jerry's key hit the latch after midnight.
Christmas came without a tree or tinsel gifts.

Martha draped the dog with baubles, star on his nose
like Rudolph. Jerry found her one night in the alley
dragging the dog through the snow and weeping,
trying to cram that velvet dog in a dumpster
with other trash, fluorescent in moonlight,
its buckshot eyes bouncing each time
she shoved and punched it in the face.

[Previously published in *Counting Survivors* (Pittsburgh: University of Pittsburgh Press, 1995).]

The Meaning of Flat Fields

Landscape never tells us how to live.
It never moves, is moved, shifted
in sandstorms, silted by floods,

thrust up as mountains and cliffs
millions of years ago. Nothing
that old teaches us how to cope

with hate. We tell a landscape
what we hope it means,
invent rich sounds wise

as well as ancient and give those
mournful names to landscapes—
ocean, horizon, stone. Nothing

that long ago knew what to do
but kill and flee from being eaten.
We've hurled the fear in ourselves

to the moon, our longing for peace
into sunsets. Hawks are no wiser
for watching the world from above,

no safer than rabbits balled up
in burrows, crouched with wide eyes,
not knowing when to run.

[Previously published in *Pequod* 26, 27 (1989): 29 and *Counting Survivors* (Pittsburgh: University of Pittsburgh Press, 1995).]

Coming Home

Mother knows I'd break my neck
to be here for her birthday.
Soapsuds in her eyes, hands
winding themselves dry
in her apron, she hugs and hurries
to the car to kiss my wife,

at last her arms grabbing
the grandkids. They disappear
inside her spongy belly,
giggling and clinging. For days,
she chases them like a nanny,
pots steaming on the stove,

dinner for kings. She slips them
peppermint sticks the way
she spoiled my father. Gone,
like the last passenger train
from the roundhouse. Nights,
while kids play games outside,

I squint to make stars move
like Pullman windows that winked
on their way to Houston when I was five,
the year my father died, when I knew
it was never my father's run
but waved anyway at the lights.

[Previously published in *Poetry* 143, no. 2 (1988): 101 and *Night Landings* (New York: Harper & Row, 1989).]

Charts

We didn't believe the stars
slashing across our years meant anything
but Orion hunting seven stars he never found,
a parade of unattainable maidens
and the tilted dipper pouring nothing.

We claimed we understood the hunger
of a bear lumbering under the North Star,
longed for the dawning of the age of Aquarius.
With luck we survived a war, the raising
of children and monthly debts, so far.

And now we've come this side of sixty,
a puzzled hunter stiff in the joints
and faithful wife stumbling somewhere
under a maze of stars, Polaris only a name
for navigation, whose mutable charts

we can't use, wherever we're going, dippers
tipping us toward the grave. Father of light,
we can't dread darkness where burning stars
hurtle outward, a gallery of myths,
but praise you for this vast created world.

[Previously published in *Tar River Poetry* 29, no. 1 (1989): 40 and *Counting Survivors* (Pittsburgh: University of Pittsburgh Press, 1995).]

Valley of the Shadow of Death

Barbed wires on rusted nails
can't hold lone bulls at home.
When they sniff greener pastures
they thrust their bone skulls
under barbs, tongues out,

quivering for a taste of strange,
and shove until the post gives way.
Days later, we find wires sagging,
reset the post and tighten bent wires
like a fiddle, and rope the worn-out bull,

wishing there was only a fence
between us and our wild desires.
Someday, a posse with spurs and a rope
will find us, yelling and cursing
on horseback, and gaining,

after our family and friends,
dragging us wide-eyed and frothing
into that dark arroyo, a valley of shadows
far from this sun-bleached yellow range
toward glorious whirlpools of wings.

[Previously published in *College English* 53, no. 8 (1991): 908 and *Counting Survivors* (Pittsburgh: University of Pittsburgh Press, 1995).]

Uncle Philip and the Endless Names

Uncle Philip hated work, walked off a dozen
jobs before thirty. Wide jawed, he sported a wiry moustache
and smoked, believed the sisters from Bovina

who called him handsome. He remembered their names
when he was eighty. His mother died when he was ten,
years before he enlisted. Never mind the war, he scoffed,

the Kaiser's army of millions. Uncle Philip won it,
he bragged again and again, his doubled fists like tanks.
Smoking, he coughed what he swore was mustard gas

in trenches of France that killed him. He lingered
sixty years with cigars, the pension he never got
stuck in his craw, his quarrel with the war the rage

that saved him from steady work. I remember the tilt
of his cap in pictures, a swaggering doughboy in Paris,
caught with some girl he bragged about. He taught me

to flip flies between logs in streams, hard to hook
brown trout in ponds. He taught me to drive, slouched
in his truck and smoking, coached me to shift big gears

like butter, don't lean into turns, but trust 18 wheels
would follow. When I glanced back, they followed.
I remember his eyes in the rest home. I followed his stare

to the ceiling, the shapeless water stains. Sobbing,
he called out dozens of names like a roll call, soldiers
I'd heard of, girls from Bovina, "Momma!" "Momma!"

[Previously published in *The Missouri Review* 14, no. 3 (1991): 135 and *Counting Survivors* (Pittsburgh: University of Pittsburgh Press, 1995).]

The Invention of Courage

The slam and cable whine of dawn,
the rumble and bang down alleys.
On side streets and loading docks,
trucks tug and bump the morning
out to sea. We rise and drive to jobs,
checking the clock, the clock,
amazed another day has gone
as if last night we passed the date line.
At drive-in movies in Dumas

in high school, on hay scattered on beds
of pickups, we sprawled side by side
watching monsters with fire and scales
invading cities, devouring battle tanks
and girls. Restless on straw, we watched
robots explode on the screen, time
to comb straw from our hair like rubble,
blinded by lights at intermission, hungry
and wild to be around our kind again.

We were kids inventing courage
in kindergarten, playing with sticks
like spears. Big brothers insisted witches
and wolves stalked the halls, and stars
were the eyes of ghosts. We didn't
and did believe. That night, to stop
their lips and lies, we chased each other
around and around the bonfire,
shouting, swinging our blazing sticks.

[Previously published in *The Missouri Review* 17, no. 1 (1994): 74 and *Counting Survivors* (Pittsburgh: University of Pittsburgh Press, 1995).]

My Cousin and the Widow's Ranch

"Bizarro Gonzo," I called my cousin
who swallowed snails and goldfish.
Joe wasn't slow, but bold with muscles,
always a broken nose or ribs, the other guys

worse. Aunt Lou gave up switches
when he was ten, since nothing she did
could tame him. Joe turned Marine at fifteen
when Uncle Ed faked Aunt Lou's name,

who stayed at home while Mother and I
waved goodbye to Joe on the bus. For years
I watched black pins on Aunt Lou's map–
Guadalcanal, Saipan and Guam, my cousin

island hopping with MacArthur toward Japan.
Joe came back without a scratch in '45, duffle bag
crammed with grenades and bloody flags
and knives. For years, he fed me souvenirs

and silence, shared nothing about the war
but playful punches and Japanese ears for birthdays
and Christmas, pictures of body parts and bracelets
made of teeth. At fifty, Joe married a widow

with a ranch, sold his hotdog stand and disappeared,
not even a call or postcard. One summer
he came back with Nelda and their adopted baby,
a blind and three-thumbed orphan from the slums.

Joe and Nelda run a ranch outside Fort Worth,
ten miles of fertile prairie flat as the past,
a hundred orphans and horses. I've seen Joe
hold five giggling children on his lap

and saddle, laughing with them on his Appaloosa
trotting to the corral with hardly a tap of reins,
all cowboys on the ranch sunburned and massive
like a battalion of retired Marines.

[Previously published in *Image* 29 (2000–2001): 96 and *Faith Is a Radical Master: New and Selected Poems* (Abilene, TX: Abilene Christian University Press, 2005).]

Sausage in the Mess Hall

Nights, my skiff stalls in the fog
until I swing legs down and wade ashore,
disgusted. At dawn, black coffee

to drown the dreams. No keg of beer
for breakfast–this is yellow Texas sun
like eggs over easy, not Vietnam.

Songs of daily bread belong to finches
giddy in the sycamore, feeder packed
with pounds of sunflower seed.

I'm back at my fighting weight. On the deck,
I'd rather sing than eat, no arias of ham
and grits, thick bacon and imported cheese.

Doves coo like maple syrup
over Willie Nelson's twang on the radio.
Rocket attacks came back last night,

crackling like static from Saigon.
In the shower, I throw my head back
and shout old bawdy squadron songs,

no one to stop me. I try to wash it
down the drain, memories of sausage
in the mess hall after the night's attack,

more bodies in the morgue, somebody
splattering ketchup over eggs and steak,
pumping up for battle, hot food to die for,

Billy Joe and the Outlaws blasting songs
on the jukebox, fat cooks shouting
and big lids slamming down.

[Previously published in *The Drunken Boat* 3, no. 2 (Summer 2002) and
A Thousand Miles of Stars (Lubbock: Texas Tech University Press, 2004).]

Who Swears the Last Blind Beggar's Doomed?

We touch you one by one and mumble,
words stumbling on our tongues,
stunned in your blurred living room,
hours after your lab report: a little lump,
a mass of bulged, malignant cells.
Telephoned, we've come to hold you.
The ghost who walked with mourners

to Emmaus may be in this room.
We are mere mortals, all. We don't know
anything but that. Who knows
this winter drought will last? Who swears
the last blind beggar's doomed,
no spittle for his lids? Who calls down
fire from heaven and isn't seared?

[Previously published in *North Dakota Review* 60, no. 4 (1992): 149 and *Faith Is a Radical Master: New and Selected Poems* (Abilene, TX: Abilene Christian University Press, 2005).]

Buzzards and Uncle Douglas

Old Uncle Douglas taught his dogs to chase off
buzzards in the sky. He cursed their black apparel,
their bowed necks praying for the dead.
He wanted them starved above his dying trees.
Trees died faster than he could haul them off,

nothing but dogs in his heart after Aunt Wanda died.
Douglas was Pharaoh of dying aspens, without a son.
Fungus killed all aspens on his farm, nothing to do
but cut them. He dropped his chain saw down
and stacked them, his skies still haunted by slow

whirlpools of wings. The old man loved his dogs
but never let anyone see him pet them, never mind
the moon, the nights we fished together, the black bass
fighting for their lives. He taught me the feel
of hard earth underfoot, the way to cast far out

for lunkers. He hated anything that grieved in public.
From his woodlot we watched buzzards like a dark
mobile of mourners that never cared for something
while it lived. He cursed them all, an old man
lost in a forest who hated every day he wasted

while Aunt Wanda lived. Gruff, he taught me to aim
at buzzards with a shotgun, but I always missed.
In August, he harnessed the mule and let the road
to the depot keep us both from choking, holding me
tight as a son before my train pulled out.

[Previously published in *Manca* 2, no. 2 (1990) 11–12 and *Counting Survivors* (Pittsburgh: University of Pittsburgh Press, 1995).]

Aunt Emma and the Spoils of War

When she found the herd bull dead,
Aunt Emma said, "Now everything makes sense."
She accepted when the pastor was fired,
when cattle went up five cents,

when my sister's appendix burst.
Every success and death, she shook her head,
another worry bead for her rosary–
her husband's jungle rot, the long Pacific war,

the Bomb. We're thread in the eye of a needle,
she believed, beasts in a fable called fate.
I saw the grainy photograph of her as a bride
in the hall, red-lipped laughing girl

of sixteen, weeks after Pearl Harbor.
After the honeymoon, Uncle Roy shipped out.
She swore she'd die childless if he died
in combat. After the land mine

flattened him, she swore he wouldn't die.
They shipped him back, patched up and whole
except what mattered most to him.
Aunt Emma taught him the rhythm

of rocking chairs and cards, helped him
until he could ride a horse without flinching.
She talked adoption, brought the first
blind child back home in her arms

while Uncle Roy drove, tight jawed
and tall as a stallion. For years, I watched him romp
with his kids, five orphans everyone loved–
three-thumbed, clumsy cousins who hugged

and clung to Uncle Roy, mellow as Emma's jam.
Aunt Emma set extra plates for my sister and me
on visits, humming, counting children like beads
and nodding, now that everything made sense.

[Previously published in *Seneca Review* 33, no. 2 (Fall 2003): 73–74 and *A Thousand Miles of Stars* (Lubbock: Texas Tech University Press, 2004).]

Hammering Ice to Slush

Wind flings snow over stalks like cobblestones.
Cattle wait out the storm in windbreaks
far from barns. They know when it's over
we'll drive out on tractors, hauling hay
and hard alfalfa pellets. They fear no evil,
since every dawn we come and hammer ice to slush.

Nights, we rock on the deck and watch the dark.
Children we raised are safe in cities lit
by a billion kilowatts. We know spring runoff
will water summer's hay, we'll own the ranch
someday, if luck and hard work save us,
knowing these dusty plains are home,
our south and north, a thousand miles of stars.

[Previously published in *Archipelago* 5, no. 3 (2000) and *A Thousand Miles of Stars* (Lubbock: Texas Tech University Press, 2004).]

Splitting Wood for Winter

"What we have here is smoke. Think of these logs
as smoke, and heave the axe the way I saw you
smoking bark behind the barn last Sunday.

Up and back, swing high and hit it, don't bend
your elbow like some bum puffing a butt.
Reach back and grab some fire and smoke it. Now!

See how they split?" That's how my father taught me
thrust when I was nine, the most power I'd held
in my life, two-bladed axe honed silver, heavier

than rifles that boomed and knocked deer down,
and fierce, able to split imported piñon in one thrust.
Now, swinging his axe grown lighter in my hands,

I feel the dry wood shudder, most logs the same,
hot summers short, green leaves turning brown,
snow clouds blooming sooner every year. I teach

my sons the arc of most deflection, the way
wide thrust can slice hard wood like cheese. One
by one they lift my father's axe and raise it back

and try to guide it like a kite. I hear some other voice
in my voice coaxing, "Here, you boys, reach back
and grab some fire. All logs are anyway is smoke."

[Previously published in *Prairie Schooner* 61, no. 1 (1987): 24 and *Night Landings* (New York: Harper & Row, 1989).]

Filing Systems

"I have that written down," she said,
"somewhere." And she always found it,
though it might take weeks, digging
through stacks of brittle clippings and notes,
some bent with the corners gone.
It all was there, the unassembled diary
of her life and all she cared about—

Armistice Day, the Dionne Quintuplets,
the night Daddy fell off the ladder
and only bruised himself, the date
of her third grandchild's seventh tooth,
the night the Lindbergh child was kidnapped,
the dawn she saw the sun after surgery.

While Daddy lived, she stored it all in stacks
against the wall. Later, the stacks multiplied
like kittens, litters on every chair and footstool
in the house. She hobbled happily for us
and lifted them from the floor like lazy cats,
her hands inches away to make sure they stayed.

My sister bought two filing cabinets and studied
notes for months, no way to order them all—
the first time Mother gave blood in World War One
had on the back a partial list of cousins
who had died. Mother knew where the others were,
a graveyard without stones, locked in the mind

of one who had dug there for eighty years.
Other cabinets had quilts she made for children
of grandchildren she would never see.
Her last months, she found most facts
we asked about, sifting stacks we handed her
in her rocking chair. Sometimes her eyes

went blank. "It's here," she said, "somewhere,"
and we had no doubt it was. Later, we found
on the back of a bill the exact hour of her pain
and, in more hurried cursive, which dress
to choose, which mortuary to call. In her parlor
afterwards, not knowing what to keep

and what to throw away, we crated them all
and stored them like urns in my sister's attic.
For years, she's emptied the musty crates,
keeping photos already faded, throwing most
of the bills away. Someday, I say, others will burn
them all. She smiles and goes on quietly filing.

[Previously published in *The Georgia Review* 32, no. 4 (1978): and *Night Landings* (New York: Harper & Row, 1989).]

The Middle Years

These are the nights we dreamed of, snow
drifting deep in mountains, enough stacked wood
and meat to last a week, alone at last
in our A-frame, isolated, without power,
high in the San Juan. Our children are safe
as they'll ever be, seeking their fortune in cities,
our desk and calendar clear, our debts paid

until summer. The smoke of piñon seeps back
under almost invisible cracks, the better to smell it.
All day we take turns holding hands and counting
the years we prayed we'd make it—the hours
of skinned knees and pleading, diapers and teenage rage
and fever in the middle of the night, and parents
dying, and Saigon, the endless guilt of surviving.

Nights, we lie touching for hours and listen, the woods
so close we can hear owls diving. Our woods
are not our home to keep, though we hold keys
to dead pine planks laid side by side, shiplap
like a dream that lasts, a double bed that fits us
after all these years, a blunt front-feeding stove
that gives back temporary heat for all the logs we own.

[Previously published in *Cimmaron Review* 78 (1987): 30 and *Night Landings* (New York: Harper & Row, 1989).]

After a Year in Korea

Old Uncle Oscar hated cold,
hauled his lean cattle early into town
to beat the snow. Daddy kept our own steers

corralled till after Christmas,
the winter market hungry for beef.
But Daddy never froze in Korea

like Uncle Oscar's friends, near the Yalu.
I didn't know till later. I thought
he was only a friendly drunk and lazy,

staying inside by the fire, or downtown
at Earl's with honky-tonk women,
sipping draft beer, picking fights

with boys my age with beards
and draft cards they threatened to burn
to provoke him. I didn't know he'd lost

his toes and fingers. I thought he wore
the gloves for show, to make him tough.
He'd end up drunk and humming tunes

with the jukebox, the same old
country and western words he learned
before they sent him overseas to freeze,

a man with two red eyes and stumps,
without a wife, always grumbling in a coat
about a town where they'd done something

awful to the weather, maybe pesticides,
the bomb, good summers short,
the winters hard, more bitter every year.

[Previously published in *Mississippi Valley Review* 16, no. 1 (1986): 38 and *Night Landings* (New York: Harper & Row, 1989).]

Grandfather Pounding Iron

He pounded to match the mustangs' hoofs,
no four shoes the same. Fire and hammers
shaped hot iron, tap tapping to fit the form—
one mare's hoofs like horseshoe crabs, another's

curved like a hornet's body. Grandfather's muscles
bulged, the better to lift us toward heaven, his biceps
hard as tongs. Iron rods were our toys, sparks
hissing in water were Lucifer tossed to the sea.

Fire was a pit for the beast, Grandfather's bellows
the wrath of God. Oh, he was tough, rugged
as blocks of wood he carved. Squatting, shielding
our eyes, we watched iron turn to taffy

in the heat. Mosquitoes flitting around our ears
flew there and disappeared, not a *poof*. Could Hell
be hotter than fire Grandfather fanned? He branded
brimstone into the skin of iron to pound, pound

until limp metal bent, hissing when he thrust it
under water like rattlesnakes trapped in steel—"No rest
for the wicked," Grandmama said of the Devil—
nailed to a lifted hoof, a horse to tread on its head.

[Previously published in *The Sewanee Review* 113, no. 1 (2005): 54 and *Faith Is a Radical Master: New and Selected Poems* (Abilene TX: Abilene Christian University Press, 2005).]

The Winter Daddy Died

I propped the rifle by the hearth
and pulled my wet boots off.
Mother slit and ripped the hide
like skinning a chicken. If rabbits bother you,

she'd say, don't bring the dead things back.
I washed my hands, the fur, the sticky blood.
Water already boiled, the big vat
spattering, potatoes and carrots chopped.

Rabbit stew and aroma of bread
woke Daddy up, in spite of cattle snowbound
last night, his beard frozen when he stomped
and came inside at dawn. Mother whispered

"Go back to sleep." She closed the door
that creaked, turned down the stove
and poured the buttermilk, broke bread
and melted cheese. My brother shivered

until she lifted him to her lap,
and we sat eating by the fire. Flames
turned to sparks, the snow-wet pine logs
popped, steam hissing from pockets of trapped sap.

My brother reached up and touched her hair.
She raised his cup and let him sip.
Wind made the chimney moan,
the orange flames flick. Broth bubbled

behind us, and Mother hummed,
carrots and onions and wild boar.
Daddy had split enough logs until summer,
stacked high against the house.

[Previously published in *North American Review* 288, no. 2 (2003): 20 and *Great Lonely Places of the Texas Plains* (Lubbock: Texas Tech University Press, 2003).]

Windmills Like Cathedral Windows

Uncle Oscar built them, but wind set them spinning
wide as cathedral windows, platforms a man could stand on
to oil without tumbling and tighten bolts big as fists.
He dug the holes, angled up from the earth toward God,

center where blades could spin. A windmill lifts all water
Moses could ask for. Aunt Martha bathed nine babies
in the tank. Their house rambled, dark as a nomad's tent,
always towels and soap for one more. Who needs the north star

on a ranch? Wherever we are, we're home. Barbed wires
mark borders for a man, needing no compass, no sextant
to find his way back, driving calves that wandered down
steep arroyos and almost starved. Uncle Oscar rode five miles

in any direction and saw the top of the world, windmills
spinning on massive posts, foursquare gospel of waterpower
bolted to hold the blades and rudders, to aim the ranch
toward God's almighty gales, to face whatever comes.

[Previously published in *Great Lonely Places of the Texas Plains* (Lubbock: Texas Tech University Press, 2003).]

Prairie Was a Tableland of Praise

Unlatch the table leaf, cracked piece of Ohio craft,
and fold it down. Quakers who knew how far,
how close to the heart God was, my great-greats
came to the plains when a river crossing took faith

in God's rod to part water. Mahogany that dark
fed them quail and leavened bread over trails
to this rattlesnake prairie, their wagon wobbly all day,
the bull-necked oxen hot. Each night, they jerked

this table out of the wagon and lifted the leaf to eat,
daily ark of their covenant to praise whatever bread
remained. All winter, until their first box house and harvest,
they slept in a scorpion dugout, raised the leaf each meal

to feed eight shivering children, then lowered it
for feather bedrolls. Let it down, leaf of a keepsake,
gently, leave it here, even scarred, in the entry,
history we pass in our hallway to the hearth.

[Previously published in *New Texas '99* (1999): 260 and *Great Lonely Places of the Texas Plains* (Lubbock: Texas Tech University Press, 2003).]

Uncle Howell and the Magic of Moonlight

Out of the kingdom of wood blocks,
coyotes crouched as he carved, elk heads,
the flicker of windmill blades.

Uncle Howell made barn owls stare,
made roosters rise and crow.
That old man fed shavings to the fire

at bedtime, tossed candy we gobbled
although we'd brushed our teeth.
Shadows flickered over goblins and lions

on the mantle, caught in the forest of Oz.
My sister swore he didn't whittle,
but caught rattlesnakes and hawks

and stuffed them, the fangs and beaks
too real—"Check out those beady eyes,"
she whispered, "real snakes in every room."

She feared he would turn them out
from stumps and silence in his house—
Aunt Sarah dead, the buffalo long gone,

herds no one could save, not even him,
no matter how many nights he carved
blocks of live oak into eyes.

[Previously published in *The Florida Review* 27, no. 1 (2002): 125 and *A Thousand Miles of Stars* (Lubbock: Texas Tech University Press, 2004).]

The Perks of Being a Greenhorn

The foreman smoked a cigar and drove a Jeep,
not the trail boss I bargained for.
The horse I drew from the remuda
was a gelding, not the palomino stallion

I'd fancied since first grade. Each time I took
the bridles and saddle horn and mounted,
his withers trembled. Was he ashamed
of being a gelding and fat, or of me,

the greenhorn? All summer, I rode alone,
the new guy banished to far arroyos,
the haunt of buzzards and the dumbest strays.
I mended fence and hauled the lost calves home,

turned back and found my place at night,
a bedroll under stars. That fall, high school
was all I hoped it would be and more,
girls in church and at the lake on weekends,

dreamy with lipstick in chemistry,
the equestrian club over-enrolled
with girls in love with saddles
and horses, any old boy who could ride.

[Previously published in *Descant* (Canada) 334, no. 4 (Winter 2003): 20 and *Great Lonely Places of the Texas Plains* (Lubbock: Texas Tech University Press, 2003).]

Hardscrabble June

I miss the dull routine of rain,
corn bogged in fields around a town
in Iowa. Here, rattlesnakes

hear the skin of cactus stretch
like leather: no wonder rattlers
love drought that boils the odor

of mice. Months without clouds,
the ranch is awash in mirage,
a rich man's tongue in torment,

horses I'd trade for camels.
Plunder is all bobcats
and starving coyotes do to barns

and chicken coops. Roosters,
watch out: they know who rules the roost,
and you're dead meat if caught asleep,

your hens dragged off to pups
or dusty caves for kits with wide
wet eyes and teeth already sharp.

[Previously published in *Nimrod* 46, no. 1 (2002): 137 and *Great Lonely Places of the Texas Plains* (Lubbock: Texas Tech University Press, 2003).]

Making Book on the Aquifer

Witching on dry land is prophecy,
and drilling a well, creation.
Pipes of our neighbors' wells dry up,
and they auction all they own.
We seed each angry cloud
and dance each dance with weather.

When it's time to irrigate dry crops,
we crank an old Ford engine
and pump the sweetest water
up from nothing we've ever seen,
gambling our luck on fields
flat as the moon.

The Ogallala aquifer drops
three feet each season,
and nothing we know brings water
out of stone. Home is a casino
of chance and choice,
four arms that hold each other.

[Previously published in *The Sewanee Review* 97, no. 1 (1989): 28 and *Counting Survivors* (Pittsburgh: University of Pittsburgh Press, 1995).]

Getting It Done

I've watched amazed the same
burnt sienna land we live on
begin to glow under her brush,

patches of ocher sand glinting light
she invents from nothing but tubes
and bristles. Weaving a delicate balance

down arroyos, she gathers and blesses
turquoise, obsidian, anything to bring color
to copper, making gardens of stones

and cactus. Even me, she polishes nightly
with the roughest of kisses, giving up
on nothing she's started, taking years

and three children to paint this scene
in the desert where we live, only brown earth
and sky and in between, all that matters.

[Previously published in *Visions* 14 (1984): 1 and *The Flying Dutchman* (Columbus: The Ohio State University Press, 1987—winner of the 1987 George Elliston Poetry Prize).]

Out in the Pasture at Dusk

We leave barn windows wide for owls,
but ignore coyotes that woo the moon,
complaining they own it all. Skunks waddle by,

sniffing for meat. Granddaddy taught me
north and south through his pastures,
past bulls to windmills and muddy tanks.

He slapped a dime-store compass in my hand,
turtle with a tin head wobbling on a pin.
Miles from his barn, I climbed crossbeams

and saw the plains through spinning blades,
a round horizon without a town. Buzzards
patrolled in slow motion, and coyotes loped away.

I thought I'd never be lost on a gelding
trotting home. In jungles outside Saigon,
even a compass lied, no directions out. Now,

after that war a world away, the ranch
and cattle are ours, no trains on tracks
laid out by crews long dead. I swore

I'd ride the range and never look back
too long for friends missing in action. Goats
claim the ranch, butting each other off

as if they own the troughs. At dusk, we rock
on plains we'll harvest tomorrow. Heads bowed,
the cows lie down, worshipping only now.

I know my compass wobbles like an old man
on a high wire, but Carol's blue eyes know
dark from dawn and lead us always home.

[Previously published in *The Old Red Kimono* 26 (1997): 2 and *Great Lonely Places of the Texas Plains* (Lubbock: Texas Tech University Press, 2003).]

Tasting the Night Air Gladly

We race the harvest moon past barns,
the highway and barbed wires
strung between towns, hours on the road
and still two hundred miles. Jackrabbits

hit the lights and vanish, sometimes an owl
we leave behind with coyotes. We see it rise,
flapping wide wings away. A lonely woman's song
calls us to the world of others, radio waves

that ricochet all night. Grandchildren we adore
are sleeping in Dallas, arms around big pandas
and baseball gloves we gave. A week
is never enough, gone like asphalt miles

behind us. When we pull over to stretch
and let the other drive, we taste the night air
gladly under stars, the vinegar-sweet aroma
of mesquites, the tang of cactus. And there,

out there in darkness, a flash, another light
we'll puzzle over, enough wonders
to marvel at after all these years, taking turns
behind the wheel, chasing the centerline.

[Previously published in *Borderlands* 8 (1996): 59 and *Great Lonely Places of the Texas Plains* (Lubbock: Texas Tech University Press, 2003).]

Pleasures of Coffee Together

"They'll have to shoot me
if they shoot me down,"
our colonel swore.

He leaned back, sipping,
and sighed: "I'd kill them all
for coffee." How that man

could fly and teach a tight
formation, trying to save us
from rookie mistakes

and missiles. Captured
when his luck ran out,
he lasted years in solitaire

and beatings, bones never set.
After they dumped the corpse,
they shipped his dog tags back.

Now, past sixty,
I can't stand coffee at dawn
without my wife beside me.

I'd quit this habit without her.
God knows what I would do
if she were gone.

[Previously published in *Phi Kappa Phi Forum* 82, no. 4 (Fall 2002): 43 and *Great Lonely Places of the Texas Plains* (Lubbock: Texas Tech University Press, 2003).]

Boys with Chihuahua Dogs

Chihuahuas the size of mice
chased cicadas in our backyard
under willows they entered
like doorways draped with streamers.

We argued what they'd do if they caught one,
yip-yipping and leaping, tumbling
and running, clumsy as rocker horses.
Dogs we wore in our pockets

kept us in trouble at church,
Sunday School no home for creatures
hopeless, without souls. Once
they scampered like devils down aisles

while the pastor convinced us all
we were starving for mercy, choking back laughter,
dying for benediction. Our father
who was in trouble with the board of deacons

left us alone with our dogs
and conscience, preaching a gospel
to all creatures small enough
to enter the kingdom of pockets.

Hairless like Mary's lamb after shearing,
they followed us often to school
and on bicycle errands for parents.
What can you say about dogs

too dumb to read stop signs,
too slow for cars in a speed zone,
too small for a shoebox,
too hopeless for a cross.

[Previously published in *The Florida Review* 18, no. 1 (1992): 94 and *Counting Survivors* (Pittsburgh: University of Pittsburgh Press, 1995).]

The War in Bosnia

Under darkness of stars our son flies
over Bosnia, keeping watch over snow.
Apache gunships will be out tonight.

The moon on foreign snowfields highlights
bodies running under trees, friend or foe.
Under darkness of stars our son flies

with star scope and rockets and wide eyes
over war zones bitter enemies know.
Apache gunships will be out tonight.

What keeps a nation armed and justifies
air power is such a killing field. We know,
but under darkness of stars our son flies.

In boots and parka, someone watches the skies
and owns disposable Stingers, and is cold.
Apache gunships will be out tonight.

I conjure God to stop him, warp his sights.
I stare with the prayer all fathers know.
Under darkness of stars our son flies.
Apache gunships will be out tonight.

[Previously published in *Meridian* (Spring 1998): 89 and *Faith Is a Radical Master: New and Selected Poems* (Abilene, TX: Abilene Christian University Press, 2005).]

The Rockets' Red Glare

Waking in sandbagged bunkers,
we hummed country-and-western tunes
to explosions louder than our ears
could hear, rhythms of Nashville
waltzing with rockets, keeping us all
awake. Caught in a war we left home

hoping to survive, we slept in shorts,
sirens calling us to the noise of now.
Friends in our jungle home
were brave, even when hunkered down,
shouting George-Jones love songs
at chow and in latrines. At night,

we packed sandbags, cursing
all-clear horns that seldom came
until songs we knew were sung, and still
the sirens howled, and mortars burst
like jokes people I didn't know kept
shouting in a chopper about to crash.

[Previously published in *Poetry Durham* (UK) 16 (1987): 16 and *Counting Survivors* (Pittsburgh: University of Pittsburgh Press, 1995).]

Hauling over Wolf Creek Pass in Winter

If I make it over the pass, I park the rig, crawl back
to the bunk and try to sleep, the pigs swaying
in a steep grade, like the last curve Johnson took
too fast and burned. But that was summer. His fire

spread to the next county. It doesn't worry me.
I take the east climb, no sweat, and the rest is a long
coasting down to the pens in Pagosa Springs.
It's the wolves I wait for. We never see them

any other way, not in this business. Sometimes five,
six hauls before, propped on one arm, smoking,
I see them slinking from dark pines toward the truck.
They drive the pigs crazy, squealing as if a legion

of demons had them. Later, when I crank up
and go, the pigs keep plunging, trying to drive us
over the cliff. I let them squeal, their pig hearts
exploding like grenades. The wolves are dark

and silent. Kneeling, I watch them split up
like enemy sappers in Vietnam, some in the tree lines,
some gliding from shadow to shadow, red eyes
flashing in moonlight, some farther off,

guarding the flanks. Each time, they know
they have me. I take my time, knowing I can
crawl over the seat, light up, sip from the steaming
thermos. I crank the diesel, release the air brakes

like a rocket launcher. Wolves run in circles.
I hit the lights. Wolves plunge through deep snow
to the trees, the whole pack starving.
Revving up, the truck rolls down the highway

faster, like the last flight out of Da Nang. I shove
into third gear, fourth, the herd of pigs screaming,
the load lurching and banging on every turn,
almost delivered, almost airborne.

[Previously published in *TriQuarterly* 59 (1984): 121–22 and *The Flying Dutchman* (Columbus: The Ohio State University Press, 1987—winner of the 1987 George Elliston Poetry Prize).]

Part 3

Seconds of Free Fall and Chaos

My bored brother dragged me
away from kiddie land, shoved me
roughly to the adult ticket booth,
the line dividing me from men.

Thrilled by tickets snaking from his fist,
I entered the kingdom of risks–
the hammer and zipper, the roller coaster.
Four, I flinched when the hammer

slammed down, when the zipper toppled
and flipped us. I held the bar
in a car jerked up a track
and watched treetops and tents

fall away. My brother leaned close
and hissed how many fell
from these seats last year, flung out
over screaming mothers. He raised both hands

and made me, the cross bar loose on my lap.
Older boys tossed their hair
and laughed, the heads of girls
snug in their elbows.

Our car crawled on cables
grinding like bicycle chains
about to break, all rides of childhood
behind me, my arms high in surrender,

my skull wobbling
through tight turns, mashed down
like being born again to lights
and dazzling screams.

[Previously published in *The American Scholar* (Phi Beta Kappa magazine) 62, no. 2 (1993): 260 and *Whatever the Wind Delivers: Celebrating West Texas and the Near Southwest* (Lubbock: Texas Tech University Press, 1999–winner of the 2000 Western Heritage Award ("The Wrangler") for best book of poetry, National Cowboy Hall of Fame).]

Fifth Grade

I watched Miss Jones at the blackboard,
her chalk squeaking something I should know.
I was thinking of runways, a million acres
falling away below the cockpit, then click!

into the clouds. My boots toe-danced the rudder,
and I banked through bumpy air. Wings
balanced the needle and ball, and broke
through clouds into the sun, the wild blue

the second my teacher called me back down,
classmates along all aisles laughing
as if they all had seen those skies,
those marvelous wide wings.

[Previously published in *Palo Alto Review* 6, no. 1 (1997): 19 and *Whatever the Wind Delivers: Celebrating West Texas and the Near Southwest* (Lubbock: Texas Tech University Press, 1999—winner of the 2000 Western Heritage Award ("The Wrangler") for best book of poetry, National Cowboy Hall of Fame).]

Digging on Hardscrabble

Deep in the well, I swung a pickaxe
for another foot, so dark I aimed the axe
by feel. My kid brother leaned back
away from me. Sweat was a blessing

the body gave. Bobby called "time"
and drank, canteens the only water
we might find. I leaned against a wall,
hacked rough by the madman I was

and sipped, more soothing to my back
than to my tongue. If dirt walls cracked,
we could be buried with salamanders
after years of drought. Better clay than this

had crumbled, one cousin crushed
when I was nine—Daingerfield, pine country,
black dirt heaped higher than my head.
But here we were on parched

hardscrabble plains, digging for water
the old way. A traveling dowser
rambled over our farm and pointed
a quivering sycamore stick,

bone-dry and hollow at the core.
And though we knew three wells
out of four are sand, this was our fourth.
Kneeling, nearing the limit of our time,

I groped for the shovel, scooped fast
to fill the bucket, and tugged. Faces we loved
looked down from above and reeled,
the creak and clatter of rope and pulley

a wild hosanna. I guzzled the canteen dry,
then reached for the dangling rope
and sent my brother up,
spinning into almost liquid light.

[Previously published in *The Paris Review* 115 (1990): 51–52 and *The Digs in Escondido Canyon* (Lubbock: Texas Tech University Press, 1991—winner of the 1992 Western Heritage Award ("The Wrangler") for best book of poetry, National Cowboy Hall of Fame).]

Hawks in a Bitter Blizzard

Hard work alone can't drive blue northers off.
Nine blizzards out of ten blow out by Amarillo,
nothing this far south but flakes and a breeze
to make a man in shirt sleeves shiver.

Every few years, Canada roars down,
fast-freezing cattle in the fields, dogs caught
between barns, hawks baffled on fence posts.
Stubborn, hawks refuse to hunker down

in burrows with drowsy rattlesnakes and rabbits.
They drown in their own breath bubbles, crystal
as the sheen on barbed wires freezing in the rain.
Wood carvers driving by, grinding on chains

down icy roads, see them at dawn and envy, tempted
to haul the fence posts home and burn them,
nothing in oak or juniper they carve
ever as wild and staring as those eyes.

[Previously published in *The Atlantic Monthly* 265, no. 3 (1989): 82 and *All That Matters: The Texas Plains in Photographs and Poems* (Lubbock: Texas Tech University Press, 1992—winner of the 1993 Western Heritage Award ("The Wrangler") for best book of poetry, National Cowboy Hall of Fame).]

All the Old Songs

I never knew them all, just hummed
and thrummed my fingers with the radio,
driving five hundred miles to Austin.
Her arms held all the songs I needed.
Our boots kept time with fiddles
and the charming sobs of blondes,

the whine of steel guitars
sliding us down in deer-hide chairs
when jukebox music was over.
Sad music's on my mind tonight
in a jet high over Dallas, earphones
on channel five. A lonely singer,

dead, comes back to beg me,
swearing in my ears she's mine,
rhymes set to music that make
her lies seem true. She's gone
and others like her, leaving their songs
to haunt us. Letting down through clouds

I know who I'll find waiting at the gate,
the same girl faithful to my arms
as she was those nights in Austin
when the world seemed like a jukebox,
our boots able to dance forever,
our pockets full of coins.

[Previously published in *Ariel* (Canada) 23, no. 4 (1992): 74, *Where Skies Are Not Cloudy* (Denton: University of North Texas Press, 1993), and *Whatever the Wind Delivers: Celebrating West Texas and the Near Southwest* (Lubbock: Texas Tech University Press, 1999—winner of the 2000 Western Heritage Award ("The Wrangler") for best book of poetry, National Cowboy Hall of Fame).]

With Horsehairs Dipped in Oils

My wife's green eyes are jade and rainbows.
With horsehairs dipped in oils,
she brushes corrals and cattle on canvas,
the burnt sienna sand and pastures of our boots.
Combing October lawns like yarn,

we heap dry leaves on flames that float away,
always a breeze to make chimes clang
and jangle on the patio. Friends disappear,
and nothing we do could save them.
We store the rakes away near pups

gnawing our gloves. Rocking, we watch them
sniff the yard for bones the old dog buried.
We watch smoke drifting east
toward slow whirlpools of wings,
our neighbor's tin roof shimmering.

Prairie cattle go mad when the wind dies.
They stomp, lashing their tails at horseflies.
We survive hardscrabble drought
like spiders that spin their webs in wind
and anchor them to thorns.

[Previously published in *The Missouri Review* 20, no. 3 (1997): 42 and *Whatever the Wind Delivers: Celebrating West Texas and the Near Southwest* (Lubbock: Texas Tech University Press, 1999—winner of the 2000 Western Heritage Award ("The Wrangler") for best book of poetry, National Cowboy Hall of Fame).]

After Eden

I like snakes my own way, underfoot,
not overhead in branches draped like vines.
High on a sorrel clopping on iron shoes

I see them often at a distance, slithering away
on their bellies between mesquite and cactus.
This is the grace of hardscrabble fit for goats,

prairie where no trees grow native, nothing sweet
the old serpent can dangle from a limb.
I watch one disappearing down a hole

and pity prairie dogs, nothing I can do
to save them. Stopped at a steep arroyo
looking for strays, I prop one leg

across the saddle horn, strike a match
on a boot and touch it, smoke the one thing
dryer than the breeze. I see a steer

grazing below, but let it taste its last meal
before the slaughterhouse. I finish the butt
and crush it on my boot, and flip it,

shove that boot back in the stirrup and flick
the tip of the reins to nudge the horse
downhill. The steer sees me and stares,

chewing the last good weeds in a canyon
where it hasn't rained in months, too dumb to know
I'm a death angel come to drive him

with yells and a rope uphill to the pasture
where the loading corral is waiting
and a truck backed tight against the ramp.

[Previously published in *The Windsor Review* (Canada) and *All That Matters: The Texas Plains in Photographs and Poems* (Lubbock: Texas Tech University Press, 1992–winner of the 1993 Western Heritage Award ("The Wrangler") for best book of poetry, National Cowboy Hall of Fame).]

A Brief Familiar Story of Winter

Trees are telling the story
of harvest. The wind is listening,
murmuring "oh" and dying.
Leaves at best have only

one more month to listen.
They glitter in sunlight,
flutter like friends in a parlor
fanning themselves and flushing.

The bark has heard it all before,
thick-skinned like a snake
that cannot shed. Taproots
hear in whispers, swelling

each time they hear the old, old story.
They shove into grains of sand
and feed all they can to heartwood.
Chilled xylem lifts the last fluid up

from tips of roots like salmon
flinging themselves up rapids,
all branches eager as bears,
leaves on all limbs trembling.

[Previously published in *Kansas Quarterly* 18, no. 3 (1986): 121 and *All That Matters: The Texas Plains in Photographs and Poems* (Lubbock: Texas Tech University Press, 1992–winner of the 1993 Western Heritage Award ("The Wrangler") for best book of poetry, National Cowboy Hall of Fame).]

Starting a Pasture

Flooded with sun, this ranch looks like a rice field,
a trick of optics. Rattlers roam boldly
because their world is dust, natives as foreign
to our ways as wolves that disappeared by 1880.
Surviving coyotes sway in ballets for the moon,
heads back, worshipping only stars. We mete out mice
to cats and owls, fat from our grain sacked up for cattle.

Stuttering owls cough softly in our sleep
like goats, another herd we're saving. Neighbors
drive slowly by and stare, their windows tight.
They scoff, although we're feeding thousands,
cabrito and Texas mutton worth more than beef.
Let them laugh while little bells lead goats and lambs
to market. All week we find our cows, heads down,

praying to all the stubble they own. We fill their troughs
and call, and they come floating through a lake
of shimmering sunlight. My wife's green eyes
play homespun when the chores are done,
better chords than fiddles and sweet guitars.
After rains, fat cattle wade alfalfa ankle-deep.
It's grain, not shade, hot cattle need. Often in fields

I find buzzards, too late to save a calf
I would have gladly fed. Our sons ride the range
to keep scavengers away, gliding on thermals.
I hate tornadoes and slow whirlpools of wings.
Don't look, I say, as if blind luck could save us.
Let cattle claim our pastures, let lambs turn into wool,
let buzzards wait for city dogs tossed out from cars.

This morning in the field I found another tow sack
full of kittens. They'll grow up gladly in our barn,
making owls work harder for mice, saving our wheat
for export. All winter we sow alfalfa for livestock,
ten of each kind in a starving world, buffalo
imported from Wyoming, a flock of ostriches
that came last night by train, wide-eyed and panting.

[Previously published in *Poetry* 157, no. 3 (1990): 151–52 and *The Digs in Escondido Canyon* (Lubbock: Texas Tech University Press, 1991—winner of the 1992 Western Heritage Award ("The Wrangler") for best book of poetry, National Cowboy Hall of Fame).]

Blue Skies

Under crisp reeds, mud smooth as leather
dries out, cracks, and curves up into hooks.
Frogs caught in the drought try to crawl,
hot days drying their legs like jerky.

Bracing themselves, they leap,
believing in clouds, their throats
bruised puff by puff, the soft dust
choking. At last light, dry ponds

make heat waves seem like water.
Mourning doves flatter the dust
by gliding down, then flapping
frantically away from light

flashing on shotguns. On a cliff,
dapper in moonlight on thin legs
and four splayed feet like spats,
a coyote with his heart in his nose

sniffs, sips puddles of air. Nothing.
A breath of wind would be enough,
odor of cony, possum, raccoon
with sticky fur. Even a frog.

Better this than rain, the grit of dirt
and dry stones giving firm purchase
to scales of the belly, the leeched earth
perfect for shedding skin, long muscle

flowing, new diamonds glistening
in moonlight, fangs ready, rattle
tip-up and poised, the tongue
never so damp as now, flicking,

flicking, the tongue able to taste
aromas the wind will bring, the wind
like a god, the wind knowing where,
the wind always delivering.

[Previously published in *Southern Poetry Review* 23, no. 2 (1983): 19 and *Witching on Hardscrabble* (Peoria, IL: Spoon River Poetry Press, 1985).]

There Are No Old Bold Pilots

Young pilots at the bar are eating flames.
Blue flames burn slowly on their alcohol.
Blue blazers, they are called. The pilots

toss them down like what-the-hell—we live
in fame. Nothing, not wives, not mistresses
could make them stop. They smack their lips

and grin, their teeth burned white.
There are no fighter pilots down in hell,
they sing. Then belly-up to the bar again

and roll for drinks. Someone buys
another round, and one by one they tilt
inverted and all go down in flames.

[Previously published in *New Mexico Humanities Review* 2, no. 3 (1979): 35 and *Anything, Anything* (Spokane, WA: L'Epervier Press, 1980).]

The Winter Before the War

Sledgehammers couldn't break ice
cloudy and hard in the troughs.
For hours, we rode for cattle frozen

where they fell, some huddled
by barbed wire, some stumbling
in snowdrifts, covered with ice.

Sundown, herding survivors home,
we passed a frozen playa lake, one
whiteface bull caught in the middle.

The bull maybe tried walking on water
and broken through up to his head,
his tail raised like a flag, his horns

on a platter of ice, wide muzzle stiff,
as if he had died bawling. We fed
the lucky steers and barred the corral

to save them. At supper, we smoked
and played poker and bet how long
a bull could have bawled when the lake

gave way. We flipped our cards and drank
and cursed our luck, and tried to ignore
stiff winds and shingles banging overhead.

[Previously published in *The Kenyon Review* 18, nos. 3, 4 (1996): 185 and *All That Matters: The Texas Plains in Photographs and Poems* (Lubbock: Texas Tech University Press, 1992—winner of the 1993 Western Heritage Award ("The Wrangler") for best book of poetry, National Cowboy Hall of Fame).]

Bloodlines

Our daughter puts her hand
on my wife's belly. I came from
there, she claims. Beams at us both.
Her education sound. No, her mother
says. Remember what we've said?
How we picked you from all sweet
babies we could love? At six weeks old
we brought you home. She's heard
but doesn't understand. It contradicts
the film she saw today in preschool.
She shakes her head. Then where?
The adoption agency. Then how?
From another mommy's womb. And
what's a womb? She must have missed
that word in school. Where babies grow.
But not in you? No. Then where?
Somebody else. Then who? We just
don't know. Then how can you be sure?
It's how it's done. For even me? Yes.
Then who's my mom? Me. I mean
the one who, you know, grew me there.
We really just don't know. That night,
we hugged and tucked her in. Kissed her
goodnight. Peeped in before we went
to bed. Found her curled up, asleep,
cocooned inside her sheet.

[Previously published in *Alembic* 4 (1979): 9 and *Anything, Anything* (Spokane, WA: L'Epervier Press, 1980).]

With Cindy at Vallecito

With a flick of her small wrist,
she casts far out and reels in quick
to set the hook.

Good, I tell her, and she nods, her eyes
severely watching the bright drops
springing from her line.

It's all a matter of luck,
I tell her, and all a matter
of knowing how. She cocks her head

and grins. Be easy, I tell her.
I think you have one hungry.
She slowly reels,

not breathing at all. Daddy? she calls.
I tell her Set the hook, and she pulls hard.
The rod bends tighter than a bow.

I'm glad for her the fish is twice
the size of those her brothers caught
last night. Out of the water it jerks

as if shocked. She bites her lip
and holds the rod up high. Bring it
around, I say, and she aims the fish at me.

I catch its lip and twist the hook out.
Lifting the stringer from the lake, I add hers
to the smaller crappies. Already she runs,

her blonde hair flowing, and she calls
back to me I've got to tell! And I know
her brothers soon will swagger down

to see for themselves, and then
like losers in a poker game will cast
their own lines far, far out.

[Previously published in *One Thing Leads to Another* (New Braunfels, TX: Cedar Rock Press, 1978) and *Wetting Our Lines Together: An Anthology of Recent North American Fishing Poems*, Allen Hoey, ed. (Tamarack Editions, 1982, 105–6).]

Growing Up Flying

—for Cindy

I'd hear the car and run crashing through the door,
take off from the porch and fly to Daddy. Around
and around he'd swing me up to his shoulders
and over his head, a wild spiral that worked.

Often, nothing of the day remained but sun
setting like fire over the mountains, and magpies
formal and shiny, swirling from pine to pine.
At the steps he would swing me down, my toes

touching perfect the way he landed jets. Nothing
about that house was safe. His hat would sail
and miss the sofa, he'd scoop Mother into orbit
around his neck, Mom grabbing her dress

and laughing. Held in the air, she'd hold on tight and kiss
until I knew the food would burn. When he brought
logs in for the fireplace, I rattled off all I had learned
of the language of my father, the names of jets,

maneuvers, how to survive in the air—Thunderbirds,
Voodoos, Phantoms, and with my hands I showed
chandelles and loops, and what to do in case of fire.
Later, while he watched war news, I stood at the window

and remembered nests shaking in mountain winds,
and nothing seemed tied down, not Father or Mother,
not me, not magpies like the hours of childhood
flying by, not logs in the fireplace going up in flames.

[Previously published in *Embers* 8, no. 2 (1982): 8–9 and *Witching on Hardscrabble* (Peoria, IL: Spoon River Poetry Press, 1985).]

Fathers and Sons

Our son is not afraid of heights.
At twelve, he scaled Mount Dallas
with the scouts, attempted Pyramid alone
and fell. Splinters of his bones
stuck out below the knee like straw.
With pins and wire the surgeon
fashioned a box-kite cast around his leg,
hoisted in traction like a sling.

I climb below him, now, roped
like an anchor to a man who could climb
three times as fast alone. The route up
he takes is almost straight, the random
handholds dangerously thin. I hear him
tap tapping blunt steel pitons into stone
as a last resort. He never retreats
to try another way. Hand over hand

I give myself to the sheer face
of his will, trusting each piton
as it comes. I snap a karabiner through
and loop the rope, insert each heavy foot
and step out into space on nothing
but his piton holding me, and his rope
I climb toward fist by fist.

[Previously published in *Poetry* 144, no. 6 (1984): 333 and *Witching on Hardscrabble* (Peoria, IL: Spoon River Poetry Press, 1985).]

Sons

My son runs stubby fingers
through my hair. Fuzzy man,

he says. I shift him from one knee
to the other, and he pulls my beard.

If you shave it off, he says, I won't
kiss you again. I glance at my wife.

We both know the day will come
faster than whiskers grey when,

like his brother, he won't sit on either knee.
For the time, I hold him in my arms

and brush my chin against his neck.
For the time, I crush him to my face.

[Previously published in *Ex Libris* 10, no. 1 (1978): 28 and *Anything, Anything* (Spokane, WA: L'Epervier Press, 1980).]

Fathers and Pearl Harbor

Shoulder, hip, and boot he'd kick, then stirrup over
and sit that horse like a god, my father at dawn
on a gelding I thought was a stallion, if only
I'd known the words. Five times a week he rode off
on that great silver-blue, the only Appaloosa
in my life. I thought he'd never fall. I called goodbye
by the corral, shivering in a coat under the moon,
waving my hat at my brother, who waved goodbye,

riding off with our daddy to work. All chickens squawked
and came to the grain, pecking like prayer. All logs I chopped
splintered as oak does, the better to burn, as he taught.
Alone on the ranch with Mother, I stacked cords
and tried to ride bulls, just calves but they hated to play,
no snow but the clear day cold. At night under lights
I would hear them, coming back, clopping softly and safe.
I burst from the door into darkness, both men outside,

rubbing down, geldings tired and unsaddled, snorting,
dropping their heads. Brushes stroked the sweaty coats,
crisp bristles flicking sparks, hot horses munching
at the trough, the slurp and deep-bass crunch of oats.
I remember them mostly at night, my father taller, and boss,
but both men big as mystery under the moon and stars—
childhood a happy island before Pearl Harbor was attacked,
my father's last good winter with a son who rode off
to war on a battleship and never, never came back.

[Previously published in *Poetry Wales* (UK) 32, no. 3 (1997): 55–56 and *Whatever the Wind Delivers: Celebrating West Texas and the Near Southwest* (Lubbock: Texas Tech University Press, 1999—winner of the 2000 Western Heritage Award ("The Wrangler") for best book of poetry, National Cowboy Hall of Fame).]

Dad's Straight Razor

This old razor loves a beard, the subtle
scrape of flesh all it asks for.
It glides the moist, soaped stubble
like a water spider, sharp enough
to puncture flesh, balanced on the stretched
surface tension of skin.

I remember its touch along my jaw,
the cold Toledo steel slicing me
squeegee clean, before I grew a beard.
Opened, sharpened back and forth
on my daddy's black leather strop,
it smoothed my honeymoon face twice daily,

leaving no shadow to burn my bride.
I remember Dad's face when I flew home
after his attack, the nights in CCU,
the wave of his hand, his last request
to shave him before he saw Mom.
I remember his eyes barely wavering,

his scalp buried in the pillow,
exposing the slack stretch of his face
when I touched him, the prickle of a week's
white growth under my careful thumb
and fingers, the willing tilt of his chin,
the short, slick flicks of the blade

on his throat and jaw, floating on
blue-veined skin and bone, his face
coming clean through the lather, my own
eyes barely wavering, like nothing
I'd ever get to do again, nothing
I wouldn't have done to save him.

[Previously published in *Poetry* 156, no. 3 (1990): 147 and *The Digs in Escondido Canyon* (Lubbock: Texas Tech University Press, 1991—winner of the 1992 Western Heritage Award ("The Wrangler") for best book of poetry, National Cowboy Hall of Fame).]

Barking Hosanna

I ripped the sack and flipped the grain.
I'm not St. Francis, but the chickens loved it,
clucking for manna. Our doggie Spot
came running, soggy and shaking,

our boys like prophets out of breath. "You boys
baptize him in the trough?" Wide-eyed,
the youngest nodded, believing faith
could save him. Bedtime, they watched TV,

sleepy, their oddly named dog sprawled,
not even blinking. My wife's bare toes
played mischief with my feet. On TV,
Bing Crosby winked and wouldn't leave.

When my wife led our boys upstairs
to bed, light shimmered in her negligee.
I rose, and turned the baptized dog
outside, barking hosanna at shadows.

[Previously published in *Inklings* 4, no. 1 (1998): 9 and *Whatever the Wind Delivers: Celebrating West Texas and the Near Southwest* (Lubbock: Texas Tech University Press, 1999–winner of the 2000 Western Heritage Award ("The Wrangler") for best book of poetry, National Cowboy Hall of Fame).]

Wherever Others Are Going

When it doesn't rain, we water,
pumping the purest water 300'
up from nothing we've ever seen,

raising bumper crops on faith.
If we didn't know the world
is dying, the water table dropping

3' each year, we'd swear this water
would gush forever, like Aaron's rod
that budded without touching dirt.

Even in snow, we cuddle by firelight
and watch our fields fill up, stranded
these dark evenings between towns

and miles from mountains, but knowing
wherever others on the road
a mile away are going, we are here.

[Previously published in *Country Journal* 13, no. 5 (1986): 60 and *All That Matters: The Texas Plains in Photographs and Poems* (Lubbock: Texas Tech University Press, 1992—winner of the 1993 Western Heritage Award ("The Wrangler") for best book of poetry, National Cowboy Hall of Fame).]

One Summer Before Saigon

That summer, I strolled with Ursula to the tomb,
ducking under marble archways in the mall.
Ivy tangled down, coiling like snakes

chasing their tails. "Blonde Ursula without a bra,"
nickname I called her, silk blouse unbuttoned
to the breastbone–what would Uncle Joe

have said to that? Say "Holy buttons, Girl,"
say "Hug old Uncle Joe." That year,
I pitied Aunt Peggy's frown, "Behold,

the hussy comes." Childless, Uncle Joe
had willed me his ranch, his Purple Heart
and Silver Star, his cattle and stallions.

And so that morning after Mass, I took her
to his tomb for Uncle Joe's amusement,
knowing Aunt Peggy would sneer

and scoff inside pink marble, would have
boxed his cheeks with both big-diamonded fists,
"Down, you leacher, down!" She would know

we had been to church where Ursula
gave a kiss to the Bishop, who balked
and shook her hand, and laid the wafer there.

All that, one crazy summer after college,
before a bunch of friends and I went to Saigon.
After the war, after we married, I rode the ranch

in the dark and counted falling stars, as far from war
as cattle from cactus, "Ursula" in my arms
by the campfire under a thousand miles of stars.

[Previously published in *River Styx* 63/64 (2002–2003): 3 and *A Thousand Miles of Stars* (Lubbock: Texas Tech University Press, 2004).]

Sweet Nothings

The same old songs keep twanging back,
slurred by steel guitars and a fiddle,
tear honey for the heart. They make me young

and vulnerable again, for three minutes,
as if Saigon never happened.
Honky-tonk darlings saved us

from killing each other, gored
and stomped on all week, stubborn
as the bulls we rode, trying to ignore

the TV war. Good-hearted women led us
to the dance floor, swaying to slow sad songs
and humming. After the last good waltz,

sipping cold Lone Star after midnight,
we glowered at men too old for the draft
doing a fast fox-trot on the sawdust.

We stared through blue smoke layered
like gunfire, slouched with hollow cans
crushed easy in our fists.

[Previously published in *Michigan Quarterly Review* 28, no. 2 (1989): 179 and *The Digs in Escondido Canyon* (Lubbock: Texas Tech University Press, 1991—winner of the 1992 Western Heritage Award ("The Wrangler") for best book of poetry, National Cowboy Hall of Fame).]

Slow Times Near the River

The way the rain came down
all night like a flicker of flames
on the oak logs, slow-burning
deep in the heartwood,
the way the river flowed

near the cabin and never stopped,
at dawn the cardinals,
the stone floor cold and clean,
easy to walk on to the fire,
the way you always

had the coffee hot, my cup
waiting near the flames,
the way we always had
something to do whether
the weather cleared or not.

[Previously published in *The Spoon River Quarterly* 8, no. 4 (1993): 4 and *Witching on Hardscrabble* (Peoria, IL: Spoon River Poetry Press, 1985).]

Sunday Morning Roundup

I guide my sorrel down a steep arroyo,
cursing each crumbling step of shale, oil-rich,
if I could afford to drill it. I tell my mama's
conscience work is a virtue of godly men

on Sunday when starving cougars
believe spring calves are born to feed them.
Better here than in some high-roofed church
with robed choirs shouting Latin.

I've hummed this hymn a thousand times
and mean it, washed by the blood of the Lamb,
though I can't stand mutton. Red meat for me,
cattle and goats the only hoofs I'd have

on prairies fit for scorpions. I let the gelding
climb back to the plains, following the dog,
nothing in that valley of shadows
but bones, not one spiraling buzzard in sight

and it's almost noon, time to stumble on a big cat
sleeping it off, feeling smug as a rich man
counting his barns. The dog stops and stiffens,
wants to bay, but doesn't, breaks running

toward a weed-grown playa lake. Tapping the reins,
I gallop toward shadows, a flash of weeds,
and tug my Stetson tight against the wind,
lean down and slide the rifle out.

[Previously published in *Three Rivers Poetry Journal* 35/36 (1990): 77–78 and *Whatever the Wind Delivers: Celebrating West Texas and the Near Southwest* (Lubbock: Texas Tech University Press, 1999–winner of the 2000 Western Heritage Award ("The Wrangler") for best book of poetry, National Cowboy Hall of Fame).]

After the Flight Home from Saigon

This is the rage for order on the plains,
barbed wires from post to post. Fat cattle
are in the fields, all fences tight,

nothing to do but ride a thousand acres
and pretend they're ours. My sorrel's boss
of a herd that knows it. He's never

killed a bull, keeps no money in the bank,
sings no soft gospel songs at sundown.
He's twice, three times the man I am,

but look who rides him. With this right hand
I tap the reins that turn him. I led him
through paces as a colt, walked miles

around the corral after some hunter's
stray shot nicked him, held his head
while the vet made him a gelding. He's much

too tame to buck, to back-talk any nudge
of my boots. Slouched in the saddle,
I offer sugar cubes, oats after work,

a stall with straw in bad weather
not far from my door, each day laid out
for lucky him, easy to understand.

[Previously published in *Northwest Review* 28, no. 1 (1990): 93 and *All That Matters: The Texas Plains in Photographs and Poems* (Lubbock: Texas Tech University Press, 1992—winner of the 1993 Western Heritage Award ("The Wrangler") for best book of poetry, National Cowboy Hall of Fame).]

The Goats of Summer

The clink of steel diggers rammed
on sandstone makes pet goats easy to despise.
Without a fence, they'd "baaa" and billy-leap
wet fields of oats or cotton, nothing sacred

to their hoofs and nibbling lips.
Leaning the diggers in a hole of rock,
I wipe a wet bandana across my face
and sling my Stetson like a watering can.

Standing still at noon, I feel my boot soles burn.
What madness made me believe the silly song
of barkers selling goats, "kids for kids,"
the catchy phrase erasing the smell

of pellets, the wide-eyed grin of baby goats
and children tugging my sleeve
more whimsy than a dad could stand.
So now, weeks later, where are they,

those knee-high babies nudging for bottles?
What are these hip-high goats with deep voices,
butting the backyard gate until it warps?
Where are my kids who promised to clean

the corral reeking like Noah's privy?
Tugging old leather gloves back on,
pliable with sweat like second skin,
I raise the posthole digger and slam it down

like cracking granite, lift out chips of stones
and go on digging, two rolls of barbed wire
waiting to be strung, a dozen more dry holes
before there'll be some order to this dirt.

[Previously published in *The Atlantic Monthly* 265, no. 4 (1990): 54 and *The Digs in Escondido Canyon* (Lubbock: Texas Tech University Press, 1991—winner of the 1992 Western Heritage Award ("The Wrangler") for best book of poetry, National Cowboy Hall of Fame).]

When It Thunders

At night we hear thunder
and flash back to mountains.

Curtains aside, we see lightning
in clouds rising like peaks.

For an instant we're young again,
the cool air sweet as rain.

It seldom showers on flat plains
fenced by barbed wire.

Thunder rumbles far off.
Darkness, a million stars.

The other sounds coyotes,
the ceiling fan, your deep,
familiar breath.

[Previously published in *San Jose Studies* 17, no. 2 (1991): 100 and *The Digs in Escondido Canyon* (Lubbock: Texas Tech University Press, 1991–winner of the 1992 Western Heritage Award ("The Wrangler") for best book of poetry, National Cowboy Hall of Fame).]

Alone in a Windstorm

These are the fallen apples,
the proof of wind, the roots' labors.
All night in the storm
we lay touching, alone at last,

our children scattered
this summer weekend.
The dogs stumbled
as our rakes went back, back

under cracked branches.
We picked up apples like winnings
and counted our losses by bushels.
We touched hail-stripped limbs

and severed all we must.
After rain and raking, the grass
turned greener than we'd ever seen.
All afternoon we worked,

fatigue that saved us
for another day, no matter
how hard the hot wind blows
or if the whole crop falls.

[Previously published in *Great River Review* 6, no. 1 (1985): 145 and *Witching on Hardscrabble* (Peoria, IL: Spoon River Poetry Press, 1985).]

Beans Grown in Caliche

We live like scorpions in adobe
and eat beans grown in caliche.
Two years of drought, the brittle grass
like lichen. If we stand too long
at noon, our boot soles burn.

A clean pantry, coffee and *masa harina*
like manna from heaven.
For meat, *cabrito* and quail,
and pronghorns like fawns
we never kill. The tanks dry up

and leave chalk rings
and stumps. We feed the goats
and keep the windmills turning.
Our neighbors to the north
graze buffaloes, a hold-out herd

of eight dark beasts,
moody, hump-shouldered.
When we ride to the fence,
they turn away. We sleep
without sheets, windows wide,

although there are no screens:
snakes could burrow under
or glide down through the roof.
At night we listen to bobcats
and coyotes crying for rain.

Propped up, I try
to piece together why I'm here,
nothing about this dry flat land
like Vietnam but my own
damned eyes and ears.

I plant our chairs under the only oak
and listen to white sands burn.
All summer we watch for clouds
and let our minds idle like hawks
gliding in skies so blank we stare.

[Previously published in *Cincinnati Poetry Review* 14 (1986): 65 and *Witching on Hardscrabble* (Peoria, IL: Spoon River Poetry Press, 1985).]

After the Madness of Saigon

Today, I'm sneezes and sniffles, turn my head and cough.
Dogs slink and drop their ears and whine when I jog by.
They've seen that look on cave men flinging firebrands
from the rocks. Pockets turned inside out say to the world

I'm broke, no patience with myself, so watch it.
I might kneel and take your paper from the street, flip it
closer to your door. If there's a nail, I'll take it, too,
the worst of broken glass some schoolboy tossed

to hear the bottle burst behind his pickup roaring by
at midnight. I'll turn and fill somebody's dumpster
with trash and roadkill by the curb, and crushed
magnolia blooms from last night's storm.

Finding another old vet at my door, I'll fling
the screen door wide and loose the puma for her daily prowl.
That sad old friend and I will rock on the porch
with others who stop by, telling dumb jokes and screaming,

sipping coffee, scarfing on pizza and beer. Stuffed,
we'll cruise the neighborhood, helping up bums from doorways,
patching the widows' roofs, as if healing the deaf
and crippled, paying all people's debts.

[Previously published in *JAMA: The Journal of the American Medical Association* 280, no. 6 (1998): 492 and *Whatever the Wind Delivers: Celebrating West Texas and the Near Southwest* (Lubbock: Texas Tech University Press, 1999–winner of the 2000 Western Heritage Award ("The Wrangler") for best book of poetry, National Cowboy Hall of Fame).]

Crop Dusting in a Biplane

Crop dusting on hardscrabble,
a man keeps his eyes on a windsock.
It might be tight little pepper clouds

or dust devils on the horizon,
but if you trust to luck,
fickle winds can kill you.

On a landing strip dragged flat
by a rented grader—two headings,
east and west—you check prevailing

gusts while cranking up,
grounding magnetos, watching
the rpm fall like a barometer, the propeller

shaking both old wings of your Waco.
When the windsock flips six times
in the right direction, taxi out

and trust it as you do the gauges,
more to worry about than wind—
how many telephone wires in the way

at the next farm, how many flights
until harvest, how many turns
a wing strut takes before it breaks.

[Previously published in *Kentucky Poetry Review* 22, no. 2 (1986): 25 and *Rafting the Brazos* (Denton: University of North Texas Press, 1988—winner of the 1990 Western Heritage Award ("The Wrangler") for best book of poetry, National Cowboy Hall of Fame).]

Without Fear of Flying

When we're young we'll fly
anything with wings, step out in space
and fall for miles, trusting canopies
and luck as buffers.

Middle age hates layovers
unless hors d'oeuvres are served,
knowing warning lights may flash,
no seat belts could hold us safe
in case of metal fatigue or bombs.

Growing old is bumpy storms
at night in Minnesota, knowing
the terminal's ahead somewhere
in the blizzard, as engines strain
and we grip the armrests, lean back
and trust the wheels will touch.

[Previously published in *The South Florida Poetry Review* 5, no. 1 (1987): 27 and *Rafting the Brazos* (Denton: University of North Texas Press, 1988–winner of the 1990 Western Heritage Award ("The Wrangler") for best book of poetry, National Cowboy Hall of Fame).]

Jacob's Ceiling

These are the nickel nights, the buffalo coins
of childhood. On the carpet, kicking,
our grandson's eyes find magic

in flecked, textured swirls of the ceiling.
Lazy beasts graze the plains up there
and his eyes bulge, giggles all parents love.

Jacob in snap-pajamas tries flying to them,
kick-kick, huffing at six months, lights
and fan blades twirling his eyes around

and around. His voice coos soothing tunes,
his fists big as my thumbs rise up, a conductor
using no baton, feet kicking a jingle rhythm,

and ceiling fans keeping time with giddy
buffalo herds, and shadows going around
and around in carousels Jacob believes.

[Previously published in *Poetry Toronto* (Canada) 138 (1987): 19 and *Rafting the Brazos* (Denton: University of North Texas Press, 1988–winner of the 1990 Western Heritage Award ("The Wrangler") for best book of poetry, National Cowboy Hall of Fame).]

The Summer Our Grandsons Turned Twelve

When that fat old black lab wobbled,
we both stopped talking and watched him hobble
like a bull-beast nightmare staggering downstairs.
Creaky, spoiled-rotten Dino plopped by our chairs,
blessing us both with sour apple breath
like some old monk who knows all foibles

of the human heart, but rest assured, he loves us.
Five years after his brother died, sprayed by skunks,
battered by gout and fights with stray dogs, Dino
slept inside on winter nights, wheezing, our bodyguard
barking for treats One black eye, scarred, saw visions.
Only the other, pearly blue, could focus.

Sleeping, he snored, kicking the floor like clubs.
How fast he aged, twelve years like weeks, a pup
when our twin grandsons kicked and stared at mobiles
hovering above their cribs, cooing and twisting
when they heard those happy, high-pitched yips,
the balls of fur we held for them to touch.

[Previously published in *Whatever the Wind Delivers: Celebrating West Texas and the Near Southwest* (Lubbock: Texas Tech University Press, 1999—winner of the 2000 Western Heritage Award ("The Wrangler") for best book of poetry, National Cowboy Hall of Fame).]

Night Shuttle

We'd leave after dark, windows down
to catch the first cool breeze all week.
Three to a seat, we squeezed for elbow room,
for canteens and pillows and bags of snacks.

Before Daddy could shift the Ford to high,
Grandma raised her snuff can to her lips,
spittooning that brown sweet stink. Hands
on his knees, leg and wide elbow gouging me,

Grandpa told us again how wagons bounced
when he was a boy, no deep-pile pillows
to sit on, no sirree. Restless, without lights
to read our stack of comics by, my sister

and I sneaked punches at each other
behind Grandpa's neck, even though we knew
the first who hit him would get spanked.
For years we shuttled to Arkansas in that

black car by night to bury Ozark relatives
I never knew, grandparents asleep by us,
our mother huddled silent in the front
staring at dark plains speeding past.

[Previously published in *Widener Review* 4 (1987): 26 and *Rafting the Brazos* (Denton: University of North Texas Press, 1988–winner of the 1990 Western Heritage Award ("The Wrangler") for best book of poetry, National Cowboy Hall of Fame).]

Pulling Old Gloves Back On

This far out in the country, no one is talking.
No rescue squads row by in boats to prairie land
so dry the Ogallala water table drops three feet
each year. The digger rams down through dirt

no plow has turned. In the heat, I let my mind
run wild. For days I swore the world is ending,
the red oaks turning red again, the last geese
fleeing from the north, surviving to show us

the only hope, the tips of their arrow formations
pointing the way. So many birds, if the world
doesn't end, this may be for Canada the year
of the locust. I shake my head at my schemes

and sweat flies: cattle on cotton land. The market
for beef is weak, the need for cotton constant.
I might as well raise goats and sheep as cows,
or trap for bounty the wolves and coyotes

that claim our fields at night. I might as well
rent a steam shovel and dig a lake deep as an ark,
empty my last irrigation well to fill it green enough
for geese on the flyway both seasons. I could

raise trout and channel cat, horses and bees
like pastures of heaven, gazelles and impala
imported from deserts, two of each kind
in a dying world. Sun going down, the last hole dug,

the last post dropped and tamped tight to hold
three strands of wire, I toss the digger at the pickup
between bales of barbed wire ready for stringing,
the calves I bought last week overdue,

the feed bill mounting. My father swore a man
could lift a bull if he'd practice on a calf each day.
Pulling old gloves back on, I lift the first bale
and nail the end, uncoil the wire and nail it tight

to the posts. While it turns dark, I go on stretching
and nailing until I don't care how many neighbors
drive by with their lights high, honking,
sticking their heads out the windows and laughing.

[Previously published in *The American Poetry Review* 14, no. 5 (1985): 22 and *Rafting the Brazos* (Denton: University of North Texas Press, 1988–winner of the 1990 Western Heritage Award ("The Wrangler") for best book of poetry, National Cowboy Hall of Fame).]

Hawks, Up Close and Far Away

Steady as clocks, three hawks keep circling
mice at a trough, or rattlers, or rabbits
far from their burrows. Not buzzards,

but hawks, that always hunt alone,
until today. As long as I've been here,
whittling, they've circled whatever's near.

I could go inside for water, and soon
it would all be over. Hawks have always
been my friends, but one at a time, up high,

keeping dry skies at ease, the way
I tighten fences. Living on hardscrabble,
I keep a rifle handy wherever I ride,

time enough for scruples in the kitchen,
watching my wife cook venison or beef.
Mesquite stick finally whittled like a flute,

I push up, pulling my Stetson low against the sun,
mounting step by step our porch that creaks
too loud to hear hawks diving at my back.

[Previously published in *Outposts Poetry Quarterly* (UK) 158 (1988): 8 and *Rafting the Brazos* (Denton: University of North Texas Press, 1988–winner of the 1990 Western Heritage Award ("The Wrangler") for best book of poetry, National Cowboy Hall of Fame).]

The Songs at Rusty's

Heart-breakers sang at Rusty's, the last bar
north of Slaton. "Stand by yo'r man," they sobbed
to the swing of crystal earrings, or scowled
and doubled up ring-knuckled fists

and growled, "Ain't gonna be yo'r honky-tonk
woman anymore." Their innocent, wicked faces
were safe behind the same thick makeup.
Nests of sprayed hair floated yellow-blue

in spotlights and smoke of local men
and women groping for their lives. It's gone,
torn down like the drive-in, two midnight places
people went to get away from lives more boring

than the plains. One young singer Pearl from Austin
flirted like a schoolgirl, snuggling on every lap.
Some yelled and tossed their hats, as if
they'd stayed on a bull for eight seconds.

Up close, her eyes flared wide, as if whispering
"save me." Billy Ray crushed a beer can in his fist
and foam shot out and splattered on the floor.
Billy Ray stared at deer heads on the wall.

We knew Pearl couldn't last, trying too hard
to be human. Hard-voiced women gave us
the tunes we wanted, the same old wailing
on stage that made fist-fights and a dance

enough to dream about for days in the saddle,
roping small bawling calves to castrate and burn
with branding irons, touching our own bruised
ribs and missing teeth after Saturday night
fights, lonely and wincing, and spitting blood.

[Previously published in *Ariel* (Canada) 19, no. 3 (1988) and "Splitting Wood for Winter," University of North Texas Contemporary Poets Reading Series, 1988.]

Hawks in the World They Own

Rattlers choking down rabbits
are mascots of our eyes. In saddles,
we pause and watch the show, fat snake
all jaw, swallowing the rabbit whole,

more glutton than steers that chew
their stubble twice. Hawks glide
hardscrabble skies in spite of drought.
Steers roam the fields heads down,

praying to only grass. We scan the range
for signs, hoping for summer rain.
We can't root out all cactus in pastures
made for goats and rattlesnakes. Our eyes

unlock like jaws and swallow all we see.
A hawk needs nothing on ranches we'll
never own, so rifles are threats he ignores,
just wands directing traffic of coyotes.

Hawks go their own way, alone,
believing the wind sustains them,
the sun was made for their wings only,
the world has endless rabbits.

[Previously published in *College English* 54, no. 7 (1992): 827 and *Where Skies Are Not Cloudy* (Denton: University of North Texas Press, 1993).]

The Skulls That Eat Such Dust

The skulls that eat such dust are singing,
at last others to love them. We touch
their hollow eyes, our fingers
trained to caress all bones.

Others planted what we reap, legends
of plains people under siege,
never enough water or time to keep
whatever they hoped for—

the simple flow of bison and grain,
the endless rivers, the hope
of living another night on the earth
and others to hold them.

[Previously published in *College English* 50, no. 6 (1988): 640 and *The Digs in Escondido Canyon* (Lubbock: Texas Tech University Press, 1991—winner of the 1992 Western Heritage Award ("The Wrangler") for best book of poetry, National Cowboy Hall of Fame).]

Designed for the Shallows

This far out, bass boats designed for the shallows
wallow in waves lake-deep and lazy, no breeze,
no stars, no boats with running lights
this late at night. Our outboard motors off
and cold already, fog thick as walls around us,

cut off from shores and slumber. Deep down
under roofs of cabins and homes they flooded
to build this reservoir, fish of all sizes breed,
keeping the mountains at ease, all of us
floating in darkness above them,

needing whatever fish lie hidden. With faith
in new moons and almanacs, we've gathered
on the surface of water to let down our lines
for Junkers, believers in lures and tobacco juice
squirted on hooks to bless the barbs

with our desire and need for struggle. Fleece
of our coats keeps us warm, and bourbon
sipped from a bottle and passed back and forth
in the boat like communion, fellowship of the spirit
of fishing that calls us from the sleep of this world

to surface waves swaying our boats like a waltz.
Getting a grip on the rhythm, we cup our rods and test
the reels for tension, feed another few feet of line,
eager to feel the first hard tug, to hold in our fists
the wonder, the assurance of things not seen.

[Previously published in *Connecticut River Review* 5, no. 2 (1984): 23–24 and *Witching on Hardscrabble* (Peoria, IL: Spoon River Poetry Press, 1985).]

Out of the Whirlwind

Because the land plays out we're needed.
Nothing on the plains feeds us but dirt.
We bury barrels of iron in sand, plant
alfalfa in fields dying for nitrogen.
We plow deep rows in arid zones

and water bumper crops. After hail,
we squat among stripped stalks and squeeze
drenched cotton in our fists, shake them
at black clouds rumbling east. Something
in the sky seems foreign, sometimes sleet

or drought, never the right amounts.
We believe given the time we could reap
the moon. Out of the whirlwinds, meat.
Out of leeched clay, milk. If we believe
hard work brings cows and beans, we are fed.

[Previously published in *Puerto del Sol* 21, no. 2 (1986): 160 and *Rafting the Brazos* (Denton: University of North Texas Press, 1988—winner of the 1990 Western Heritage Award ("The Wrangler") for best book of poetry, National Cowboy Hall of Fame).]

Mercy and the Brazos River

My great-greats came to hardscrabble plains
when a quarter an acre was outrage. Quakers
from Iowa, they listened for God's still voice
in travel, a silence under stars. Their hearts
led them to prairies, a thousand miles of parchment

under the will of heaven. No trees grew native,
prairie grass enough to hold the bones of buffalo.
If they hoped for angels to wrestle for crops,
when they found this winding Texas stream,
Rio de los Brazos de Dios, they believed.

The dugout where they huddled was a cave
in white caliche. In spite of rattlesnakes
and drought, they called it home. Prairie dog
burrows pocked the farm. Even their dugout
uprooted a colony of dogs. They plugged the holes

and settled down, grass like pastures of heaven
for ox and cows that survived the storms. I've seen
the grainy photographs, held in my hands
their beaten plows. Choking down rabbits
and snakes, what did they hope for, nothing

but hawks and slow whirlpools of buzzards,
drought from wide horizons without one tree?
How could they leave their families for this?
The first deep well they dug was hopeless
and the second. Before the third well struck

the aquifer, they turned enough prairie under
for a crop and a baby's grave, their wagon
broken but repaired in time to bump down
a steep caliche canyon and haul back barrels
of water from "the river of the arms of God."

[Previously published in *Prairie Schooner* 65, no. 1 (1991): 77–78 and *All That Matters: The Texas Plains in Photographs and Poems* (Lubbock: Texas Tech University Press, 1992—winner of the 1993 Western Heritage Award ("The Wrangler") for best book of poetry, National Cowboy Hall of Fame).]

Rafting the Brazos

Downriver rocks were rapids. All summer
after chores, we dragged our tractor inner tubes,
patched like Uncle Murphy's face on Sunday,
and launched them on the swift river.

We shoved them out to the middle,
kicking our feet like frogmen. Splashing,
and dogs barking on the bank beside us,
we yelled at each other for the lead.

Someone always cheated. At fourteen
games were serious as sex. Everyone
had rules and everybody broke them.
And so the day Durwood slumped over

on his tube and dropped his paddle,
we passed him and jeered at whatever stunt
he was pulling. We watched brown water
turn into foam-white rapids around us,

each boy for himself, in hell and out again,
over and under the Brazos muddy waves.
Laughing, wiping our eyes and bragging
our ride was the damnedest ever,

we saw Durwood's patched tube bob by,
riding high on the flood, bulging like lungs
held too long, about to burst. Later,
our fathers explained the doctor found no water

in his lungs, nothing we could have done,
no matter how long we thumped and pumped
after we pulled him out, how long
we huffed and blew into his rubber mouth.

[Previously published in *CutBank* 23 (1985): 22–23 and *Rafting the Brazos* (Denton: University of North Texas Press, 1988—winner of the 1990 Western Heritage Award ("The Wrangler") for best book of poetry, National Cowboy Hall of Fame).]

Wolves in Playa Lakes

Wolves mated in playa lakes
behind our barn, a garden
of snakes and rabbits.

We watched from the roof
in moonlight. Wolves snarled,
slunk through the brush

and snapped. We seldom
saw them any other way,
not in West Texas. At night,

their eyes like wildcats'
flashed in the moon. At dawn
we prowled dry stubble

and stomped snake holes
the pesky wolves had wet.
Boys restless in summer,

we shot fat rattlers for the hogs.
Kicking tumbleweeds,
we found baby rabbits

quivering, born without fur,
and twitching with closed eyes
as one by one we backed away.

[Previously published in *Anthology of Magazine Verse & Yearbook of American Poetry*, 1986–1988 edition, Alan F. Pater, ed. (Beverly Hills, CA: Monitor Book Company, 1988).]

At the Stone Café

The waitress leans across with ketchup
for our chicken-fried steaks and beans.
Rouged, perfumed, she exposes a flared
white cleavage. She is some local boy's
Sweet Darlin'. She waltzes off,

humming some country and western tune
that makes her human. Sunlight slices
between her thighs. At the counter,
she cuts a pie for two cowboys she knows.
One rises and whispers in her ear. She winks

and flips his hat, leans back and sips her beer.
They turn and study whoever's here
without boots. Some scoff, some hunch
on their elbows, jokes muffled under fans
"whop-whopping" overhead. Some tilt

their rawhide chairs, legs crossed,
beveled boot heels cocked. They ignore us,
now, holding smokes in stained fingers
fanning out. They stare at each other,
squinting and nodding slowly.

[Previously published in *Rafting the Brazos* (Denton: University of North Texas Press, 1988–winner of the 1990 Western Heritage Award ("The Wrangler") for best book of poetry, National Cowboy Hall of Fame).]

Our Neighbor Who Kept Pigeons

Our neighbor who kept pigeons was on the road all day,
meeting his quota. At six he set them free, circling
a three-house radius. He watched them from a chair

> Up from their cages, flapping, climbing they go,
> pigeons in echelons of wings, spiraling, waving
> their delicate massive muscles, skimming

out front, smoking a pipe and pivoting like a periscope,
loving his birds. One day, he caught boys in the alley
with BB guns, shooting at them. He smashed the guns,

> past treetops and roofs, zooming up as one, flying
> the most excellent chandelles, leveling, circling in wide
> wingovers, no matter how steep or gracefully slow

grabbed both their arms and led them home. Their parents,
what else, apologized. At dusk he called his pigeons down,
feeling each one for BB shots, found one bird bloody-eyed

> never nearing a stall, all feathers functioning
> like helium, small beaks rising, tasting the breeze,
> eyes glistening and closing, following by climbing,

and gently twisted off its head. Next day, he filed a suit.
The judge threw out the case, did not approve of pigeons,
cited thousands of pests crapping on the streaked courthouse.

> tiny heads washed clean by flower-fresh currents of sky,
> gliding through shadows of sycamores and valleys
> of vine-climbed walls, wearing their feathers light,

I saw the boys days later, stalking cages with rifles, aiming
at sparrows on our fence. Our neighbor cringed at every shot,
no longer flew his birds. For weeks, he kept them penned.

> soaring in feathered formations, wing tip to tip,
> never touching, the flapping and glide like heartbeats
> in flowing turns, in climbs, in rhapsody of flight.

And then one day he sold them all, six crates soft-cushioned
in a van. I never saw him in his yard again. His work suffered.
Laid off, he let the mortgage lapse, and disappeared.

[Previously published in *Carolina Quarterly* 30, no. 2 (1978): 87 and *Anything, Anything* (Spokane, WA: L'Epervier Press, 1980).]

Consider the Lilies

I lie beside my wife and try to sleep.
The furnace clicks on, again, a record cold.
Someone in our hometown tonight will freeze.

Today we searched the parks, the alleys, streets,
found many homeless, but no fires against the cold.
I lie beside my wife and try to sleep.

The call goes out each fall for volunteers
to roam the town in cars with heaters on,
resolved that no one we find would freeze.

Clutching his cardboard home, one wouldn't leave.
He talked, but not to us, in cold, and alone.
I lie beside my wife and try to sleep.

We offered blankets and a place to sleep.
He dragged the cardboard shack back to the cold.
Somewhere in town tonight someone will freeze.

Someone in our hometown will freeze,
unless they lock him up. He wouldn't go.
I lie beside my wife and try to sleep.

[Previously published in *Meridian* (Spring 1998): 88 and *Whatever the Wind Delivers: Celebrating West Texas and the Near Southwest* (Lubbock: Texas Tech University Press, 1999–winner of the 2000 Western Heritage Award ("The Wrangler") for best book of poetry, National Cowboy Hall of Fame).]

Uncle Homer and the Cubs

Uncle Homer slapped us with his eyes,
a tap in the barn like bear cubs.
Butt first, we gave the pistols back,
not Cain and Abel. We only wanted

to copy his slow, bow-legged walk
and hold his cold pearl handles.
We asked how many men he killed.
Our dad had bragged about his brother's

badge, his limp, his hollow points.
Quietly, Uncle Homer led us outside
and spiked a round, green melon
on a post. I punched my brother's ribs,

I saw the flick of my uncle's arm
and blinked at the shot he squeezed off,
a sharp, loud flash, but flinched when I saw
the pink mush burst like a skull.

[Previously published in *Verve* 9, no. 1 (1997): 10 and *Whatever the Wind Delivers: Celebrating West Texas and the Near Southwest* (Lubbock: Texas Tech University Press, 1999—winner of the 2000 Western Heritage Award ("The Wrangler") for best book of poetry, National Cowboy Hall of Fame).]

Rattler

Coiled, it's hostile and crazy,
without a lawyer, tail rattling
like dice in a plastic cup. "Mine,"
its tongue flicks out, guarding

nothing but rocks and cactus,
its eyes squeezed tight,
still nursing a grudge, alone
and wandering forty years

in the desert, pouting
that losing the garden
was not its fault. Nobody
had to gamble the family farm

on its advice. Its diamonds
squeeze like fists of muscles,
bulged and stingy like a gut,
nothing but a mouth with fangs

and knotty, large intestines,
devouring all it can swallow,
all it can kill. I told my grandsons
never bend down by a wood pile,

never go barefoot in cactus–
but their Frisbee angled off
from the yard, wobbled and rolled
to the weeds. I saw them

and hobbled, calling, almost too late
to save them, snatched one in each arm
and leaped back, panting.
The rattler coiled and swayed

and slithered off, tiny head
weaving from side to side
as if nodding from cactus
to cactus, "Mine, mine!"

[Previously published in *Hampden-Sydney Poetry Review* (1995): 26 and *Whatever the Wind Delivers: Celebrating West Texas and the Near Southwest* (Lubbock: Texas Tech University Press, 1999–winner of the 2000 Western Heritage Award ("The Wrangler") for best book of poetry, National Cowboy Hall of Fame).]

Watching for Signs

We touched their flints and ribs,
their shards of supper bowls—this broken axe,
this skull. They counted on this canyon
between rains. This was the color of thirst
on hardscrabble, caliche white as bones
picked clean. Not much to leave behind,

but there they were, preserved in sand
it took our picks to dig. Even boys found them
shoveling forts for play, or under cut banks,
exposed when crumbling shale gave up a skull.
Wherever we dug were roots, a tree at a time.
Hawks kept watch on us all, gliding on thermals

in skies so blank we stared. Someone that summer,
mad in the prairie sun, raved to make us
bury the bones and let the shelves go begging.
He swore museums with ghosts were never full.
When the teacher in charge drove him off,
we joked, "Who was that masked man

with the silver tongue," and went on digging
for wars and tornadoes, trying to make
the simple dust yield clues. Over us
hawks kept wheeling, watching for signs.
We took a grip on brushes and kneeled,
whisking a year away with each flick.

[Previously published in *Poet Lore* 85, no. 3 (1990): 35.

In Hot, Hardscrabble Skies

Buzzards convene by the fence, a board of deacons
solemn and formal. Glistening with morning dew,
they strut and turn with the sun, drying black feathers.

One by one they rise, big bellies dragging them down,
wide wings flapping awkwardly up, then soaring
on thermals, gracefully gliding for hours. Always

they dip and circle down to something dead
in the distance. Year round, they hang in our skies
with answers, arrogant and curt as our bulls,

taut scrotums bold and shoulders massive, blunt skulls
defiant behind barbed wires stretched to bring
a stuttering fool to his knees, bulls sane unless a cow

in heat sways by and the breeze is brisk. But nothing
drives dark birds away for long. Buzzards are wise men
following the breeze, the snot and drivel of their beaks.

If we're in time, if we find the calf before the coyotes
find it, before the buzzards, and lift the injured calf
to the saddle like a lap dog, or if crows have pecked

the eyes or the belly's burst, we shoot. Those days,
before we ride home, buzzards are already down,
bowing as if in prayer, flapping, clacking their beaks.

[Previously published in *The Comstock Review* 11, no. 1 (1997): 42 and *Whatever the Wind Delivers: Celebrating West Texas and the Near Southwest* (Lubbock: Texas Tech University Press, 1999—winner of the 2000 Western Heritage Award ("The Wrangler") for best book of poetry, National Cowboy Hall of Fame).]

Rattlesnakes Locked Eyes with Me

A thousand big weeds a penny, wages I made
chopping fields when I was ten. Daddy swore
I was lucky, ten hours' pay when he was eight

an extra biscuit after sweating on his poppa's
rocky farm in Arkansas, often a belt to his back,
a cotton sack on the dirt floor for a bed. "Right,"

I thought, and miles uphill to school and back,
barefoot in blizzards and eight feet of snow.
I watched loud freight trains roar out of town,

bucks on the road, cars with places to go
and kids my age riding with windows down.
I raised my face and let rain slap me

in the Texas depression. Sun burned the mist
to sunburn and rash. Pigweeds thick as my wrist
dulled the hoe, chop and chop again.

Sometimes, with giant weeds falling in the row,
I called "Timber!" and leaped back, laughing.
A rattlesnake at times locked eyes with me,

inching slowly away "hiss hiss," back there
in shadows. I chopped and chopped ironweeds
until my shoulders bulged. I swore I'd hack trees

down someday with such swings. Wiping my face
on my shirttail, I stared at miles of cotton leaves in rows
always the same, while boys like me played ball

after school and yelled themselves hoarse or sprawled
inside the "Cactus," sipping Cokes, watching Roy Rogers
and friends ride golden stallions wherever there was to go.

[Previously published in *Arkansas Review* 29, no. 3 (1997): 18 and *Whatever the Wind Delivers: Celebrating West Texas and the Near Southwest* (Lubbock: Texas Tech University Press, 1999—winner of the 2000 Western Heritage Award ("The Wrangler") for best book of poetry, National Cowboy Hall of Fame).]

Can Deserts Like Dead Bones Live?

My great-greats claimed these acres,
trying to fatten bull-necked oxen
grazing prairie grass. From the dugout,

they watched fires burn the plains. Now,
the prairie's tamed, crack houses rampant
under smoke of fire storms. Lot's wife

has company, enough smack and salt to prop
the ozone. Aliens with outrageous smiles
ring our doorbell, burning to save the whale,

the elephant. Beggars downtown
have given up, their cardboard huts
collapsed, better bed and board in Dallas.

Strangers with picket signs own the parks.
I tell my sons don't look away. In Jericho,
the spies made friends with Rahab, the one

whore unemployed, laughing at the guards.
I think of Jonah watching the whale rise
slowly from the ocean, the startled seagulls

screeching. Can deserts like dead bones live?
Philistines gloated over blinded Samson
groaning, but heard marble columns crack.

[Previously published in *Soundings East* 12, no. 2 (1989): 21 and *Where Skies Are Not Cloudy* (Denton: University of North Texas Press, 1993).]

Two Years After World War II

Aunt Mabel was coyote ugly in grade school–
I've seen pictures–but a fox when she got to college
in 1940. She owed all she owned to nature,

no braces or cosmetics on the ranch. She beat
most rodeo cowboys on bucking broncs and bulls,
no easy barrel races for her. After Pearl Harbor,

she rode off with the Marines, first girl from our town
to enlist. She came back tall and skinny in a uniform,
nobody's darling, until Carl from a tank corps rode by,

only one arm but god! he could cowboy. My daddy
gave her away in the summer church, my big brother
handing her off to Carl while all the kinfolks fanned–

what a bride! pretty as a pin-up with a V-neck,
and a left hook a few town boys knew. When Uncle Carl
lifted her veil with his only hand and we saw how gorgeous

a Marine could be, some gasped, and all applauded,
and the old pump organ played while Carl and Mabel
turned and kissed while everyone cheered.

[Previously published in *Hawai'i Review* 25, no. 2 (Fall 2002): 24 and *Great Lonely Places of the Texas Plains* (Lubbock: Texas Tech University Press, 2003).]

Hauling on Hardscrabble

Driving fast, I watch fence posts flash by
more than cows, stalled too long at Waldo–
call it warp, a trick of optics–more posts
in a minute than a man could dig in a week.

Before Vietnam, we buzzed on training flights
ten feet above and parallel to the earth, 500 knots.
I heard the navigator hush. Cactus and mesquites

rushed under us, a blur. Our wing tips passed miles
of barbed-wire plains. A hawk flashed by, a flick
of a glimpse, but stunned steers never looked up,
not one. I held it low, the prairie a bowl

enclosing us, a swirl of dust. I lifted the nose
at last and climbed, and heard the navigator sigh.
Steers and windmills fell away, the prairie reeling
a peaceful spiral around the horizon, barbed wires

and drought, flash floods and wind-spinning vanes
with water trickling from pipes, the constant trudge
of trapped cattle grazing behind barbed wires.
Even now, when I slow the rig with air brakes,

they never look up, not even when I turn the truck
up a narrow lane between pastures, not even
when I back the truck against the loading dock
they know by now bound for the slaughterhouse.

[Previously published in *Gargoyle* 37/38 (1990): 92 and *The Digs in Escondido Canyon* (Lubbock: Texas Tech University Press, 1991–winner of the 1992 Western Heritage Award ("The Wrangler") for best book of poetry, National Cowboy Hall of Fame)]

Witching on Sand

Farming dry land, a man keeps hope
and a witch-stick handy. It might be dark
little pepper clouds, maybe a coyote
lame in the hip, cramming his head
through chicken wire and choked to death.

Something gives signs, and doubts aside,
we go witching. Ladies I know like willows,
most men trust sycamore or oak
to show where there's a well to be dug.
If Zacchaeus could find the Lord

from a sycamore, Uncle Murphy said,
the same branch ought to point us to water.
But it's maple for me, the peeled crotch
bone-white and hollow in the heartwood,
the tubes that sough in the wind persuasive.

"Go," they moan so low my doubting bones
back down, each maple bough dragging,
dragging me back, and why not–I watched
Uncle Murphy bring in six water wells
a summer, said to be one short of perfect.

It might be this sand I keep plowing, hardpan
ten feet down, eight inches of rain a year.
Coronado rode here hunting gold. I've seen wells
brought in elsewhere in Texas. With my own eyes.

[Previously published in *The Spoon River Quarterly* 8, no. 4 (1983): 1 and *Splitting Wood for Winter*, Trilobite Press (University of North Texas Press, 1988).]

Nights in the San Juan

Bed and chairs, table and stove,
home for a month in the mountains.
Because the logs are stacked,

we love them, two rooms
we call a shanty on the plains.
Cold water faucet that drips

all night. Bare ceiling, two beams
split. A board floor easy to sweep
sand through the cracks.

Curtains too short, too thin
to block out the moon. Nothing
is flush. You sleep beside me

on the uphill side, wood fire
out by midnight, the forest so still,
so dark we can hear stars blaze.

[Previously published in *College English* 48, no. 4 (1986): 354 and *Rafting the Brazos* (Denton: University of North Texas Press, 1988–winner of the 1990 Western Heritage Award ("The Wrangler") for best book of poetry, National Cowboy Hall of Fame).]

Fishing the Brazos

Fishing in hardscrabble, couples keep tackles
handy, ready to rise up and walk on water.
Rattlesnakes here are bad, snaking up
behind and shaking like saints in tent meetings,
half the congregation speaking in tongues

and quaking, many picking up snakes
and writhing, on fire in the spirit, ignoring
us kids outside and peeking. Fingertips
light as willow roots in water listen
for quivers and nibbles on the line,

and we jerk snakes that thrash, claiming
frogs and water and fish in the lake are theirs.
Better to move back and live to fish other pools
than fight old serpents thrashing and wicked,
and no fish rising to any bait for hours.

Go where the rocks are hot, where frogs sprawl
openly on stumps, crows cawing for half-eaten fish,
and there cast out our lures for trout or bass,
dangling bugs to tempt them up through weeds,
Even with stringers of fish, we still need

to reach deep down in the lake with respect
for what lies angry and hidden, to pick our way
through twigs and moss of mesquite, over stones
and caliche holes back to the car we waded from,
up to our hips in cactus, over our heads in thorns.

[Previously published in *Chariton Review* 9, no. 2 (1980): 54 and *Splitting Wood for Winter*, Trilobite Press (University of North Texas Press, 1988).]

Midnight Near Pecos

Camped in a tent in a clearing,
I heard the storm die down in time
to hear a deer splashing through stalks

in the grain field, crashing downwind
and dying, wolf pack claiming a right
to fields I lease to hunters. My pig heart

grabbed like a fist, wanting them all,
"my deer, mine." I felt hair on my neck
stiff as pig bristles. I'd gone to market

for new deer-rifle bullets and boots.
I huffed and dared the pack to try
blowing my tent down. I'd fire

point-blank and slaughter them all,
to make deer safe for men like me
and family. Mad as a feral hog, I lay back

down and snarled and slept grunting
and rooting around in the sleeping bag
for my socks, my human feet.

[Previously published in *Willow Springs* 18 (1986): 71 and *Splitting Wood for Winter*, Trilobite Press (University of North Texas Press, 1988).]

Night of the Scorpion

Night of ice packs and ankle fire,
my daddy tumbling rubble
of a chimney shifted and cracked
years ago, fierce to kill

whatever stung me. I rolled
in fever and tossed, dreamed
shadows laughing on the walls
cast by car lights, my back

and head lunging side to side,
stones and boards crashing
like ninepins in mountains.

I crawled through forests of fire,
gnashing my teeth, scorpions
hissing and scuttling away,

steam from fissures screaming
and demons reaching for me.
Spiders died, mice died in their nests,

rocks of all sizes burst. The next day
Daddy slept, unable to save me,
he thought, big fingers bloody bones.

My foot was cold and swollen,
but a foot I could stand on
here on the rubbled earth.

[Previously published in *Poet Lore* 78, no. 4 (1984): 209 and *Rafting the Brazos* (Denton: University of North Texas Press, 1988—winner of the 1990 Western Heritage Award ("The Wrangler") for best book of poetry, National Cowboy Hall of Fame).]

Dust Devils

Here is where heaven starts,
wind like the spirit of peace

blowing sand in our eyes
for weeks. Spring on the plains

is static and storms
without rain, blustery days

dry as fields fallow for years,
dust like our own souls

harrowed and seedless,
waiting to be given wings.

[Previously published in *Willow Springs* 18 (1986): 73 and *Rafting the Brazos* (Denton: University of North Texas Press, 1988—winner of the 1990 Western Heritage Award ("The Wrangler") for best book of poetry, National Cowboy Hall of Fame).]

Learning the Story of Scars

After the axe-head buried itself
in his ankle, my father clung to the log
he'd been splitting, squeezing his eyes
like fists. Twelve, he had logged those woods
all year with his father—Arkansas,
the great depression, doing whatever they could.

Groaning, he jerked and jerked the axe
like a pump handle, screamed
and went on pumping until the foot fell back,
hinged by the ankle, white and spurting.
With a bandana he held it and held it
while Arkansas flooded, and saw his father

running, his own axe, raised ready to kill
whatever snake bit the heel of his son.
I knew that scar like an oak tree
split by lightning, healed over,
knew my father had in him a boy
who had suffered alone in a forest.

[Previously published in *New Southern Literary Messenger* 2, no. 6 (1984): 2 and *Rafting the Brazos* (Denton: University of North Texas Press, 1988—winner of the 1990 Western Heritage Award ("The Wrangler") for best book of poetry, National Cowboy Hall of Fame).]

How the Records Fell

This time there seemed no stopping it,
fog for days, mist turning to rain,
to freezing rain, to crystal trees,

clear ice that cracked huge trees
that crushed parked cars. Drifts
filled the streets by noon. By dusk,

huddled with coffee mugs,
we watched snow flood the dark
so deep the shrubs went under.

All night we rose from time to time
and stared and lay back down
and held each other.

[Previously published in *Sunrust* (Fall 1986): 52 and *Rafting the Brazos* (Denton: University of North Texas Press, 1988–winner of the 1990 Western Heritage Award ("The Wrangler") for best book of poetry, National Cowboy Hall of Fame).]

Double Mountain Fork of the Brazos

Living on stones and runoff from rain
that rarely comes, this fork in forty miles
drains dust, dry mouth swearing
all it owns to the Brazos.

Whoever named it liked romance,
mountains two hundred miles away,
nothing where it begins
but a sudden drop-off in a field,

a sinkhole twenty feet across.
I've stood here, seen
a mighty river start, if I believed
in names, backpacked forty miles

and never found a stream so deep
I couldn't step across on stones.
I slept under train trestles so low
I almost bumped my head,

named creatures living on nothing
but each other, coyotes and skunks,
diamondbacks, rabbits with wide eyes,
a thousand owls.

[Previously published in *Country Journal* 13, no. 1 (1986): 55 and *Rafting the Brazos* (Denton: University of North Texas Press, 1988—winner of the 1990 Western Heritage Award ("The Wrangler") for best book of poetry, National Cowboy Hall of Fame).]

Caught in a Squall Near Matador

Thrashing through weeds, splashing mud
near the door, we burst into the shack
and threw down on all corners of the room.
Rain clattered the tin roof like rattlers.

One by one we jerked tumbleweeds aside,
the way sailors home after a voyage
flipped back the blankets. Laughing,
we slung holy water from our Stetsons,

kicked weeds to the grate and dug in our jeans
for matches to make the bunched weeds blaze.
Cobwebs thick as gauze swayed and bumped the rafters,
and weeds popped and crackled like firecrackers.

The jimmied door was half shut, but warmer
than anyone ever forced to winter here. Rain
splashed in each time the bent door slammed.
Doves we shot today bled in the creel

we stuffed them in, but no mood to eat.
Rain turned to hail, battering the tin roof
like pellets. Where weeds were stacked
we found old magazines and hunting maps.

We slapped the covers free of dust, and grizzlies
reared up on covers. Billy Bob flung them
to make flames roar. Big-mouthed bass leaped,
tails trying to shake hooks all the way to the fire.

Symbols of windmills and shelters on maps
led to this sheepherder's fireplace, and deep
in the dust, a calendar, a pastel maiden
praying beside still water, hoping the shepherd

whose hands first find her will let her kneel
on the magazine's stone with little on
after countless seasons alone, exposed
on her knees above a pond long gone.

Joe rolled the calendar, the cover soft
as old vellum, and lay it on the creel of doves.
When the storm moved on and we were home,
feasting on dove breasts dark as hearts,

we thought of living alone in a cabin,
glad we were far from weeds and wolves
outside our doors, our ladies of the lake
blessing their husbands home.

[Previously published in *Colorado Review* 13: 1 (1985): 55–56 and *Witching on Hardscrabble* (Peoria, IL: Spoon River Poetry Press, 1985).]

Where Seldom Is Heard

Tired cowboys when the wind is wild make music
with their ears. Slouched in saddles, they twist
their heads like antennae, picking up squeaks
like the twang of mouth harps, songs from Nashville
Saturday night. Hawks hear music all day long,
squeals of mice and tympanum of claws,
wheeling, gliding back to catch the song,
the slightest sound. I watch a goshawk dive,

one more sad song recorded with the eyes.
Rattlers go their own way, alone, flicking
split tongues like tuning forks. All prairie cries
worth hearing they can taste, tongues stiffening,
their fangs and beady eyes like crystal sets
they tune the old way, twisting between feast
and famine, rhythms of the heart, the breath
of cottontails the only song they need.

Coyotes make music on the moonlit ridge, howls
that turn their hunger into moans. Lower, slower,
another sways on a carriage of legs, tarantula
haunting the shadows of cactus, wild eyes
and curved furry legs that climb the skulls of cattle
and drowse in the echo chamber of the brain,
laying eggs, needing at most one meal a day,
a little night music, a careless squeaky mouse.

[Previously published in *SLANT* 12 (1998) (the editors of *SLANT* published this poem after a dedication page, which reads, "This Twelfth Edition of *SLANT* is dedicated to Walt McDonald for singing in a unique voice the music of our humanity") and *Whatever the Wind Delivers: Celebrating West Texas and the Near Southwest* (Lubbock: Texas Tech University Press, 1999–winner of the 2000 Western Heritage Award ("The Wrangler") for best book of poetry, National Cowboy Hall of Fame).]

The Neighbor

One spring, he lay the plow down like a fork
and almost made it to the porch.
Under the siren, his heart stopped,

paramedics pounding, pounding him alive.
His chest was bruised for days, his room
in the west wing like a hot-house, green leaves

and glucose draining his brain. Lying alone
at night, trying not to call for another shot,
he dreamed of letting the cat out, of plowing

the last rows, then putting the plow away
until winter, turning mustard greens
leaf by leaf for aphids, and finding them

clean, gathering strawberries, tomatoes,
Kentucky Wonders, bearing bushels
to widow friends all over town, and later,

snapping the beans, the cat purring in his lap,
children of neighbors running to him,
begging a story, a blessing, anything.

[Previously published in *The Texas Review* 4, no. 3 (1983): 66 and *Witching on Hardscrabble* (Peoria, IL: Spoon River Poetry Press, 1985).]

Black Wings Wheeling

The danger more than wolves
is hardpan caving in,
tumbling down an arroyo
alone and bawling,
bone snapped, stumbling,

unable to stand. No cows
claim calves that won't follow.
They thrust their stubborn horns
down over prairie grass
and graze for hours,

collapse under mesquite shade
and chew their cud,
their round eyes fixed on lakes
shimmering in the distance.
If they see black wings

wheel down a slow
whirlpool of air a mile away,
heat muzzles them.
The hunger of calves nuzzles
and punches them awake,

heavy hindquarters
and brittle forelegs shoving them up,
tails swatting at flies,
one wide-eyed cow
wandering from calf to calf.

[Previously published in *Three Rivers Poetry Journal* 25/26 (1985): 39 and *Witching on Hardscrabble* (Peoria, IL: Spoon River Poetry Press, 1985).]

Found in an Alley Dumpster

Bury the sack, and let more cats
make kittens. Only a fool
would kill blind kittens
with a stone. But there they are,
carved out of fur and blood,
their teeth like zippers
that won't close. Whoever bashed

and dumped them in the trash
had in mind silence, the fastest
way to fix unwanted cats
simply to beat them with a brick.
Their fur and blood are crusted,
their tiny eyes shut tight. We're sure
they never saw a human face.

[Previously published in *North American Review* 273, no. 3 (1988): 45 and *Where Skies Are Not Cloudy* (Denton: University of North Texas Press, 1993).]

High Plains Orchards

These twigs may be an orchard yet.
Grow peaches on the plains most years
and be satisfied with leaves. Bindweed
and Bermuda grass are the certain crops.
All prairie dirt is blow-sand
trampled by hooves, herds on the prowl
thousands of years for water scarce as trees.

My great-greats came here trying to choke back
bull-necked oxen, backs bowed west
and gorging on prairie grass like pastures.
Here they stopped, refused to budge, or died.
On land so flat no wonder people pray. Bad luck
explodes next door, tornadoes that swirl down
out of clouds black as Bibles. With no mountains
to hide behind, homes are glass and love goes on.
Trees are our only valleys.

My neighbor's horses picket my gate
for their daily pears. For luck, I promise apples.
Each winter, I jab down arrows of new trees,
mound up the dirt and wait for buds
here in a zone so dry no trees grow native.
Last March, somebody with a buzz saw
killed all pecans in my neighbor's orchard.
Lord. No one need offer an excuse for trees.

[Previously published in *South Dakota Review* 21, no. 2 (1983): 63 and *Rafting the Brazos* (Denton: University of North Texas Press, 1988—winner of the 1990 Western Heritage Award ("The Wrangler") for best book of poetry, National Cowboy Hall of Fame).]

Spending the Night Near Matador

Deep in the game preserve,
night coming on, I sit in the car
cursing a battery that crawled out here
to die. Did it hope to find privacy
dying far from its kind, miles
from the nearest town, no way to call

for help? The wind has gone away.
I haven't heard a shot since noon.
Thousands of mesquite trees
stand around pretending to be
flamingos, their skinny trunks
supporting the ugliest branches

I expect to dream about tonight.
They did nothing all day but scratch
themselves, flouncing about in the wind,
cackling like crones. Dove breasts
I cleaned at the stock tank
are bunched on ice in plastic

like a bag of hearts. I would cook them,
but I have no skillet, no fire
but the car lighter, and the battery
is dead. I would eat them raw
if it were dark and I weren't mad
and didn't need the breasts to buy off

wolves tonight. I've done nothing but hunt
in season. I consider flashing my license
to the nearest tree. My sixteen-gauge is empty,
but there's no need to load it, not under a moon
this full. I would try the battery again,
but I never disturb the dead this time of night.

[Previously published in *Beloit Poetry Journal* 35, no. 2 (1984–1985): 5–6 and *Witching on Hardscrabble* (Peoria, IL: Spoon River Poetry Press, 1985).]

The Beach at Kitty Hawk, the Long Ride Home

Seagulls fall and caw like crows,
soaring between sand and clouds.
Here come flocks of pelicans, skimming
over waves as if they could ski. No need,
wind never fails at Kitty Hawk. Simple,
just spread their wings, birds fly, rising

and angling away with wingtips flexed,
like that gull tacking against the wind,
the right wing straight, the other buckled
like a hawk's. Whatever they see pitched up,
gulls eat, or drop like rocks if children
pitching bread toss hollow mollusks,

seagulls gliding off stiffly as if indifferent.
On the Outer Banks, we're either cold or hot
at Christmas or August, ribs often bruised
by grandchildren's hugs. Stiff wind never matters
except storms that knock beach houses down,
hurricanes that wash Kill Devil Hills

close to the ocean, like the sands of time.
Last month when Father died, we hurried home,
driving fast across swampy Georgia,
bypassing Birmingham, ignoring casinos
of Shreveport, nothing for us up to Utah
but hawks and crosswinds for a thousand miles.

[Previously published in *Ascent* 23, no. 2 (1999): 63.]

High Plains Drifter

After years of buckshot and sandstorms,
a man turns sour, no more Mister Niceguy,
all grouch and red meat, "Dang,
why don't you dust?" Riding at noon

he hears rumors: women from town
ride over dunes at night with wineskins,
smiles on their faces. Herding strays,
a man begs for tunes after days on the plains.

Cactus alone can't make a shade,
out hunting for supper. Killing takes timing,
leading a quail by the barrel
down a valley of cactus. Squeeze,

and the shot hurls hollow. Stunned, the quail
falls tumbling down steep angles of the wind.
At dusty supper at campfires, a man longs
for honky-tonk songs and women

in deer-hide chairs. He imagines fiddles
and strumming, laughter and clinking of glasses,
locked in each other's arms. Rattlers
and coyotes circle the camp and lie down,

wary of flames and dancing. Meanwhile,
his wife has a daily affair with the wind,
southwest and lean, the silent type,
a whistler who taps on the glass, slips in

and strokes her sweaty neck. Slowly
he swirls her auburn curls like corn silk,
leans back and rolls a smoke, watching her
glossy lips twitch and whisper while she dusts.

[Previously published in *New Texas* (1995): 120 and *Whatever the Wind Delivers: Celebrating West Texas and the Near Southwest* (Lubbock: Texas Tech University Press, 1999—winner of the 2000 Western Heritage Award ("The Wrangler") for best book of poetry, National Cowboy Hall of Fame).]

Moses, at Jordan

As close as he can ever go,
that soil hot through his sandals,
rocks scattered like bones

of those who died in the desert.
His hips ache, he wants to rest,
but he'll never see this far again.

These olive groves are theirs
for the taking, thatched roofs,
the first rain falling in months

like grace. Between him and calm
is a stone path steady as faith.
Hills upon hills of grapes roll on,

layered with clouds like wool.
If he had shared God's holiness
spread like a table before him–

this land flowing with honey–
he could at last have found peace
under a roof of olives all his own.

[Previously published in *America* 156, no. 7 (1987): 158 and *Rafting the Brazos* (Denton: University of North Texas Press, 1988–winner of the 1990 Western Heritage Award ("The Wrangler") for best book of poetry, National Cowboy Hall of Fame).]

A Distant Relative

We hardly know him. He rolls our crystal in his hands
as if he came to repossess, not merely visit.
He tests each chair, selects my favorite. I offer him
the TV guide. He shakes his head. I'll nap awhile,
he says. Call me for dinner, please. We set the table

and glance at him reclined, at home. He seems asleep.
Long fingers crossed on his chest. He brought a bag.
We wonder if he means to stay the night. Our dog
has not yet noticed him. My wife tells us it's ready.
I hesitate, then touch his shoulder bone. His eyes

without lids roll slowly toward us. "Dinner," I say.
Bones creaking, he rises from the chair and follows.
Without waiting to be told, he takes the head of the table.
My wife and I bow our heads. I hear teeth clicking,
food being swallowed. We both pick up our forks and eat.

We stare at his jaw without lips consuming food
like a cutaway machine that shows us how it works.
"Eat," my wife whispers to me, "keep up your strength."
Finished, he shoves the chair back and stands slowly up.
We wait, knives flashing. Thanks, is all he says.

He goes toward the front door, knees clicking together
like sticks. "You're not staying, then?" My wife and I
hold hands. Can't, he replies. Have others to meet
tonight. "Is business good," I ask. She stares at me.
About the same, he says. It's steady work.

[Previously published in *Forum* 17, 3 (1979–1980): 18 and *Anything, Anything* (Spokane, WA: L'Epervier Press, 1980).]

Billy Bastrop and the Centipede

Bastrop was his name. We called him
Billy Bastard. He slashed window screens,
tied cats' tails together with wires,
set fire to the garage next door.

He stole a scalpel, tweezers, alcohol.
We crowded around his specimens
pickled in jars, grasshoppers,
garter snakes, a tarantula

floating like a baby octopus. Once,
he caught a centipede eight inches long,
dangled it over a jar of alcohol.
Took out the scalpel, cut off some legs.

Wiggling, it crawled away.
He tweezered it and sliced more off.
Put down, the creature still could crawl.
"You stop it, Billy Bastard!" Winona said.

His lips cupped the slightest grin.
He shaved away more legs, curved and dark
like eyelashes. "I'll tell!" Winona warned,
and began to cry. Each time he let it down,

it dragged its back half like a sled.
He sliced the last legs, and it writhed,
rolled over on its back.
Some of us stayed, looked on.

He sliced it then like sausage, piece
by piece till all that lived
were stumps, a head, two eyes
that bulged, that saw us all.

[Previously published in *Burning the Fence* (Lubbock: Texas Tech University Press, 1981).]

Teeth Know

Teeth know the devil lives.
Teeth gnash and grind, bite
into fruit forbidden or not.
Fall out at an innocent age.

Grow back sharper,
two like a serpent's fangs.
We call them "canine"
to disguise the truth.

Between the teeth, we lie
and curse, pour whiskey
past the teeth until there's hell
to pay. Teeth stain, decay,

need to be crowned, and pulled.
We joke, the road to hell is paved
with good dentures. Grinning
at each other we say you devil, you.

[Previously published in *Tar River Poetry* 19, no. 2 (1980): 11 and *Anything, Anything* (Spokane, WA: L'Epervier Press, 1980).]

The Girl in the Mackinaw and Panties

The girl in the mackinaw and panties
thumbs at you staring at her legs,
gives you the finger as you hesitate.

Backing up, you see her waiting,
a passive gal after all. You open
the pickup door and she climbs up,

ripped panties showing. "Hi there,"
you say, shifting up as you go. "You live
around this way?" "Just take me

the other side of Slaton," she says,
her tone hard as her knees.
You try steering your eyes

off her legs to keep from crashing
you both. "Lose something
in a poker game?" you try to joke.

"Listen," is all she says, "shut up
and drive." She keeps
looking back. "Faster," she says.

[Previously published in *Alembic* 2 (1978): 8, *Anything, Anything* (Spokane, WA: L'Epervier Press, 1980), and *Washing the Cow's Skull*, Dave Oliphant and Luis Ramos-García, eds. (Fort Worth, TX: Prickly Pear Press, 1981).]

Hit and Run

She's loosening my tie
with the softest hands,

fingers that fan out
slowly through my hair.

I try opening my eyes,
but thumbs warm as lips

glide by. The siren
coming through snow

is for me alone.
My knuckles are bloody,

freezing on bricks.
The ambulance arrives,

blue light flashing,
flashing. This dear lady

leans down. I lie calmly
in her arms this enchanted

night in snow I feel myself
becoming. When she

goes away, I try to rise,
but they're lifting my feet

and shoulders to a bed
too narrow for anyone but me.

[Previously published in *Confrontation* 37/38 (1988): 202 and *Rafting the Brazos* (Denton: University of North Texas Press, 1988–winner of the 1990 Western Heritage Award ("The Wrangler") for best book of poetry, National Cowboy Hall of Fame).]

University Library

Banyan and bougainvillea sprawl in the foyer,
fountains splash syllables of sleep. Students
in far corners stretch out together, smoking,

exit bars clicking each time another leaves.
Librarians index astounding bound books
from everywhere. The elevator's packed

with people of all ages going up, going down.
Deep in the stacks in fourth floor carrels,
graduate males massage slide rulers

backwards and forwards, mastering bodies
of knowledge by degrees, and dreaming
beyond facts of the incredible design of wives.

[Previously published in *The Spoon River Quarterly* 5, no. 2 (1980): 40 and *Burning the Fence* (Lubbock: Texas Tech University Press, 1981).]

Bermuda Grass

Root-rot and winter kill,
still the old grass comes back,
cracks in the drive and sidewalk
caulked with green, pale blades
shoving up under layers of weeds
and leaves rotting to mulch, Bermuda
rooting runners everywhere in connected
directionless sprawl, all crawling to seeds
breeding in the wind, scattering both lawns
with spawn that eat peat moss, chaff, and thrive,
that neither weeds nor drought, root-rot nor winter kills.

[Previously published in *Visions* 4, no. 7 (1981): and *Burning the Fence* (Lubbock: Texas Tech University Press, 1981).]

Flamingos on the Plains

Often in fields I see mesquite trees
balanced on one trunk, pretending to be
flamingos. Wind in the west does that,

ruffling their leaves like feathers.
Cactus and snakes beg it'll never rain.
These dry, bone-scattered plains

go on forever. Trucks on highways
pound pelts so deep in hot asphalt
not even buzzards can resurrect them,

armadillos or coyotes, whatever
in their last appetites crossed the road.
Living on thermals, a hawk rises high

toward heaven, blessing each shadow
with feathers of each wing, seeing
a rabbit hop into sunlight, and diving,

wings stiff and wide, totally silent.
All is as it will be, in a desert.
Even the trees are balanced.

[Previously published in *The Malahat Review* (Canada) 82 (1988): 34 and *Rafting the Brazos* (Denton: University of North Texas Press, 1988–winner of the 1990 Western Heritage Award ("The Wrangler") for best book of poetry, National Cowboy Hall of Fame).]

Boys and the Laws of Mercy

Under the hat racks, under the drip
of plastic raincoats, I showed Billy Ray
the bat, huddled by rain boots,
nose like a puppy's, wings folded

like a cape. Billy Ray pulled off
his shoe and scooped it. The eyes,
the throbbing throat
gave it away, limp and wheezing,

holes in its breast like buckshot.
It must have flown through a door
like a cave, wobbling through halls
to our room. Billy Ray and I

took turns stroking the fur,
the ears that twitched
when we touched them.
After someone told the teacher,

before the rest came running,
it simply died. Billy Ray lifted it
in his hand and stood there holding
the bloody shoe, daring anyone to laugh.

[Previously published in *The Digs in Escondido Canyon* (Lubbock: Texas Tech University Press, 1991–winner of the 1992 Western Heritage Award ("The Wrangler") for best book of poetry, National Cowboy Hall of Fame).]

Hunting the Pasture

They've done it again, gut-shot a cow
in our pasture. Signs don't stop them,
miles from the nearest ranch leased
for hunting. At night I might forgive

someone trespassing hardscrabble brush
and spooked, stalking a wild hope
of stumbling on antlers, shooting
when something slides by his boots.

But whoever climbs a fence in sunlight
risks more than fangs. If she feels me kneeling,
blood muzzles her, her bossy eyes glazed
on distant mesas, her black barrel heaves.

[Previously published in *Prairie Schooner* 62, no. 3 (1988): 52 and *The Digs in Escondido Canyon* (Lubbock: Texas Tech University Press, 1991—winner of the 1992 Western Heritage Award ("The Wrangler") for best book of poetry, National Cowboy Hall of Fame).]

Dawn of the Bitter Blizzard

Bulky in coats, we entered a world
below zero, in flurries blinding us
again. Barbed wires can't hold

blue northers back. Gusts swerved
on the snow, in sunlight slanted
on diamonds. Our boots crushed

the stubble of stiff alfalfa. Raw wind
ripped shingles loose, the whine
and clatter of tin on the pump house.

Our dogs plowed snow with muzzles,
ice-happy and barking. Not one sullen
hog hobbled grunting to the trough.

We found them buried, tons of lard
under snow. Buzzards perched
on power lines, watching.

After the last cows found the barn,
we dumped hay bales to save them,
trusting our stubborn goats

outside the barn to keep ringing
their bells like a challenge
to stiff winds wailing overhead.

[Previously published in *Poetry Northwest* 31, no. 4 (1990): 40 and *Where Skies Are Not Cloudy* (Denton: University of North Texas Press, 1993).]

Goats Imported from Austin

Goats stumbled on shale, a rocky mesa
Daddy fenced for kids imported from Austin.
He swore *cabrito* would be worth the smell,
a market killing, but hated goats–

cattle the only odor for a man. Coyotes and rattlers
roamed those acres until he claimed them.
Goats climbed the hill like bighorn sheep,
playing king of the mountain, bold on the bluff,

staring at greener pastures. Other goats popped up
like penguins, searching for all he saw in the distance.
My brother and I fed goats by hand, lugged oats
to kids with nubbin horns, bellies that bulged

and muscles butting us for buckets. After chores,
we dragged our wagons to the top. Where the cliff
dropped off, we risked the bumpy ride downhill,
tumbling, bending the wheels and tongues.

The goats ignored us, picking their paths
up and down like angels. After frost,
our father slaughtered them all and hung them
one by one from rafters, smoking the meat

for winter, the market for cattle and goats
collapsed, the start of the Texas depression.
Drinking windmill water from cans,
we chewed tough jerky for months,

salt-cured and stringy. We learned to curse
the dust of a ranch that failed
and played field hockey without a stick,
kicking the tiny hoofs like pucks.

[Previously published in *Poetry Durham* (UK) 29 (1992): 19, *Where Skies Are Not Cloudy* (Denton: University of North Texas Press, 1993), and *Whatever the Wind Delivers: Celebrating West Texas and the Near Southwest* (Lubbock: Texas Tech University Press, 1999—winner of the 2000 Western Heritage Award ("The Wrangler") for best book of poetry, National Cowboy Hall of Fame).]

Searching

The same soft stomping every dawn,
our son's grown ferret dancing for food,
seeking the way to say what's on his mind,
his dark eyes blind with rage for meat.
He grips the bacon in his teeth

and snarls, arches his swan neck and rips
the fat, lips high as he smacks, big eyes
staring beyond this meal, this day,
already worried about the dark, if dawn
will come, if there'll be meat tomorrow.

Previously published in *Poet Lore* 80, no. 4 (1986): 231 and *Witching on Hardscrabble* (Peoria, IL: Spoon River Poetry Press, 1985).]

The Snowplow Driver

Most follow along like sheep, single file,
snow spouting an arc from my plow.
When I turn on side streets, most follow
around the block rather than risk the road

unplowed, but some can't wait
to get ahead, bumper to bumper
like stock-car racing and me
the pace car. Some of them shoot past,

one after the other, slipping like kids
learning to skate. I've seen cars spin out
into trees, crash into trucks creeping along,
or simply stall. One time a guy too reckless

jerked his midget car out and around,
cut short and hooked the blade.
The curved point peeled him like a can.
I hear his screams like claws on a blackboard

each time my blade digs down on streets
too dry to plow. Whoever heard of people
forty years back dying in drifts, thousands
stranded, old people freezing in their homes?

So much depends on keeping these roads clear
I can't quit. I won't let anyone freeze,
not on my streets. I'm like a shepherd.
When I look back, they're following.

[Previously published in *Kansas Quarterly* 17, nos. 1–2 (1985): 68 and *Witching on Hardscrabble* (Peoria, IL: Spoon River Poetry Press, 1985).]

The Last Five Acres of Timber

They've cut the last trees down, loblolly pines
the color of money. We take the sun for granted
on the plains. Sunlight ripens pine sap
heady as a mountain still. We wade through stumps

and kick old trunks, tall pines that die of bites.
They poof like toadstools, dust to dust.
They'll rise again as seedlings, too late for us,
all bark we own killed by a million beetles,

condemned, flames the only way to save infested trees.
Rangers faithful to their tasks have bulldozed
stacks of logs, a slash-and-burn salvation. Each fall
we drive from Texas to trees more costly than cash

they earn, leased to loggers. We've waged
this tree-house dream for years. Our children
pretended goats were ours. Little bells led goats
to pasture through these woods, a neighbor's herd.

Now stumps are ours, and fungus. Blue jays
are gone, the men who felled the logs are home.
After the whine of chain saws, it's silent.
Those who'll burn the logs are miles away

in smoky bars, planning tomorrow's fire storm.
It's best to torch them all—mushrooms
and fallen logs, scallions and truffles, down
to slow-burning brush, the last miraculous tree.

[Previously published in *The Digs in Escondido Canyon* (Lubbock: Texas Tech University Press, 1991—winner of the 1992 Western Heritage Award ("The Wrangler") for best book of poetry, National Cowboy Hall of Fame).]

A Thousand Yards Downhill

Embers blaze-back nights
of bonfires ice can't echo. Wild nights
and days when our children skied
linger in blinks of slides
fierce light without sound projects.

A river tumbles underground
and comes back up for air
a thousand yards downhill. Foam
is its only note, it holds it all day,
gushing up from that deep cave

and babbling resurrection.
When we backpack halfway
between eagle and otter,
we never climb the same trails
twice, sliding on shale most steps,

the eyes of all things wild
straining to see who's here.
Our children with children sleep
in distant condominiums, skiing
when it snows enough for powder

deep as dreams we cling to, these
brief nights, enough for two-log fires
to rock by, hours after we hoped phones
would ring, "Hello? Hello?"
In this cabin, we two are not alone.

This calm could be thunder
to a stethoscope, gongs to the inner ear.
Imagine the softest saxophone note
you've ever heard, diminuendo.
For now, for us, silence is enough.

[Previously published in *Poetry Wales* (UK) 27, no. 4 (1992): 29 and *Where Skies Are Not Cloudy* (Denton: University of North Texas Press, 1993).]

Weeds, Barn Owls, All Nibbling Goats

We chop these weeds with hoes
filed shiny. Nothing but rain could save
these puny roots. Enough of killing weeds
for a hobby. Wrong, maybe, trying
to make hardscrabble sand say "beans"

as well as "grass," the nearest lake
a hundred miles away. Bless weeds
that wring hard water from this dirt.
We'll throw the gate wide open
and let goats graze until they bloat.

Even a stunted pasture feeds them.
The days of miracles may not be gone.
Too old to start over, we watch for signs,
a front, a steady shower. An inch of rain
would yield Kentucky Wonder beans

to freeze. Neighbors could pick their fill.
Even that weedy dried-up playa lake
could be a pond. We could breed ducks
imported from swamps. Afternoons,
we rock together on the porch, sipping iced tea

from depression glass, watching mirages
for hawks, the shimmer of heat waves
breeding whirlwinds but no angels
in the clouds, sometimes an owl blinded
by sunlight, weaving from barn to barn.

[Previously published in *Threepenny Review* 11, no. 4 (1990): 19 and *The Digs in Escondido Canyon* (Lubbock: Texas Tech University Press, 1991–winner of the 1992 Western Heritage Award ("The Wrangler") for best book of poetry, National Cowboy Hall of Fame).]

Taking Each Deep Breath

Rain, the long arm of thunder, reaches us
at last. After months of drought
and shimmering mirage, so much staccato fuss
to make one pond. Steers wade the pasture

and stare, lower broad muzzles
into grass and shut their eyes, and why not,
about to be hauled off in trucks when the rain stops.
Propped on the back porch with coffee,

we watch the prairie fade in a squall line,
hard rain like the days of Noah. The breeze
is fresh honey in the hive. We are two bees
in a pasture. The steers go under in the haze,

even the barn, only this porch swing
dry in the downpour, an ark we rock on,
gliding under the crack of thunder,
taking each deep breath to let it go.

[Previously published in *America* 162, no. 6 (1990): 144 and *The Digs in Escondido Canyon* (Lubbock: Texas Tech University Press, 1991—winner of the 1992 Western Heritage Award ("The Wrangler") for best book of poetry, National Cowboy Hall of Fame).]

Pools Under the Campus

Crawling through tunnels, a man keeps his compass handy.
It could be fierce little fish in a pool, without teeth
but vicious, nipping wrists and thrashing as if he was food.

Or bats suddenly above him, soft breaths, eyes closed
in the glow of his headlamp. Somewhere under the campus
he's paid to keep comfortably cool, he may stumble,

lights blinking off, without landmarks, the polished stone
perfectly innocent of dust, without tracks. If he crawls
two cautious steps and pauses, marveling at rocks,

the whorls of stone tunnels lovely, like sliding through arteries,
he may lose his way until later. It may be pools he's waded,
stalagmites he held in his hands to wiggle past, or the same

dripping stalactites he lay under, maybe, and thrust on his back
to squeeze past. It may take hours, puzzled, that maybe
his watch stopped or sprung a leak when he fell. It may be

totally colorless fish in shallow pools he's read about,
fish that don't shrink from light, eyeless, with stubborn
carp-like lips opening and closing in silent, absolute darkness.

If he lifts the compass to his eyes, or finds a sole shaft of light
at his feet, it might be the difference between the needle's dark
and silver points, the long dark tunnel in, and out into the light.

[Previously published in *Prairie Schooner* 61, no. 1 (1987): 26 and *After the Noise of Saigon* (Amherst: University of Massachusetts Press, 1988—winner of the 1987 University of Massachusetts Press Juniper Prize).]

Steeples and Deep Wells

No sense of guilt: that must be
what they sought, driving bull-necked oxen
to the plains, teams stubborn as mules
grazing swaying grass knee-deep all day,

wagons stranded like crippled buffalo
a thousand miles from Kentucky loam
and lakes, pleasures of the flesh
where sin came easy. Here they found

no trees, no stones to hide behind.
If any came blameless, here their faults
were plain. No wonder they shoveled dugouts
first, somewhere to sleep out of sight.

On land so flat they dug deep wells
and raised plank steeples fast,
as lightning rods. If they worried
about chances left behind, the sun

burned the truth of what they were,
a crop away from being meat for buzzards.
Rain fell like manna twice a year
and saved their starving crops.

Believing signs of saplings all winter,
they doled out grain and shivered.
They shared their meager corn
with dogs and ate the flesh of snakes.

[Previously published in *Fiddlehead* (Canada) 166 (1990): 18 and *Where Skies Are Not Cloudy* (Denton: University of North Texas Press, 1993).]

Where Skies Are Not Cloudy

We hear old heartache often on the plains.
The whine of steel guitars and songs
of lonely blondes escape from pickups
passing by. Whoever's driving waves,
and I wave back. My dogs trot out to ask

if I'm all right, wagging their lazy tails.
They're blinking from the barn, squinting
in sunlight to prove they're loyal dogs.
They wet a stalk and trot away
to nothing but shade and daydreams.

Watching a hawk, I hear another whine of tires.
Soon I'll hear the tune, the same old fiddles
sobbing in a neighbor's truck, some singer
swearing these empty plains are all she knows,
pleading a stranger's arms are all she needs.

[Previously published in *New Virginia Review* 9, no. 2 (1992): 42 and *Where Skies Are Not Cloudy* (Denton: University of North Texas Press, 1993).]

Releasing the Hawk in August

Say something sober to a hawk
and he'll rise flapping,
curved talons eager
to tear our hearts out.

He had that stare
the scalding day we found him
by a cactus, wing drooped,
grazed by a hunter.

After weeks of feeding him
giblets and mice he snatched
with curved beak and ripped,
we knew we'd never be friends

up close, too much alike,
his wound a temporary scratch
of nature, the shape of genes,
his way of saying save me.

[Previously published in *Oxford Magazine* 7, no. 1 (1991): 53 and *Where Skies Are Not Cloudy* (Denton: University of North Texas Press, 1993).]

Picasso and the Art of Angels

What if the day Picasso died,
he dreamed he saw an angel
and wept he could never paint her,
marvelously complex,

the skin tones perfect,
her flesh angelically erotic,
nothing at all like humans,
but skewed, cubistic angles

of the actual. Would he know
as he reached for his brushes,
watching her folding towels
as if to drape herself

inside a perfect canvas,
did he know she was only
his morning nurse, a local woman
working for pay?

[Previously published in *Maryland Poetry Review* 9 (1990): 27 and *Where Skies Are Not Cloudy* (Denton: University of North Texas Press, 1993).]

Steers in Blizzards

Overnight, the ice froze so hard
we couldn't smash it loose.
We thawed the pipes with torches,

brought buckets of water
to stock tanks, and urged
cold steers to drink

while they could. At first
they didn't drink, as if they believed
they were dead. Glazed steers

circled the tank like hours
on a clock. Frost muzzled them,
and snow frozen on one side

showed how they had leaned
all night against the wind.
Under tall white firs,

one old snow-covered steer
was down. He couldn't move
when we prodded him with boots,

with rifle butts. Even his flanks
didn't quiver, but horns snapped back
with the shot his eyes never saw.

[Previously published in *The Pennsylvania Review* (1985): 23 (received *The Pennsylvania Review* Poetry Award in 1985 under original title "The Norther") and *Witching on Hardscrabble* (Peoria, IL: Spoon River Poetry Press, 1985).]

Lockett, Where the Water Quit

This town is like a brother broken by the war.
Never mind which war, it's haunted.
The school is boarded up. Farmers
who kept four stores in business died

or lost their fields at auction. The aquifer
dried up under most of the county,
plains where it rains two times a year.
Hands who guard the bankers' herds

drive now to Clovis—a mall, flea markets,
a hundred fast-food shops. Hunters with guns
stop in Lockett for Coors and gas
and joke about the town's cock-pheasant

fading on the billboard. The old man still takes
dollars or credit cards but gives away too much,
the same complaints he always had,
sad country songs sobbing on his jukebox.

Tumbleweeds bounce into town each fall
like teenaged drivers on drugs, the last
paved road out of town abandoned. Sandstorms
invade, and empty houses let them. Windows

we wanted to smash as kids are smashed.
We wonder when. One store holds on,
but nobody buys in a town but young couples
showing surprising defiance, rose bushes

and latticed green vines, fresh-painted
porch swings on chains hanging straight,
new garage doors easy to raise, mailboxes
shiny, and tall flagpoles in the yards.

[Previously published in *Berkeley Poetry Review* 23/24 (1990): 124 and *The Digs in Escondido Canyon* (Lubbock: Texas Tech University Press, 1991—winner of the 1992 Western Heritage Award ("The Wrangler") for best book of poetry, National Cowboy Hall of Fame).]

Stars and the Laws of Motion

These trees yielded networks of buds,
an expanding universe. Stars we believed
enough for love and navigation were never true,
flung forever outward toward black holes.
Computers predict in a million years

Orion's stars will become the scorpion
that stalks him, his straight belt bowed
like legs, the stars that were his sword
raised like a stinger. Years ago, we loved oceans,
blue-phosphorus balloons of jellyfish

bobbing ashore. Seagulls wheeled above us,
moon-white and silent, like memories of those
we've loved and left, when it was over.
Tonight, after weeding the garden, we rest
in lawn chairs under stars vanishing at dawn.

[Previously published in *The Fiddlehead* (Canada) 159 (1989): 67 and *The Digs in Escondido Canyon* (Lubbock: Texas Tech University Press, 1991–winner of the 1992 Western Heritage Award ("The Wrangler") for best book of poetry, National Cowboy Hall of Fame).]

Windmills Near Escondido Canyon

Relax, it's Friday, nothing to do but chop
the ground until iron weeds are dead, the hoe
filed silver-thin, gloves frayed and molded
to our fists. Grow sorghum when it rains

and feed a prairie black with steers, fat Angus
glistening like whales. This month, our dry steers
stumble to the barn at sundown, coughing,
jaws grinding from side to side their latest cud.

This is a week in summer on the Plains, eating
red meat, praying for rain, kicking chalk-white
caliche dust to tanks moss-green and empty.
Climb up and grease the windmill bearings

one more time, connect the rods and duck
when the rudder swings and starts the pump.
Climb down and watch the water troughs fill up,
shove back at cattle nudging to the pump,

stiff breeze reliable, more comfort to the steers
than rain. Buzzards soaring on thermals keep watch
on us all, lost in time and sandstorms. At noon,
we drag cane-bottomed chairs to the only oak

and watch for clouds on wide horizons. Cold beers
condense more moisture for our fields than clouds.
We feel like hawks, scouting the skies, hoping dry wind
keeps coyotes loping to caves. Squinting, shooting

buzzards with our fingers, we face the sun and wonder
how many heads of maize we can harvest, how many
steers to a bushel, how many gallons spin on a windmill,
how many times a pump goes around in an hour.

[Previously published in *San Jose Studies* 17, no. 2 (1991): 99 and *All That Matters: The Texas Plains in Photographs and Poems* (Lubbock: Texas Tech University Press, 1992—winner of the 1993 Western Heritage Award ("The Wrangler") for best book of poetry, National Cowboy Hall of Fame.]

Driving Home to the Plains

Now it begins, the endless golds and blues,
no forests, no mountains anywhere. Sunshine
sixteen hours a day, nothing to shade us,

not even an eclipse. Parched lips seek
each other for escape, the cracked bruising
oozing blood. Fields this flat sprawl

like the moon, like Mars. Nothing about it
resembles home. On land this flat no wonder
people pray, left out all night like babies

that fell off wagons heading west,
weeping all night for bottles, blankets,
nothing forever but sky, ten billion stars.

[Previously published in *Poet Lore* 80, no. 4 (1986): 229 and *The Flying Dutchman* (Columbus: The Ohio State University Press, 1987–winner of the 1987 George Elliston Poetry Prize.]

One Thing Leads to Another

Sometimes two hands take mine, or even ten.
Some nights, all nine grandkids mount me
like a camel, hanging on humps of shoulders,
tugging my beard, the littlest fist

gripping my lip like a sultan's spoiled
family camel, patient while the children play.
We pose for the birdie on birthdays, always
some grandson making horns with his fingers

above a cherub's head, another giggling
and squirming, one sneezing, the pose clicked again,
again. I never failed at math as a schoolboy
but struggled, adding up answers on fingers

under the desk on tests. Now I'm over sixty,
stunned by how fast men and women multiply,
how one turns into two, then three, then doubled,
and now fifteen. Birthdays, I'm surprised

by "Here is the church, and here's the steeple,
open the door and see all the people,"
toddlers wide-eyed on my lap watching magic
of my stiff hands that lock and open like a door.

[Previously published in *Tex!* 1 (1998): 19 and *Whatever the Wind Delivers: Celebrating West Texas and the Near Southwest* (Lubbock: Texas Tech University Press, 1999–winner of the 2000 Western Heritage Award ("The Wrangler") for best book of poetry, National Cowboy Hall of Fame.]

The Last Saloon in Lockett

Bulky in coats, we hummed the old songs
badly after days of riding herd, barbed wire
and steers too dumb to know deep snow

could freeze them. At big old Uncle Earl's,
rouged women gave us the songs we needed,
the swing of crystal earrings pumping our blood

uphill, a loud and smoky dance hall never closed.
We broke our backs for cash to shove those
swinging doors. Tall mirrors lined the walls,

moose heads and posters of laughing girls
in feathers and stiff red petticoats. When Earl
moved heads and all to Austin, he left us alone

in our pickups, driving around and around.
They've torn the tavern down, another place
we went to get away from skies more lonely

than ourselves. Call it an order on the plains—
Tear down the honky-tonk walls, who needs them?
That part of me that needs a mob drove by

most nights for weeks to watch the wrecking crew,
nothing but echoes of hard-voiced singers
and the clink of friendly bottles, sweethearts

in spotlights moaning the songs we longed for.
They've hauled the last beams off, bulldozed
the parking lot and banished all ghosts

with throaty tunes and flash of starry earrings.
Never mind the moon, the vacant field.
Nights when I drive by, they're gone.

[Previously published in *Manoa* 5, no. 2 (1993): 111 and *Whatever the Wind Delivers: Celebrating West Texas and the Near Southwest* (Lubbock: Texas Tech University Press, 1999—winner of the 2000 Western Heritage Award ("The Wrangler") for best book of poetry, National Cowboy Hall of Fame).]

The Ogallala Water Table

Anytime from March through Fall
on the Plains, irrigation engines
like mosquitoes syphon the purest
water a hundred, three hundred feet

up to the surface, turning our desert
into crops. Nights as a boy I lay
waiting for water to soak its slow way
down the rows, the smell of earth

and cotton leaves easy to breathe
in acres of oxygen, the breeze
blowing the news of water on its way,
the giddy smell of dirt turning to mud,

thousands of acres living on nothing
but transfusions from below. Now,
stretching through hundreds of miles
of sandy aquifers squeezed like sponges,

the Ogallala water table drops three feet
each season. Pipes of the wells go deep,
and some dry up. Sections of land
go back each year to sand and blow away.

My brother with no choice changes oil
in his engines, tightens the nuts
and starts them up again. He waits,
the wells suck deep, the water flows.

[Previously published in *Ascent* 4, no. 2 (1979) and *All That Matters: The Texas Plains in Photographs and Poems* (Lubbock: Texas Tech University Press, 1992—winner of the 1993 Western Heritage Award ("The Wrangler") for best book of poetry, National Cowboy Hall of Fame).]

Anniversary Six Miles High

My wife tries sipping champagne in turbulence.
Thunderclouds make us sway and bump
with plastic glasses balanced on our laps.
A down draft jerks us up, then slams us down.

Juice splatters on our trays, our laps. She glances
at me wide-eyed, and laughs, and seat-belt signs
flash on. She glances out at clouds, at lightning.
The jet slams hard, doors pop open and luggage

tumbles out. Up front, a woman screams.
The captain's voice comes on, a mellow baritone,
"Folks, lean back and enjoy the flight,
and we'll have you in Dallas right on time."

She dabs a wrist that's damp from the ice.
My own glass sloshes, so I lean near to toast us
with the ounce of fine champagne that's left,
and lift it to her chin, her dazzling lips.

[Previously published in *The American Scholar* (Phi Beta Kappa magazine) 64, no. 2 (1995): 240 and *Whatever the Wind Delivers: Celebrating West Texas and the Near Southwest* (Lubbock: Texas Tech University Press, 1999—winner of the 2000 Western Heritage Award ("The Wrangler") for best book of poetry, National Cowboy Hall of Fame).]

On Losing a Child

We understand autumn,
its easy tears, why cattle
keep grazing till sundown,
why leaves die splendidly,
trembling in disarray
after such brief seasons.

All fall we stroll arm
in arm through leaves,
and if we feel like weeping,
we match our chatter
to leaves crunching
underfoot, as if nothing

at all is falling. Nights,
we hold each other longer
before drifting off, knowing
one of us will wake in the dark
and pull the blanket
when the first snow falls.

[Previously published in *Hardscrabble* (1984): 12 and *Witching on Hardscrabble* (Peoria, IL: Spoon River Poetry Press, 1985).]

Hosannas Dangling on Strings

The sun burns silver in your hair,
flash of green light in your eyes.
Shadows left this mountain hours ago–

dusk, the start of what we all call night.
We like the private hours of midnight,
the stars flung out to wide horizons,

always a breeze to make chimes ping
and jingle on the patio. We don't need light
to touch what matters most, the rising up

and falling of the sun, the blaze of lavish hours
together, the swift and playful nights like wild
hosannas dangling on string. I love the halo

of your hair, the simple mystery of your eyes.
I'm stunned by more on this screened porch
that shudders when I walk and fall back

with you on the swing, extravagant kisses
I adore, secrets familiar, within reach, even
the kind and steady squeezing of your hand.

[Previously published in *Tex!* 1 (1998): 19 and *Whatever the Wind Delivers: Celebrating West Texas and the Near Southwest* (Lubbock: Texas Tech University Press, 1999–winner of the 2000 Western Heritage Award ("The Wrangler") for best book of poetry, National Cowboy Hall of Fame.]

Where the Trees Go

In time they all rise up
and glide away. For years
they lie where they fall,
leaves brittle, branches

twisted like fists. In time,
even the bleeding stops,
the stumps seared dry by sun.
The others learn to go on

without them.
They watch the wings
they were always too near
to notice, from learning to fly

to flying. Birds
seem never to die. They fly
away—they simply
fly away. The trees lie still.

Silent for years,
they dream of leaves, of wood dust
light as feathers. They dream
they pick up their beds

and walk away. They've found
where the birds go. In time
the other trees look down
and find them missing.

[Previously published in *Poetry Northwest* 25, no. 4 (1988–1989): 43 and *All That Matters: The Texas Plains in Photographs and Poems* (Lubbock: Texas Tech University Press, 1992—winner of the 1993 Western Heritage Award ("The Wrangler") for best book of poetry, National Cowboy Hall of Fame).]

It's Still the Same Old Story

Often I rang her doorbell after midnight
in my mind, hat in my hand and hoping.
If a man answered, all hair and husband
in his underwear, what would I do?

A year since she flew away, taking her hand
like a house key. Coiled in an Air Force cockpit,
I fed on dials and dog fights, emerged months
later with a chest of wings, and longings,

highballs and takeoffs at dawn the way to strut.
Pilots worshipped the god called luck,
two-headed Buddha called throttle and stick,
power we wielded with our fists. I thought of her

often after lights out, and alone at 40 thousand feet.
Once, I cursed an engine fire at night, spiraled
and set it down at the base in her hometown,
time enough for a telephone. I flipped to her name

and there it was. I remembered the number,
even the lick of the tongue of her dachshund.
Taxi idling behind me, I stared at that doorbell
and almost stalled, reached out and pushed.

All that, decades ago. Someone I flew with
has gone to the moon and back, others shot down
near Hanoi and Laos, the endless guilt of surviving.
But here is her photo in a golden frame,

her paintings on every wall, our grandkids
laughing, clattering pans in the kitchen,
and when I rise and go there, she's leaning down
and hugs them, watching them roll the dough.

[Previously published in *First Things* 88 (1998): 29 and *Whatever the Wind Delivers: Celebrating West Texas and the Near Southwest* (Lubbock: Texas Tech University Press, 1999–winner of the 2000 Western Heritage Award ("The Wrangler") for best book of poetry, National Cowboy Hall of Fame).]

Part 4

Hunting First Drafts in Vinny's Place

I come here to think, the corner diner
with the stiff menu, cramped counter
and booths like bookends. The aroma of toast
mingles with bull-necked sausage smoke,
sweet sleeves of waffles and heated bagels
coaxing me to eat, don't talk with your fingers,

don't even think. Tongue, do it with your tongue
and sticky lips, hot syrup and butter
oozing down your chin. What the body needs
the teeth can taste, all this smack
and sucking of tooth like a cave of pumas
cracking bones. Here is the odor of work,

words I can taste, sweet buttered cinnamon buns
in this passenger car from the forties,
omelets and sizzling breakfast steaks
steaming the windows, something to sink my teeth in,
grease and coffee stains on paper. A man nearby
lets go a small explosion muffled by his fist,

paper sack popped like a balloon. His other fist
shields biscuits and bacon smothered in gravy,
hash browns fried in dairy butter, the real stuff
before going to work, real work. His muscles bulge,
like a wrestler's a decade or two ago,
brogans with bulged steel toes. His buddy

sops big eggs, sunny side up, the runny taste
of gold before hard work, nothing to do
in Vinny's Place for half an hour but eat,
no matter what's ahead, time enough
for one more steaming refill and thoughtful
toothpick before swaggering outside.

[Previously published in *The Pikeville Review* (1998): 47–48.]

The Second Sign

Ink scattered on a notepad frazzles my brain.
I'm stumped by something I wrote on the nightstand,
baffled like a janitor filling in at the switchboard

for Myrtle, who stepped out for a smoke or the washroom.
What reminder rolled me on an elbow at two,
what appointment have I missed, since I can't read it?

I never learned this tongue, but hours ago,
I wrote it. Code breakers from World War II
might crack it months from now, but it's today,

a message I dared not, sleeping, forget–secrets
of perpetual motion, a formula I can't decipher
for growing hair? I've heard "forgetful" is the first sign

of aging. If there's a second, it's Sanskrit,
squiggles. "Wash spittle from spigots? Wham
thimbles for Shirley?" Who waits for me at the airport

or Starbuck's, fifth cup of Espresso cold,
lifting wristwatch to listen, about to leave?
What lawyer did I promise to meet, or sweetheart

from high school in town for an hour with a pouch
of photos of us one summer, her children, grandchildren,
the lout she married instead of me?

[Previously published in *California Quarterly* 28, no. 2 (2002): 17.]

Banjo Saturday Nights

Picking a mean, mad banjo
is half showing off, half teasing,
more rhythm than brain waves.
Old Uncle John was skinny and six-five,

half man, half rubber plant,
long fingers around a banjo's neck,
plinking tight strings and tapping
fast as teenage dancers' feet.

Sprawled on a folding chair
in a ballroom or VFW hall,
Uncle John was all knees and neck
with a Stetson flipped back

to give him room, dueling head down
with a hot guitar, cowboys and wives
twirling each other, old couples
clapping time, watching Uncle John

at ninety playing the way God made him,
slapping the strings with fingers
and half a thumb, not many years to live
but faster than most of us could twirl.

[Previously published in *The Oklahoma Review* 3, no. 1 (2002).]

Jostled Pods of a Yucca

We listened to voices ringing on the rails,
swapped rumors of babies and girls, wars
uncles fought, weapons and dried tongues
hidden in attics. Raised on the plains,
we taught ourselves to draw,
that perfect slap of leather

and wavering whine across miles of pastures.
We shared flat cactus fields with coyotes
then tried to shoot them with toy pistols. They knew us
and kept their distance, complaining to the moon.
We shoved our boots into bedrolls
on the same cool sand with rattlers.

Billy Joe swore he heard one, only jostled pods
of a yucca. We wondered what bumped it,
werewolves or ghosts we believed in
under a moon that full, our wide eyes
watching mesquite trees like witches
waving a thousand arms.

[Previously published in *The Nebraska Review* 20, no. 2 (1992): 24–25.]

Sandlot Baseball, Before Pearl Harbor

"Get off the fence!" old Mrs. Wilson screamed.
I tossed the ball out of her yard and leaped,
barbed wire snagging my sleeves and knees.
My big brother's buddies howled like mad dogs,

not afraid of her husband, old man with a badge
and gun, night watchman at the town's one bank.
They scoffed, "Who could sleep on Sunday
after lunch?" Sometimes, from the sandlot,

I heard Mr. Wilson coughing, windows up,
old couple alone. Five mocking boys in the alley
that day never came home from World War Two,
shot down or drowned, tangled in concertina wire

and machine-gunned, buried at sea or in coffins
on Normandy or Guam. After my brother came back
from France, we never talked about the neighbors
or played ball again, not even catch.

[Previously published in *Louisiana Literature* 20, no. 1 (Spring/Summer 2003): 43–44.]

After the Long Flight Home from Seoul

Toast was the most he cooked.
Why bother, when take-out tasted great?
Years as a POW made batter
fried on fatty wieners a feast.
After Korea, Uncle Oscar tried them all,

the street from his house to town
a carnival of barbecue and fish,
quick pizzas and kosher beef on rye,
bagels or egg muffins for breakfast.
Oscar's wife was gone when he came home

from war, his old job waiting at the bank,
a special place to park. His legs, titanium,
rode an elevator to the top, but for lunch
he climbed two flights of stairs
without a cane to the snack bar,

pastrami in cellophane, mustard
in a little tub, and a Coke. Sometimes,
at night, when his stumps hurt,
Oscar took off the legs and locked
the wheelchair by the door

for deliveries of pizza and tuna salad,
even cold cuts from all-night delis
across town, drapes shut, eating alone
in the dark with the TV off, ignoring the phone,
the doorbell, the sirens wailing by.

[Previously published in *Poem* 89 (May 2003): 34–35.]

At the Football Stadium

Last night, beyond the flooding
stadium lights, up through a cloud deck
in skies almost too dark to see,

the moon emerged, a round orange tunnel
in the east. Our son, his oval eyes
responding, reached for the case,

squeezed black binoculars together,
focused the night
through dark scoops of space.

Silent, under the savage crowd noise,
beneath the lenses and his fists
he mouthed an O.

[Previously published in *Mississippi Review* 5, no. 2 (1976): 20.]

Town Girls When I Was Nine

Kids envied our ponies, how we trotted to town
from the ranch, the horses we rode every day
on the plains. New kids in town since our one-room
school shut down, I let boys stroke and talk

to the gelding, then rode to the stable and left him
and ran to catch up with my cousin at school
two blocks away. Bobby envied their bikes,
the store-bought cigars they swiped from daddies

who kept boxes of cigars and didn't miss any
his spoiled kids sneaked. Bobby choked
on most, but I didn't smoke after cigars of bark
we had crushed and rolled in toilet paper and lit.

What I liked about Eddy and Earl and their gang
was what they could see any day, even weekends–
pretty girls in a town of hundreds, those teasing
blondes and brunettes, classmates who turned

in their seats to see us. They watched us both
like mavericks, batting their eyes and flirting
over sweet, up-lifted shoulders before the teacher
made them stop and face the front.

[Previously published in *Pennsylvania English* 24, nos. 1–2 (Fall 2001/Spring 2002): 148.]

Doctors, Lawyers, Undertakers

Boys couldn't tell turtles from knuckles
in soup. Sue worked with worms,
turned some boys and girls

away from baseball and hopscotch
to biology. "See that?" she asked
and stepped back from the microscope,

so we, lined up, could look,
a bit of tissue from inside her lip
displayed naked on the stage.

"That's how we look to worms,"
she confessed, "our sticky cells
tasty enough to eat."

Sue patted us on the back
and looked us in the eye,
examining our brows, the shape

of our gritted jaws and skulls,
forecasting our futures.
She made us call her Sue,

our classmate in love with flesh
and the leveler worm, even us—
some of us peeking "Wow!" into worlds

of microscopes and slides,
some flipping fingers
behind her back,

not knowing what to say
but snarls or gritted teeth,
some simply green.

[Previously published in *The Drunken Boat* (July 2001).]

A Bowl, A Little Skull

Suddenly, this skull, a girl's, the cause of death obvious
and swift, a diamond-shaped incision through the brain.
Shape says she fell face down, bowing under the same

tornado sky we worship. Summers, we scrape layers
of dry caliche down through rocks and pottery,
hoping to know these people, our picks flicking bones

of buffalo and wolves. Carefully, we resurrect her.
What did she see, those last few hours? Alone
at this dry playa lake, plains people kneeled this deep

in the canyon, nowhere else to turn. They might
have sacrificed lame sons to keep them safe, nothing
to cover them but skins of whatever they could kill,

bison and antelopes with dark eyes and rapidly
beating hearts. On land this flat, if they wondered
about gods, when they stumbled on this canyon,

they believed—a spring-fed stream, rabbits and quail,
enough flint for fire and arrows. Did they ever feel
nothing threatening, not even the wind riffling, feathers

of an arrow about to kill? She was more than a bowl,
a little skull we stroke and photograph, and probe
for an arrowhead trapped in the brain's hard dust.

[Previously published in *The Fiddlehead* (Canada) 153 (1987): 48–49.]

Climbing Geometry

Our Lady is always awake,
we joked about Ms. Oldham in eighth grade.
If we dared pass notes to Emma
batting her eyes, the witch was there,

sparks in her hair and hand,
wadding our offers of love for the trash.
Doze off behind geometry books,
Widow Oldham packed us off

to the blackboard blank as our minds.
Old biddy who loved us, she ripped
ignorance like ticks from our brains.
She kindled and ice-packed our skulls

with formulas, dragged algebra
out of seventh-grade lockers, tacked hints
of trig to our skulls and made us stretch.
She was worse than Coach Gunny Moore

with his drill-sergeant clipboard
and whistle, his fat slick ropes
dangling from the ceiling in gym,
no mats on the hardwood floor—"C'mon,

McDonald, climb! don't die on me today."
Squeeze and kick, climb like half-dead spiders
up strands we didn't spin. Then came
Ms. Oldham's dreaded last class of the day,

the old gal we loved shouting hosannas
about angles, drumming deductions from curves
and magical unknowns, square roots
to girls we yearned and studied for.

[Previously published in *Locust Magazine* 16 (December 2002).]

Hoping the Playground Would Notice

When blue-eyed Trudy sauntered by,
we threw our knives at trees
and shoved each other—"My blade
went deeper, mine." Sixth grade was bluff

and gas, gross-out the way to impress girls,
we reasoned with our jeans. We stumbled
and cursed, gobbled obscene drawings
someone stole from his brother, desperate

to make girls see who tossed the spitball,
whose paper plane grazed the teacher
in study hall. We crossed streets without
watching, hoping girls on the playground

would notice what bold boyfriends
we would be. That's what Durwood
with the cool clothes must have thought
when he jogged out between parked cars.

[Previously published in *Ontario Review* 59 (2003): 115–16.]

Sounds in the Mountain Cabin

Proudly, the owner rips the insulation back
and points–"Not mice making that clatter
in the attic." Then, scurry of tiny toes and gnawing,
and he balks. I say again it's annoying
while I'm trying to write. Noises upstairs

sound like games or fun, or hunger. So now
it's one man banging around with a lantern.
I watch him sweating up there, teeth clenched,
breathing the dust of droppings and rot. Cramped,
he moves a pole like slow-motion shuffleboard,

and four hair-trigger traps back wobbling
until they touch the wall. The mice are silent.
I leave, and hear him tug the trap door back into place,
I hear it clunk. My wife hugs me and smiles. Tonight,
the clicking of my laptop will start. A thousand pines

have never been so still, the jays this quiet.
A green-backed hummingbird stops and sips
at a berry bush. I see contrails of a jet too far away to hear.
Above jet roar I know is there, I hear
the patter of claws, a sniff, a nibble, and *snap*.

[Previously published in *Connecticut Review*.]

Against This Winter

Thousands of geese glided down, squadrons
of perfect V's floating over willows without leaves.
Back from Canada, they fanned out

over the ranch, eating whatever geese eat
after thousands of miles on the flyway.
Downtown, we found them flocked in the park

like cobblestones. Families tossed scraps of bread,
surrounded. Toddlers turned their backs,
hands to their heads, giddy, but begging for help.

Later, we crossed the hospital parking lot
and watched dogs parting the flocks,
their masters calling. Hundreds of geese

flapped away, but not far, banking back
to the lake, feathers and bowed necks dipping
and feeding, the whole world honking.

Across the road at the rest home, old people
in wheelchairs lined the porch, wheels locked
and alone, or pushed by their children or aides.

Some pointed and waved. Most merely slumped,
heads bowed and limp, as if praying, or asleep,
now that they'd seen these wild, exotic wings.

[Previously published in *Defined Providence* 4 (1996): 25.]

After Living a Long Time Alone

She reaches high in the pantry,
no ladder, but tiptoe on a kitchen chair,
a pirouette at eighty. The top shelf topples,
her leg twists, snaps, and she's down,
back broken, no phone she can reach.
Many to call, but how, and so many,
but anyway she calls, the pain calls,
the wet jaw opens and she calls.

Aunt Pearl never screamed, but now
she cries. In pain and feeling dizzy,
she gasps, can barely breathe. She begs,
but no one comes. Dear Pearl, if only
you'd called 911 or neighbors, or us
your nieces and nephews, always
with cell phones dangling from our belts
like pistols—"Dang, we're tough."

If only we'd choked on sweet rolls,
jumped up and run to whoever's truck
was close, tugging at ties, a dozen
cell phones and not one buzzed. All that,
hours before I knocked and shouted,
peeked and banged on your window
and rang and rang your bell
then kicked the back door down.

[Previously published in *King Log* 6, no. 1 (2003).]

Well I'll Be Damned,

he says. My second jury summons in a year.
What do they think I am, retired? I can't afford
another week. He shakes his head.
Turns back to his office. Stops
and sips his coffee. Goes in and shuts the door.

Mark and Maureen run a pharmacy. Take turns
at the store, and home. One has to be
with Joel. Maureen always wanted children.
Intended to have four. Tried to be good.
Obeyed her doctor. Took faithfully a prescription
from their own pharmacy: thalidomide.
Joel has no arms, no legs. An active mind.
Seal-like: a torso and a head.
After his birth, Maureen had a hysterectomy.
Mark, a vasectomy. Taking no risks.

Kyle is a doctor. Three children. For sixteen years
his wife died in their home. M.S.
Unconscious the last eight weeks. Within a year
he took another wife, plain, an old friend, perfect
as a mother for his kids. One left home
within a week. The youngest calls the new wife "Ma'am."
Sometimes shakes his head. Cries at night.
Cuts school. Sits in the park all day. Kyle
is a doctor. Takes care of people's pain.

Four houses down from us the Jenners live. Or used to live.
The wife last week drove toward her parents' home
in Idalou. The children rode in back. She may have,
angry, lunged to swat them. And lost control.
Or only a blowout. No one knows. Only that the car
jerked down into the median, rolled twice, stopped
on the opposing highway on its wheels. A cattle truck
smashed over the hood, sliced off the top
and Jan Jenner's head. Dragged the crushed car
a hundred yards. The car tank exploded first. Both
truckers lived. The diesel tanks burst into flames.

Men crawled under the wreck and tried opening a door,
a window, anything. They saw a bloody torso.
Blood-splattered kids. Eyes pleading louder
than screams. Both tried until they caught on fire.
Ran desperately away. Some people knocked them down,
rolled out the flames. Most of the cattle burned.
The smell of diesel fuel. The stench
of burning tires, of cows. And something else.

Ray and Nadine retired at sixty-two. No children.
Took tours to England, Paris, Rome. The Holy Land.
In Spain, Ray had his first small stroke. Next spring,
they cruised the Caribbean. Back home, at sixty-six
they worked two months assembling five-thousand slides,
splicing ten-thousand feet of 16 mm movie film.
Invited friends to come and see. The Bates declined,
infirm. The Woods were out of town. A dozen others
had lost mates, didn't feel up to fun. The young couple
next door stayed half an hour, the man checking his watch.

Next week Ray bought tickets for the Orient.
In Singapore Nadine suffered insulin shock. Back home,
Ray had another stroke. Could only move his eyes.
Nadine showed movies on the ceiling. After a week,
Ray closed his eyes when she turned on the film.
Had seen enough. She nursed him for three years.
Died suddenly one day out shopping in the Mall. Police
found Ray in bed and moved him to a nursing home.
It took Ray four years more to die.

Carl and Lucille were college sweethearts. Practical.
Waited three years to marry. After graduation, waited
three more, saving, then bore a child. Three more
to have a second child. Beautiful frail girls.
Their skin almost transparent. The first
lived to be four. A rare disease, transmitted
through the genes. The second died at three. Carl
and Lucille went celibate for years. Considered divorce,
and suicide. Went to psychiatrists. Lucille wrote
three hundred letters to editors, begging young people
not to marry, to have no sex. None of her letters
published. Carl had cancer of the lungs at forty,
welcomed it as penance. Lucille looks no one
in the eye. Wears no make-up. Tries to look old.
Looks forward to menopause. To death.

Life expectancy in Bangladesh is twenty-eight.
Infant mortality, one in two. Names: Bangladesh,
Uganda, Ghana. Statistics have no arms, no legs.
A torso and a head. A world of pharmacies
and disease. Millions of movie feet. A child sits in a park.
Sometimes shakes her head. The truck sliced off
the top. The stench of burning tires. And something else.
A jury deliberates. Looks no one in the eye.
Wears cancer like a curse. Wants to be damned.

[Previously published in *North American Review* 263, no. 4 (December 1978): 14.]

What Clark Taught about Cockpits and Sonnets

Stun us, the Colonel taught—old pilot, joke-teller,
boss. Toss more at us than catalogs, more than facts.
Don't waste our time. Write clanging sounds
or songs, flints clicked together to make flames
that linger, that take our breath away.

On takeoff, don't bother about rhymes or the taste
of sounds. Keep your eyes wide, find what's in the skies.
You might see lightning or jet fighters diving
out of the sun. First drafts are wild abandon,
trying to spook up a poem, to lasso something weird

to haul snarling and kicking back to the screen.
Later is time enough to whittle words into birds
or wildebeests. Labor a lot. Indulgence tempts us
to lower our goals, to go easy on ourselves, winking
at mediocre lines, thinking "That's good enough."

Don't cup your hands and smirk, "Guess what I've got"
and not show us. Poetry's not a 3rd-grade game
of keep away. Welcome us to your world, make us
see. If not, "Well, keep it, Jerk," we'll probably say,
walking away. *Poems* that boast "How deep I am"

are calculus. Poetry's a dog fight in the sky we feel
in our spines. Slam flat abstractions down and stomp them,
kick, stab them to death, gouge out their eyes. If they still
crawl up your legs and beg with mushy four-syllable words,
save them for later to throw away. Hold all drafts to fires

and burn the chaff, the sounds and sights that don't save
or scare you. Tinker and tighten each line again
and again, like outboard motors that won't crank,
just sputter or cough. Take stanzas apart and put them
back, but slant, tugging the cord until it starts.

[Previously published in *The Drunken Boat* (Winter 2002).]

Finding a Cracker-Jack Surprise

Each time I swear I'll let my subscription lapse,
I stumble across a poem and wonder
"where has this been all my life!" What a poem,

what a lucky, talented editor to find it
inside a stack of manuscripts–what a break
after months of smudged bifocals, coffee cups,

rolling her eyes "Oh, brother," groaning
over another "moon/June/spittoon." Just now,
Maria, I found your poem in a journal,

expecting another tin ring or penny whistle
like in Cracker Jacks when I was a boy with a dime,
but finding treasure, delight, real surprise.

Hunched on elbows over this issue, reading
your amazing poem, I knew when it was over,
perfect, and didn't even turn the page.

[Previously published in *Borderlands* 16 (2001): 53–54.]

Ponderosa of a Thousand Fires

Logs draw from the window's inch and pop,
pine blazing splendors of a winter fire.
This mountain cabin's cold, and rafters creak.
Breeze seeps in from snow and a frozen stream.
Granddad hauled big logs for decades

after Grandmother died. Summers, I watched him
carving claws from oaks, his thumb
and knuckles flicking shavings into beaks
of hummingbirds, the somber scowls of owls.
He watched me try. A dozen goat-like carvings

tumbled from my hands until I stopped.
He crammed his hearth and mantle with eagles,
angels, bats and coyotes, owls of a thousand nights,
flocks he shaved from blocks of oak and mesquite,
aviaries he gave to neighbors and my sister and me.
I'm partial, but I'd swear those birds could fly

if he had cut claws loose from logs he carved.
He taught me the feel of Toledo steel, the taste
of xylem before it's ripe. I'm moved by aromas
of all wood I've ever held. Granddaddy's tools
are mine, now, my thumbs less stiff than his.

But how does a man match Granddad or Disney?
Most hawks I carved shiver like featherless parrots,
why I burned most birds or put them away like bowls.

[Previously published in *Phi Kappa Phi Forum* (formerly *National Forum*) 82, no. 1 (2002): 38.]

A Clown Fired from a Cannon

—John 3:16

Sleet taps the screens, bounces like pellets
dipped in buttermilk by clowns, shot at a crowd
with pop guns. On the porch, bundled up,
I watch the clouds for signs, a hint of angels.

My luck again, two-fisted braggart on the ropes.
I fold, unlucky in cards, starving for faith.
No sense in betting baby's food on these.
Crumbs, I'd stoop for crumbs. Go on,

kick me with doubt, I'll bite like a bulldog,
I'm foaming, I won't let go. Lately,
I've taken to the streets, trotting after cars,
barking, nipping bumpers and tumbling,

a hound with no master, hoping for faith, mad-dog
dreamer pretending to be sane. I need only a bone,
not a flash slashing from Heaven, not thunder
parting the sky, more like a hint than a rainbow.

Let it linger in the brain, an after-image,
synapses snapping salvation of clowns fired
from cannons to nets fragile as grace, echoes
beyond space awaiting answers, "over, over."

[Previously published as "Faith Is a Circus Act" in *The Midwest Quarterly* 37, no. 4 (1996): 412.]

The Oldest Nurse in Our Hometown

She never scolded, not even for taunts,
not hollyhocks broken off, never pebbles
tossed at her walls to make the crippled
witch leave. Miss Armes allowed boys

to be boys that fought wars, that marched
away in leggings and sailed back gassed
or lame. She was the last shipped back
with fever after a year bathing doughboys.

She helped them hobble with canes or walkers,
all who would try. She taught the Bible
and Braille at old soldiers' homes, but a stroke
left her bedfast behind walls her father built,

ten rooms without a telephone, without a cat.
Widows from church looked in on her for days,
fed her and changed her bed. When she tottered
downstairs by herself, one foot flopping

and left hand hanging down, they went away.
That's when rumors of witchcraft started, big boys
wicked enough to blame anyone over thirty
hiding up there quiet behind the glass.

[Previously published in *Event* (Canada) 30, no. 2 (2001): 27.]

A Woman Titian Would Love

Aunt Ethel looked fat in the saddle, two-fifty in boots
and Stetson, bossing her herd from a stallion
too stout to canter. She hugged us both on her porch,
lifting my sister and me like dolls. Her ranch was dust
and cactus, a petting zoo, spring calves that sucked our thumbs,

our pick of the ponies, big breakfasts at sunrise
and inch-thick steaks at night. Uncle Ed was dead,
all cousins grown and gone. All summer she spoiled us,
tucked us in with cookies and milk, turned out the light
and let the coyotes howl. Each dawn, she called us

to cocoa and hugged us, wide belly bulging. *Eat up,*
she whispered—*work to be done, and it's up to us.*
She ruffled our skulls with both big, tender fists,
heaped stacks of pancakes and ham as we yawned
and rubbed our eyes while our pet calves bawled.

[Previously published in *Tattoo Highway* 8, vol. 6, no. 1 (January 2004).]

Uncle Oscar's Trophies

Uncle Oscar shot them all, elephants
and elk, grizzlies mounted in his den
like family. My brother and I wondered
how that grouch ever scaled mountains,
ever cared about anything enough to track it.

Old man with rifles, he ignored us both
behind dark glasses, bald head forever cocked.
We stared at trophies on his walls, male lions
and big horn sheep with bronze horns curled,
eyes like enormous marbles. Webs sagged

like spittle from cougars and tight-lipped goats
he killed before his only son died in Korea.
While Uncle Oscar rocked outside with Dad,
we prowled his attic trunks stuffed with photos
of Model T cars, Uncle Oscar and his son

in hunting clothes, posed in African brush
like buddies. We found a box of medals,
a folded flag, three combat boots, a picture
of his only son in uniform, wearing ribbons
of many colors like codes we never cracked.

[Previously published in *Blue Unicorn* 18, no. 1 (1994): 24.]

Belling the Cat

Slash never looks back, once he rasps "meow,
let me out, now." Fat cat aloof on his rump,
curling that long, slow muscle of a tail
around him, blue-furred Buddha staring
at the door. He has no use for laps or snacks,
not now, he's through with us, old Russian Blue
locked behind slits of jade. Before he was fixed,

he was a hot wire rigged to explode, his eyes
like rifle scopes. He hated sunlight, lived
for the ear-splitting combat of alleys, insane
on the odor of orchids under the tails of females.
Not the kitten he was years ago, yowling
one dawn at our door, gray rack of fur purring
gladly at a glance. Now, he's fat and sassy,

fluff on his face hiding a turquoise collar,
belly almost round, the easy wisdom
of one beyond regret, but after hours inside,
sprawled on whatever lap or chair he desires,
he's off again somewhere, driven by habit,
keeping his prowls a secret, cold eyes blinking
in sunlight, his furry claws still sharp.

[Previously published in *Concho River Review* 10, no. 1 (1996): 30.]

If Owl Named the Animals

Buzzards roosted on oaks, scratching
fat knees and grumbling like old men
whittling and spitting. Old buzzards sighed.
Sly, they envied naked Eve, kittens and lambs
she fed by hand, stroking furry bunnies.

Big gorilla stomachs growled. At dawn,
the horned owl closed his eyes, wiser
than Eve and Adam, who named the whole
world wrong. Owl called the eagles
"Squirrels," the rabbits "Ours." He called

the clumsy humans "Who," stuttered to make
them afraid of the moon, thereafter. Owl
flew quietly at night, the first stealth fighter.
Someone had to die, or why have claws?
Hawks stalked all saucy rodents below them,

two-legged meals off limits, swaggering,
beasts called "people" ignoring raptors
above them, talons obediently tucked, sharp
beaks created for tearing. Months of the same
bland weather, same grapes and perfect figs.

Roosters and lions ambushed Adam at lunch,
teaching him swagger and pounce, the mind
of a braggart. Owl followed dreamy Eve
around the orchard, hawks and bald squirrels
above her, watching. Buzzards licked their beaks

like old men ogling a stripper. Otter hissed
in her ear, flicking his tongue, calling her "His."
Eve patted his scalp, hairless as foreskin, and
flipped him with her foot, strolled back to Adam
still hungry at lunch, licking his bloody lips.

[Previously published in *Lullwater Review* 8, no. 2 (1997): 11.]

My Brother's Photos from Okinawa

That giggling boy in the picture
was me, riding my brother's shoulders
like a stallion with massive flanks,
unable to fall. My pudgy fists
turned him, cupping his ears
like reins. Roy glanced back

at the camera and whinnied
like a stallion, as if saying, whenever
I held the photo, "Wasn't this fun?"–
taped in a scrapbook by this pose
of him in the paper after boot camp
in World War Two, my hero,

a local Marine overseas. After he died,
more photos of Roy with buddies
arrived in the mail after battles, rifle
slung over his shoulder in one, muscles
where I used to ride, his prance
and big-brother whinny just for me.

[Previously published in *First Things* 33 (May 2003): 54.]

What I Can't Promise

No trees stay green all summer here,
heat-stressed, blighted, full of drought,
a zone so rough no trees grow native.
Nothing thrives by itself without
what I can't promise—wind gusts

within reason, rain more than twice a year,
enough birds to eat the leaf lice. The wind
is foreign, and even with silver iodide
and prayer, it rains only when it rains.
Birds fly over every year, a desert

between snow and tropics. We coax them
with baths and feeders in the yard
high off the ground above the dogs.
In winter, since dry land never freezes,
we dig down through sand to white caliche

and throw in loam like pennies, lift
bought trees balled up in burlap
and bury them deep like treasures.
The only way these trees survive
is like love, faithful to roots

in the ground like blessings
against the storms, pruning
what isn't required, soaking them
over and over with water
pumped from our own deep wells.

[Previously published in *Oxford Magazine* 3, no. 2 (1987): 47.]

Grandfather and the Boys He Knew in School

Old men argued and whittled oak for hours.
Grandfather led them, flick, and flick,
and old friends followed like a rhythm band.
Down on the county square, on benches of iron bars
straddling fat roots of elms and hemlock,

decades before the high-rise jail or seniors' center,
the spit-and-whittle club punched the clock
like bankers' hours, nowhere to go but home—
a Dodge sedan with the seat down, or a shack—
Billy Earl and I played jackknife with those men,

mumblety-peg, blackjack for matches. One by one
we watched them cough into bloody handkerchiefs
and die or disappear, praising God or Roosevelt one day,
then gone. One year, I found park benches empty,
nothing but squirrels on the county square,

and most of those looked old, hobbling like dogs
on all fours, not hopping. Never mind
that some old men wheezed, "Help!" strapped down
in nursing homes like Grandfather, fed by college boys
like me, to pay tuition. Sometimes I see arms

around bars of the ten-story county jail
where the courthouse was, where squirrels
and toddlers had roamed, where old men wailed
about the drought and taxes and shook stiff knuckles
at each other, their last remaining friends.

[Previously published in *JAMA: The Journal of the American Medical Association* 281, no. 5 (1999): 402d.]

The Range Looks Flat to Cattle

Our cattle colonize islands when it rains,
natural selections of chance and downpour.
The ranch is harvest all year long,
even grass grazed down in August.

The range looks flat to cattle
wandering the world without fearing
they'll fall off. And then the floods.
Nobody's Noah, I drive them to high ground

if I'm in time, before thunder scatters them
too widely for a horse and a man in a poncho,
both of us too old for a stampede.
Before the gelding sinks like a stalled pickup,

I turn him, leaving dumb steers on knolls
I forgot are there. Cattle wade and slosh
until they stop, hard ground like islands,
stranded five or fifty together. The first flood

years ago, I watched them with binoculars,
huddled oddly on islands, docile as fat men
at bus stops. Steers want only to survive,
don't panic unless they have to, nothing as bad

as hunger. They wait for rescue, won't wade
for help unless their island swamps, content
to starve an hour. They chew their cud,
don't know enough, but hope I'll row out

with bales of hay to keep them safe
until the water drops, until the pasture dries,
until mud is hard enough for trucks
from the slaughterhouse turning off the road.

[Previously published in *Hampden-Sydney Poetry Review* (Winter 2001): 23.]

Tugging Bull-Necked Oxen

My great-greats rolled west in wagons
maybe on a dare, tugging bull-necked oxen
over plains so flat they balked, the last

sweet lake days back. Nothing led them
but faith in folded handbills and the sun.
On land so dry, no wonder they believed—

dug wells, capped them with windmills
hauled board by board from Dallas,
begged circuit-riders to come each fall

and dunk their kids in troughs. This stream
kept tribes alive. Now, after deadly tornadoes,
we've hauled away all trash, the canyon

a perfect dump, tons of rubble bulldozed
flat as a road. Like Moses we can walk
across dry land. Drought can drain a river,

drove people wandering on foot toward snow,
leaving nothing but sand and shards of bowls,
sharp flint wedged tight in bison skulls.

[Previously published in *Carolina Quarterly* 42, no. 2 (1990): 20.]

What Uncle Don Saw on Guam

Old Uncle Don fought war with a bottle,
Guam in the palm of his hand, wrapping that map
around our ears, that mad, forgotten war,
a drunk with cash who taught us all to laugh,

gaunt cowboy with a handlebar mustache
who flattered single women with a drawl
as common as hundred-dollar hats.
Don never married again after Donna

died, always in a bar after midnight.
He said he never killed without a cause.
A thousand sisters teased about that smile,
tilting his whiskey with a wink. He always thought

they thought him handsome, but he didn't know.
He swore he knew when dead friends came
at night and whacked him on the back.
He still called their names, shouting for quiet

and pointing, ordering another round
for women no longer friendly. Ghosts
listened to Uncle Don: the one about
the captain and the cabin boy, the raw

half-eaten dogs, the soldiers burned alive.
One cowboy slouched, one turned a deer-hide
chair around and scoffed about that fire,
about the thousand starving babies Uncle Don

found with bellies split. One tilted back his chair
and howled. Coughing, Uncle Don leaned close
and frowned, rubbing his face. "Can't you see them
now?" he whispered, gouging his own eyes.

[Previously published in *Writer's Forum* 23 (1997): 3–4.]

Things About to Disappear

In Escondido Canyon, pronghorns the size of fawns
dip down and drink. There's no more water for miles,
the next shallow canyon on the plains.

If they sense odd bones diggers find each summer,
thirst muzzles them. They stare, antelopes on thin
stick legs, faster than a horse can run.

From the car, we count two dozen, holding field glasses
steady as we can in cold wind gusting
from the north. Thousands of ducks fly over,

doves, Canada geese in arrow formations, pointing
the way away. A car backfires, or a shotgun.
Antelopes bolt away to high ground,

the flat plains settled and surveyed. They gallop off,
they never pause, before our eyes they fade
like legends and run for miles.

[Previously published in *Night Landings* (New York: Harper & Row, 1989).]

Uncle George and the Farm Aunt Martha Bought

Bull horns and twisting body torque
turned Uncle George to crutches at thirty,
the last concussion bad, the last hip fracture.

Since middle school, George rode muscles
wadded into bodies of bulls, mad dragons
snorting fire, back bulging, ready to explode

when the gate burst open and spurs kicked
for the crowd, cowboy gladiator Christians
cheered. Bulls were the devils he stayed on

five rides out often his last long months
in coliseums, seldom a belt buckle
but often in the money, paying for splints

and split britches, dusting his Stetson off
and hobbling, holding his busted ribs
or broken shoulder after he left the ring.

[Previously published in *Southwestern American Literature* 28, no. 2 (Spring 2003): 75.]

Night Watch

Before the war, I went out nights with lantern
and clipboard on Granddaddy's ranch and oil field,
swinging a beam through fumes thick enough
to swim. Gas might explode if it didn't burn.

Always I found all gauges in the green, tapped them
to be sure and logged them. After high school,
age was a shell game easy to win, but now,
death's sleight of hand keeps me guessing.

Uncles and aunts disappear, black phone that rings
and rings. Answer with the one good word I know,
"Hello?" Cancer of this cousin, that wreck,
this old friend's kid so bitter he ran away.

I meet them for coffee, and they hold tight
and cry. Sometimes, my eyes are wax and wicks,
easily lit by grief. Sometimes they're marble slits.
Nights when memories of war rush back,

I fix my stare on the road past accidents, like bulls
that go on grazing whether one or a dozen calves
are missing. My first month back from Saigon,
I bounced down steep arroyos, honking an air horn,

chasing a bull that gored the foreman and broke loose.
What drives a foaming bull is fear. When he charged,
what could I do but bump him? He faced me
exactly as I would, his eyes wild in the headlights.

[Previously published in *Sonoma Mandala Literary Review* 21 (1994/95): 90.]

The Farm at Auction

It's gone, let garbled voices auctioneer
no more. The one bold gavel gags us, "Sold!"
Don't give them tears, it's over. Blunt men

in denim, dealers, bidders not from here
run fingers around our heifers, like strangers
reaching under my own wife's dress,

neighbors looking on in silence, our children
standing by themselves and staring.
One grown farmer could raise all cotton

dirt could grow, if banks would let him,
if markets stayed the same, if diesel
didn't turn to gold. Something turned its back

on us overnight, something we've cursed
but worked for all these years—threats of hail,
too little rain before harvest, the reasonable

gamble of sweat in all seasons. How many times
can strangers sell all we own to low bidders?
Eighty dollars to take that ditcher off my hands?

Thank you for nothing. I paid a thousand new,
and the paint's not scratched, the blade
is silver clean from clay I broke it through.

I should be used to this by now, plowing
flat fields for nothing we can keep. Come,
lift up your end of this oak hope chest

and heave it aboard. Woman, there's room
in the pickup for this and more, but not for tears.
Lift up our city heads and look around: it's gone.

[Previously published in *Colorado Review* 14, no. 1 (1987): 60–61.]

A Player that Struts and Frets on Stage

The skin remembers its shape for twenty years
and then forgets, needs to be prompted,
rehearsing the same proud lines. At first,

a blemish, a wrinkle above the brow. We say,
"Nobody does it better, playing me."
Around the eyes, crow's feet appear,

puffy lids water pills can't fix. We tug
stretch marks over cheekbones, wondering
what happened here, which makeup artist

let my liquid skin-tone dry? Even lavish,
half-ton curtains ravel, have to be clipped
and scrubbed, and raised for the public,

no place to turn but face-lifts, snips,
exotic creams, aging exposed by stiff
gnarled knuckles and liver spots,

less like our hands than our parents'.
Arthritis is a fan that has caught our act
a thousand times, picky about each move

we make onstage, able to spot any change
of pace, the forgotten or lazy line,
demanding the same old, aching bow.

[Previously published in *The Southern Review* 39, no. 4 (Autumn 2003): 716.]

Cousin Eddy and the Packed Chapel

Eddy was everywhere, tall boy with fast legs,
our school's medal-man girls loved to hug
barefooted at the beach. Nobody's toes

kicked sand in a race like Eddy's—"Hey,
Scoops!" the girls yodeled. He loved it,
long flippers better than Bill's big nose

or Arnold's elephant ears. Before Saigon,
Eddy was also a banjo marvel in college,
taking charge of parties, parting the sea

of fried chicken, the first boy aunts and cousins
served. He led a dozen of our class to Vietnam,
walked point in jungles for his platoon.

We buried Eddy last winter with the casket
closed, family and friends from all around
the county, coaches and cousins, coeds he dated,

the pastor asking us all to move over,
please sit close, make room for others
outside the church to come in from the cold.

[Previously published in *Red River Review* (February 2003).]

Riding the Range for Strays

Far off, a coyote hobbles after a mouse
that scurries, zigzags, and stops, playing him
like a trout. I've lost the field mouse
with wobbling binoculars,
then watch it scamper past cactus

and other mice, a tag-team match.
The coyote hops like a dog
with a thorn, squats down
and sprawls, exhausted. I let
binoculars dangle by the strap,

no calves in sight, no black wings
wheeling, all fences tight,
the gelding patient and sweaty,
a steady mount that waits
until I tap the reins.

[Previously published in *Connecticut Review* 23, no. 2 (2001): 48–50.]

Scanning the Range for Strays

Granddaddy roamed these fields
in a pickup, scanning the range for strays
lost in arroyos. If a steer was alive,
he'd find it. Roped, it balked

but followed that smoking truck uphill,
walleyed and frothing. They don't make trucks
that crude anymore, no radio,
a bench of steel coils covered by quilts.

There it rusts, stranded on blocks
where we hauled it. I remember
Granddaddy's white mustache,
the scar where a roped bull hooked him.

I remember the boulder the truck straddled,
chugging up the canyon. Caught,
he must have bounced on the bumper
until his heart stopped. We found him

face down in the dust, the steer
snugged to the truck and foaming,
no longer jerking, the rope
so tight we had to cut it loose.

[Previously published in *The Missouri Review* 17, no. 1 (1994): 70 and *Counting Survivors* (Pittsburgh: University of Pittsburgh Press, 1995).]

Mother's Hand-Stitched Seams

Sister and I hauled handbags to market,
a winding corridor of shops. We laced
a teakwood stick through the straps,
four feet of dangling leather bags. Rich
women turned to watch waifs walking off

with goods they themselves might buy.
Some followed, as if they'd cry, "You, boy!"
Buyers from Dallas to Atlanta helped us
hoist the bar, displayed on a swing
like meat hooks. They knew good stitching,

things ladies liked to touch back home
in stores with names exotic and in gold.
One buyer our grandmother's age picked two,
saw the price and took two more.
Big men with pencil-wax mustaches

rubbed our mother's zippers, stroked the welts
like monograms, like Mother's calluses,
her hand-stitched seams. Slowly they turned
her straps of evening gowns, slipped them off
and picked two purses up, rubbed the bottoms

between their fingers and thumbs,
making the sign of merchants' Esperanto,
money, money. By noon, all purses sold.
My sister bought cheese and sourdough
San Francisco bread. I liked the word

baguette, the taste of travel. By fountains
with thousands of coins, we ate the cheese,
the bread. She let me pitch a penny in,
let me bounce a stick horse from the mall
across broken bricks, riding that stallion home.

[Previously published in *Windhover* 8 (2003): 119.]

Leaving the Middle Years

Boldly they show us how to go,
pelicans cruising for fish
inches above the waves,
long beaks and bent wings

wide as faith. Sometimes,
they glide like prairie hawks
back home, but suddenly
fold wings and dive,

pouches bulging
when they bob up for air,
rising, flapping away.
We rock on the deck at dawn,

sipping hot tea,
a thousand miles from grandkids
scattered in distant towns.
Even after hurricanes, palm trees

on the beach grow back.
Neighbors install new glass,
haul trash and stripped leaves away
and boil their water.

The shrimp-boat fleet's already out,
gulls swarming a scow growling its way
through the harbor, the glint
on waves so bright we blink.

[Previously published in *New Texas* (2000): 267.]

Pastures on the Plains

We bulldoze cactus for pastures.
Burning the stumps, all we have left
is smoke, no coals, not even ash.

Think of those flames as gold,
Granddaddy said. Sow oats
and watch them grow, and ration water

worth more than oil on hardscrabble
fit for goats. Granddaddy dug these
wide, deep wells to last, walled them

with bricks and steel rods pounded
through bedrock. Now, they're boarded over,
the iron cranks fuzzy with rust. Skunks

outlast the months, waddling down rows
as if they own them, spraying our dogs
each fall, each spring. Sneezing,

dogs roll and quarrel in dead leaves
and dust. We find skunks often
on highways, pelts flat as raccoon hats,

faceless unless we stop and stare.
The eyes of all roadkill astound us
in globs of tar. Some months, we lift

one of our own dogs off the road,
hoping its eyes weren't crushed
by eighteen-wheelers or pickups.

Our tightened barbed wires sparkle
to wide horizons. On the porch swing
at dusk, we rock slowly until dark,

watching cattle in shadows of pastures,
knowing these dusty plains are home,
our north and south, a thousand miles of stars.

[Previously published in *California Quarterly* (2003).]

Ars Poetica, Pilgrim

I want you lean and hungry, dude, I want you mean.
Don't take "Good enough" for an answer, trust
no one's gospel but Paul's, who learned to see
when he closed his eyes. Wranglers are what we
are, wranglers of poems, who don't know what we'll say
today, so ride the only horse you own. Don't worry

about how to start. Type the first word that comes
with others hiding behind cactus, shout "Coyotes!"
and watch them scatter. It's your ranch, just start,
type the word, the phase that floats by, grab it,
write it down. If it's "When," type "When . . ."
and whatever follows becomes your first draft.

You probably won't know where it's going, but follow
the path that unfolds like jungles in Tarzan movies—
if "When," maybe "When . . . Uncle . . . Bubba . . . brought
the lamb home . . . from school . . . the one Mary lost . . ."
That's a start. Don't toss it out, if your mind
saw the lamb and your fingers enjoyed leading it home,

safe from cars and poachers. You've begun a poem,
not a bible—an ugly nag, but someday, a mustang.
Don't worry about "writer's block," there's no such thing
unless you drop the reins. A good horse moves
if you click your tongue and let it trot or gallop.
Whatever wobbly you find in the brush, take,

break its legs, beat flabby abstractions to death
with John Wayne's steel Winchester or Charlie Chaplin's
cane. Abstractions bore. Slash flabby fat. Trust sounds
like sonar as if you're blind as a bat. Listen to rhythm,
and launch from the sounds of lines—believe whatever
comes will lead you past the fence to all wild meat

you need and back into the caves. Corral first drafts.
Don't send them out. Let them rest a month or more,
then make them better, make them jump through hoops
while you and your mustang turn back to blank pages,
the untamed ranch you own. You won't have to beg
good poems to run. In time, your stallions will gallop.

[Previously published in *Southern Poetry Review* 41, no. 1 (Summer 2001): 69.]

Night of the Steep Arroyo

Brave men gamble with their lives
and ride down dark arroyos for strays.
That's what they said, my first winter

in the bunkhouse. I'd heard about snipe
hunts all my life, and cherry boys,
and nothing they said could make me

volunteer for that, unless they ordered me.
They never did, so I hoped I proved no fool
lived in these bones tough as their own

behind wind-burned hide and stubble.
Until the night old Earl went down
riding back from Lubbock alone, in a blizzard.

We didn't know what hit us, wind banging
everything not nailed down outside, coffee
almost freezing on the stove with the fire out,

night riders shivering in our bunks.
So when the foreman called for volunteers,
I went, knowing Earl was fair and never

tried to make a greenhorn seem a fool.
We found him in the canyon, steep trail
no danger in daylight down the caprock

winding to gullies of this prairie ranch.
Earl's horse was alive, but buried in snow,
leg snapped, quivering in bitter wind.

Earl died where he fell, frozen, neck broken,
his heavy sheepskin coat and gloves
within reach, but strapped to the saddle.

When the foreman brushed back the snow,
we found Earl's eyes still open, like marbles
with tiny beads of bubbles frozen, the last view

he ever saw. While some men bundled
and lifted the body to the gelding we brought
along, others saw to Earl's horse, which never

had a chance. Without a choice, we stood there
silent in haze and freezing wind, our flashlights
blinded him. He never saw the rifle raised.

[Previously published in *SLANT* 1 (1987): 79–80.]

With a Woman Who Looks Like Crystal Gayle

Listen too long, and you know it.
Your tired ears reach for the sky
like bad guys, enough, enough.

Eyelids sag after loud, sad notes
dance by in this dark, smoky bar.
Nothing stops country songs wailing

through speakers tall as coffins.
Belly up to the bar and order Coors
or Bud, and watch them bring you

Lone Star. No matter, my darling's
at the table, waiting, sweet lips amber
as her long straight-hanging hair.

Grab three cool necks in one hand
and flick pale ashes with your thumb,
waltzing slowly and sliding down

in a calf-skin chair beside her, feeling
loved enough to listen to fiddles
and humming sweet tunes in her ear.

[Previously published in *The Journal* 11, no. 1 (1987): 9–11.]

Ten Miles of Coyotes

Uncle Oscar was boss, and all of us his boys,
mostly old men of forty broken down like nags
and cousins from town like Billy Joe and me.

How simple life seemed between wars,
riding horses all summer in high school,
ten miles of coyotes and rattlers.

Lucinda poured mint juleps for the boys,
she called us, no hunting parties like her dad's.
She flirted with us the most, no risk

in vanilla wrists being twisted behind her back
by wranglers, with Uncle Oscar there. We swore
she used us both like dolls, rag dolls she hugged

and waltzed to her hums around the wide,
mahogany porch, taught us to follow her arms
like dancing bears. Prettiest cousins marry,

and after we flew off to war, Lucinda did.
We see each other once a year since Vietnam,
Uncle Oscar dead, the bunkhouse closed,

all cousins busy in cities, a frenzy of details
and children, no hunting parties in years,
no guns, no good times on the porch.

[Previously published in *Parting Gifts* 15, no. 2 (Winter 2002): 8.]

Dawn in Montana

Brother bear up there
waddles around boulders,
skinny after winter, big-boned
bachelor alone.

Cougar lolls in clouds
above 9,000′,
sleepy with squinted eyes,
flicking her dark-tipped tail.

She knows elk cows will calve
when snow fields thaw.
Deer with tiny jaws
glance about for coyotes,

bow down and nibble,
jerk their heads up
and stare, flag twice
and bow again to grass.

Hawk keeps watch over all,
wings wide, gliding above a mile
of meadows, tail feathers
flexed to turn in thermals

like a wand, presto! a flash
of tan—chipmunk or pica
forgetting what's above
might fold its wings and dive.

[Previously published in *Connecticut Review* 23, no. 2 (2001): 49.]

That Night and Others Like It

Round like wagon wheels, the moon rose orange
and massive around the plains, Comanche moon,
moon of twelve thousand years of people huddled
and wandering, drawing models of the moon,

so many pictographs, crescents and bulging bellies,
arrowheads and antelopes and bears, anything
killable, ready to be skinned and lived in, eaten
or worn–bison and deer, woolly mammoths,

the shaggy shawls of wolves and necklaces of teeth.
In 1880, my great-grands wobbled down from Ohio,
following tracks of coyotes and God's bright book
of stars. Wolves sniffed their cows at night, red eyes

flashing by campfires, then gone. This warped
and split-wood wheel is all we own, their clock
and trunks of treasures burned to ashes, tent fires
they survived without albums, not even Bibles.

The moon was often huge, a pockmarked ball
afloat over Estacado, a village gone, now. Decades
ago, my pilot-friend Charles Duke walked on the moon
on Apollo 16, gathered rocks and practiced golf swings,

leaving a flag, a moon rover with piano-wire tires.
Days after Big Granny climbed down from the wagon,
the range looked nothing like the moon, dugouts
and buffalo dung, and valleys where they kept cattle

near cliffs and caves with ancient symbols of deer.
She and her boys pitched tents for their kids at night,
coyotes howling at their cows and crackling campfire
under a moon going down across a thousand miles.

[Previously published in *The Midwest Quarterly* 40, no. 4 (1999): 451.]

The Noise of Jukebox Steel Guitars

Saturday nights, we headed for the bar,
dropping quarters down some dead singer's blouse
in the jukebox. She sang like a windup toy,

sad honey for the heart. Who cared
what draft dodgers wrote about in songs?
We came back from Saigon and Da Nang,

we couldn't claim anything but that. Our wives
knew when time came to let us out like lap dogs
in mountains in spite of cougars

glaring from caves. We seldom made toasts,
too many old friends gone. Like the Wall
at midnight, we said their names under noise

and blue smoke layered like gunfire.
Jukebox steel guitars slid and glissandoed
at the end of songs, with recorded applause

when they were over. We named our buddies
to stay sane. We forgave enemies,
most of us. Forgave–some of us–ourselves.

When Elrod's cigar burned down, two inches
of ashes sagging, somebody slapped the table
near his elbows, and ashes fell. Some nights

before they closed the bar, we might stop
fights outside, and jumpstart cars stalled
between street lights, fix flats old widows feared

to change, then helped our drunk friends home
and found our own shacks by midnight,
dogs barking and porch lights always on.

[Previously published in *Other Poetry* (UK) Series 2, no. 20 (2002): 57.]

Loaded for Bulldozers and Bears

At last we're back in Montana, ready for glaciers
and bears, zoom lens and packs of Kodachrome.
There go the trucks and bulldozers, jockeyed

by men with hard hats. They've built a fence
above McDonald Falls and posted bold signs,
KEEP OUT. They don't hurry, pouring tons

of cement over boulders and crushed, pink granite,
pounding a path through cedars and hemlock.
Panting, we've hiked a mile to find the river

we camped by on our honeymoon. Torrents,
we want torrents of foam-water tumbling,
Montana thunder, cold as Montana snow.

We're old, far from home in Arkansas.
A sign says "Duncan McDonald's waterfall
is for all to see, but later, when it's safe."

Hurry up, then, get it done. Other signs say
"Landslides aren't safe for seniors," as if we all
haul oxygen tanks and walkers. Grizzlies,

watch out, we're old, afraid of nothing,
a thousand miles from home, too close
to Uncle Duncan's falls to turn back.

We've hiked this forest for sparkles and spray
through decades of babies and teen-aged rage,
and after Saigon, the endless guilt of surviving.

We're stubborn and tired, we don't need signs
to follow the tumble of bubbling Montana water
whether we see this river again next year or not.

[Previously published in *Three Candles* (June 2001).]

Looking for Dry Land

"Water, water, everywhere . . ."
–Samuel Taylor Coleridge

The dogs drove one dove off
the first week out. No crows come back.
The condors stare at each other,
at us. For weeks the soaked ark moaned,
wood creaking above waves. Each dawn

I paddle out on a bale of tobacco leaves
the shape of coffins, my legs in the water
for balance. I watch for dry land and fins.
The ocean's a sewer. Something nibbles my feet.
Dolphins follow, our playful neighbors. Dusk,

I paddle back. At first, she spread our bedrolls
in the aviary, set out lilies and ferns
in loam under the birds. Vines climbed the hull,
berries blood-red, birds warbling and cawing
over all green stalks. Now, lice cover everything.

We scour the fruit to keep from gagging,
grain blighted, cattle bony with scurvy.
Our bored sons wake up late, staring at skies
without clouds. All day they lie around,
slip down to the hold after dinner, smoking,

squatting and grinning, seeing visions and shouting.
My daughters-in-law flee to my wife, weeping,
begging to be held. I hear her whisper,
"Keep sending the birds out that will fly
and pray the pitch holds us afloat awhile longer."

[Previously published in *Berkeley Poetry Review* 20 (1986): 133.]

Nearing the End of a Century

Night of the comet, space without angels,
unless our eyes can't find them.
The stars are rose ember over coals

already gray. Orion rises angry in the east.
Night after night, he prowls the same
black forest of stars, tracking the spoor

of nothing he remembers. In zipped
twin sleeping bags before Saigon,
we claimed billions of stars to wish on,

perfectly foreign, the absolute absence
of meaning. We counted myths made up
by others needing to believe in something,

projecting filaments like spiders spinning
delicate webs to turn stark fear to faith.
Somehow we survived that war and raised

our children who've moved away. Nights,
you turn for me to hold you, faith and hope
and love, if not the answers, enough for us.

[Previously published in *The Antioch Review* 45, no. 4 (1987): 437.]

Faith is a Beast and Blessing

Let go of that sick pygmy,
doubt. The fall can't hurt him,
even if he tumbles thousands
of nights before you die.
A breeze makes him appear
to breathe, dangling on the rope
you cling to, needing
the substance of things not seen.
There's nothing you can do
to reel him up on those thin
threads his body keeps unreeling
like a spider, like corpse hair.
Your hands are tacky with it,
faithful to their task. Believe
it's over, and let go.

[Previously published in *Poets On* 18, no. 1 (1994): 19.]

Billy Cox and the Rocket

We called Billy Cox "firewheel, yellow hand,
hot socks," after his first rockets fired. "Don't hold it"
was the middle-school's motto, should have saved
the district from paying a teacher's aide
to take his notes that year. Teachers told it

before spring break, old Mr. Gordon announced it
daily on the P.A. with a voice like God's.
"If you have to shoot fireworks, put them down
and run, and only out of town." That month, all boys
wanted bottle rockets, but mainly Moon Shots

that cost a dollar at firework stands with flashy signs.
We grabbed all we could buy through boards
that slid back like windows in speakeasies.
For nickels and dimes, we wanted more,
whatever the slimeball was hiding behind his back,

maybe magazines and toys in plain-wrapper packages
from China, like nothing in dusty Lubbock.
Billy Cox was rich and rode a Harley. The tips
of his jacket collar dangled like Brando's cigarette.
He got his boots and watch chain free

at his daddy's pawn shop, the biker's gloves
he wore when his slouch announced *Watch this*
on the school ground. He held the long rocket
like a club, like a rattler behind the jaws,
as if he'd slap it to his other fist

and milk the venom. When he lit it, we all
stepped back, but Billy stayed, thick glasses
that saved his eyes when the rocket exploded
in his fist, flames fizzing like mad dogs, smoke
and schoolgirls screaming while Billy burned.

[Previously published in *Pennsylvania English* 24, nos. 1–2 (Fall 2001/Spring 2002): 146.]

Night of the Bonfire Club

They whispered stars were sparks
and we believed them, afraid
of our brothers and their friends
our first night out. Tumbleweeds

tossed to the fire blazed fast
like kerosene, their faces bronze,
their eyes like tiny flames.
They dragged us one by one

into the dark of the Bonfire Club,
said we'd all kiss witches tonight
on third street and take them to caves
a mile away. We had to promise

we'd never tell our mothers.
They fed us raisins they swore
were Spanish flies that would die
in saliva and burn holes in our eyes.

Close to the fire, they made us stare
at each other for minutes of silence
without laughing, and it was true,
we could see the flames.

[Previously published in *Mid-American Review* 6, no. 1 (1986): 85.]

December after World War Two

Cold weather came, a foot of snow on plains
where dustings of snow are rare. Around town,
lines snapped and big limbs broke, but nobody cared.

Dogs running with heads down sniffed and slid,
mine sweepers following a scent. Good neighbors
waddled to the park, Jack Frost stalling cars

already old before the war. Ranches froze
like the South Pole, but now, a wonderland.
How now, brown cows in the pasture, blanketed

white as Brahmas, bowing to grass they know
is theirs. Old couples ambled by on Main Street,
slower than they'd strolled in years, gloves snug

and cheek bones pink, waving greetings to all
and shouting, their breaths like little clouds.
Most ladies hugged every Santa they passed,

happy fat men with beards, real beards that year,
selling joy to the world on sidewalks and singing
to all who danced by, and ringing, ringing the bells.

[Previously published in *The Gettysburg Review* 16, no. 2 (Summer 2003): 333.]

The Tongues of Birds

Birds sing because their world
is saved in seed fields, a garden
of stored provisions. They either toil
or spin. They have their seasons.

Birds are risks of their world,
their only reasons for living.
Their beaks are often empty.
Wings are their dreams

when daily pursuit is plenty.
Trees are the heaven they cling to
when they're weary. They sing
because they have tongues.

[Previously published in *Mississippi Valley Review* 19, no. 1 (1989): 3.]

Midnight Near Ralls

Boys found them in the stiff stalks
of grain fields, beheaded, three bulls
a mile apart, so little blood. Some said

wolves could do that, starving
but startled off. Some blamed the cults,
the devil worshipers. Some guessed

a grizzly, lost from a circus, confused
and famished, attacked the bulls.
A posse of farmers mounted up.

We jerked the reins, rifles raised
against our thighs. One woman
couldn't convince us she saw it all

three nights last week. She swore
it hummed like a helicopter skimming low
over winter wheat, red glow in the sky,

jet-powered, shaped like a shark.
We called it "Grandma's saucer." She claimed
it circled over farms a mile east,

shot one sudden blinding beam
like a laser, hovered, and disappeared
in a shimmer of twin blue flames.

[Previously published in *Oxford Magazine* 3, no. 2 (1987): 46–47.]

Someone I Hadn't Thought of in Years

I know what you do in the night.
I know where you place your hand
to slide into your car or a cab,

but never again with me. That's taking
a back seat to the past, which any fool
could regret. You're warm in another's arms

tonight, if you're alive, or baking cakes
for grandkids, maybe. So many years ago.
I've never dreamed of you as you wash pans

or drive to church, or if so, it's only memory.
I've tried to imagine you old and brittle-boned,
but I can't. You're locked in the photo

I carried to war and lost long ago.
Not even nineteen, you were another's wife
when I came back–no letter in the box

you sent overseas to me with the ring,
no return address, but whatever state,
it was thousands of miles away.

[Previously published in *Connecticut Poetry Review* 21 (2002): 31–34.]

Toulouse, Maurice, François of Tulia

They came to make a name in towns
without beauty parlors. Wives mad
for Dallas styles kept them alive

for a while—Francois, Maurice,
Toulouse of Tulia. In Venetian silks they snipped
and squeezed, soothing aging ladies

with creamy shampoos, scalps pampered
with exotic oils and sprays of phosphates.
Men without pasts massaged and gossiped,

smoking weed, sending groomed women home
reeking of secrets and cannabis to bedrooms
fogged with cigars. Husbands sniffed

as if the wind from feedlots had shifted.
Drive by any day and see the store closed
for months, glass shattered, signs sprayed

with graffiti and buckshot. Barber shops
in town stay open late again with razors
for shaves for husbands who talk and wait

for wives down the street at the widow's,
good customers who return for a wash
and set, a trim, the usual perm.

[Previously published in *Urbanus* (Summer 1997): 39.]

To All Friends Fast Asleep

Rest, heads twisted severely
on your necks, or muffled face-down
or on your sides, jaws
drawn to the chests, legs up,
bones of shoulders and hips

burrowed into pine needles of sleep,
or staked out flat on your backs,
chins slack, exhausted
by the weight of space
shoved down, shoved down all day

on hands that lift
and pat each other on the back,
or simply grip and squeeze,
handshakes that mean "Hello,
hold on, it's over, it's okay."

[Previously published in *The Seattle Review* 17, no. 2 (1994/1995): 12 and *Counting Survivors* (Pittsburgh: University of Pittsburgh Press, 1995).]

Strokes

Till I was ten I lived in fear of evenings.
Nights brought the beast with bad breath
in from the carport, my dad banging
on the screen door till Mother gave up
and let him in, or the bolt broke.

He never laid a hand on me. I grew up
swearing if his knuckles struck her
I'd break his nose, like Humpty Dumpty,
with bottles he smashed like lightbulbs.
Shotguns couldn't have cured him

faster than my mother's stroke. For weeks
he sat up turning cold cloths on her face
like seven veils. When he let me help,
washcloths from her brow were hot.
I'd run to the sink and rinse them

and run back. Huge fingers that could lead
bulls to slaughter unfolded the cloth
like pearls and placed it softly on her face.
The night I staggered home and fell
face down in the carport, my mother

switched the porchlight on. That's all.
When I woke at dawn, I found Dad
above me on the bottom step.
I watched his hand come down, and flinched,
and almost missed the blessing.

[Previously published in *The Fiddlehead* (Canada) 139 (1984): 58 and *Witching on Hardscrabble* (Peoria, IL: Spoon River Poetry Press, 1985).]

After the Fall of Bataan

Two of us would do, though he hired more boys
for special sales. He kept us waiting by his pre-war car,
clumsy in short pants, biting his nails. Counting coins,
he loaded canvas bags with flyers announcing sales

and shoved them on us, squinting, a butt squeezed in his lips,
wheezing, veteran's tag taped to the door. That summer of '46,
we lugged a ton of circulars, stores stocked with Army tins,
the town flooded with surplus. Mr. Martin parked before six

under Chinese elms, eye sockets hollow, thin as a corpse.
Starved three years as a prisoner of war, he came back to a wife
who left him. I didn't know what that meant to him until I married.
He was thirty, old man to us. His hands shook when he coughed,

spitting into rags. He picked his yellow teeth with a knife,
scowling, counting flyers or adding up coins with a pencil stub,
wet lips mumbling something about Bataan, about his wife–
then shoved us away with his fists, screaming "Hurry, hurry!"

Hours later, when we ran back with empty sacks, he hissed
and snatched them, cursed as if we'd dumped them in the trash.
He grabbed, and jabbed his shivering jaw in my face, his fist
without nails stabbing my palm, pressing the sweaty cash.

[Previously published in *Connecticut Review* 20, no. 2 (1998): 14–15.]

Catfish Farm on the Brazos

In the river, bass flipped each other fin
to lip during drought, stranded on sandbars
in the Rio de los Brazos de Dios.

Some months, miles of the Brazos
were mud going nowhere, fish bones
picked by buzzards. Docks dangled

splinters like barns after tornadoes.
Grandfather hauled hay to cattle
and locked the gate, the bank too steep,

the river sludge. My cousin and I netted
ponds and hauled catfish to market,
barrels thrashing, some fish barely alive.

In rain, Grandfather swung the gate
and drove cattle into shallow floods,
cows shoving, mounting each other,

wading up to their udders, wide muzzles
guzzling, nothing as urgent
as the "River of the Arms of God."

[Previously published in *Pennsylvania English* 24, nos. 1–2 (Fall 2001/Spring 2002): 146–49.]

The Last Unstocked Stream in Colorado

Ruby sonics, Florentine spoons,
anything to lure cutthroat trout
to light flashing faster than lips.
We give them time that breeds
believers in mountains. This far
upstream, flies we designed
flick lightly on tiny lines to pools

behind boulders. This game's so easy,
fish fall for any compelling treat.
Even our vests are wrong, red vinyl
fish should see, refracted. Cast by cast,
we flick shimmering flies to ripples,
to trout lips stubborn and opening,
easy. The story we'll tell, this time.

[Previously published in *Prism International* (Canada) 24, no. 1 (1985): 40.]

On Taking a Small Son Hunting

Only later, as he approaches,
expecting nothing breathing
in feathers he had aimed at

or something dead but flat
on the highway—fearing no evil.
At least with its eyes closed.

And most lay still.
Woodcarvings.
Nothing like doves.

In his sleeping bag in the camper
all night he saw
the one dove bleeding

with eyes like a kitten's,
the throat rapidly beating,
the dark, bloody pearls.

[Previously published in *Blue Unicorn* 7, no. 3 (1984): 18 and *Counting Survivors* (Pittsburgh: University of Pittsburgh Press, 1995).]

Ejecting from Jets

Holding the arm rests, I watched the sergeant
who had shot a thousand men take aim at me
and squeeze. My skull slammed my helmet

like a gong on a midway. Spine jammed
by the ejection seat's cannon, staring at space,
I stuck thumbs-up at him and my buddies,

all of us glad to be flying. Practice saves
no one but the blessed. I could have crashed
like Lawson, on takeoff, or exploded far

from base like Wally, or wallowed low
like Kirk, trying to hold his F-100 with power,
but flared too low and flipped and burned.

We wondered if he died in an instant.
We found his head in his helmet
and a hand holding the trigger of a gun.

[Previously published in *Mississippi Arts and Letters* 2, no. 3 (1985) and *Night Landings* (New York: Harper & Row, 1989).]

Reasons for Taking Risks

I could have died when I was ten
on the Brazos, diving blind
in water dark as dirt.
I might die old, after long silence,

the sad way we say of fathers,
at last he's at peace.
I could have died climbing
Long's Peak last summer,

trying hard to release
my son's looped rope.
Pitons and karabiners
like the tightest bonds

break loose. It was dark
when we reached the summit.
We stood a long time together
wishing the night would never end.

[Previously published in *Prairie Schooner* 60, no. 1 (1986): 42 and *After the Noise of Saigon* (Amherst: University of Massachusetts Press, 1988—winner of the 1987 University of Massachusetts Press Juniper Prize).]

Driving Rampart Range on Our Honeymoon

I flicked it with my boot off the highway,
rattlesnake flat as a chili pod scooped hollow.
No need to crush it with my heel, not even
a wiggle along it, nothing that quivered.

Tread marks, maybe an eighteen-wheeler
caught it crossing, or some sicko in a pickup
out for kicks, burning rubber and roaring over it
again and again. I squatted by the highway,

the snake a streak of wet blood and dust.
My bride jogged over, arms folded against wind
lashing the mountains like a fire hose no one
could hold. I slipped my winter flight jacket

over her shoulders, and she saw the snake
long as a broom, fat as a rabbit, but flat now,
its rattle chopped off to keep by the trucker
or the pickup hick, the snake's head missing

also, severed like a bloody thumb. Under aspens
turning gold on October mountains around us,
I gave her our binoculars, focused on stunning peaks
in the distance, not the rolling, blurred valley

down below—not brush fires, but whirlwinds
of dust from a pickup roaring down that bumpy
county road to a saloon in town, to strut and brag
to the crowd and pass his latest rattle around.

[Previously published in *Event* (Canada) 26, no. 3 (1997): 95–97.]

Harvest

Nine bulls out often were a waste, no fatted calves,
no pedigrees. We made them steers

and fed them well for meat counters, months after fat
alfalfa pastures. Without a calendar

or cows, steers in shades by the pond thought all this
was theirs forever, grain in the troughs,

and salt blocks. Artists of the tongue,
they carved delicious salt and waddled off to wade

and lap the lake, lazy tails flicking the pesky flies,
not bothered by wind or showers, or shouts

of cowboys by the corral, the blast of air brakes,
trucks from a slaughterhouse backed tight
at loading docks.

[Previously published in *The Gettysburg Review*.]

Long in the Tooth and Tame

The lake we camped by decades ago
is slush, a mulch of ice. We've seen it
frozen so thick trucks drove on it loaded

with boulders, no sign of trucks this month,
no boulders, or piles of charred rocks
of campfires. The inch-tall tundra blooms

chartreuse and mauve, tiny buds about to burst.
Marmots are already fat, and coyotes trot by,
taking their time. Dall sheep that used to

stare us down ignore us, now, as though
they know we're long in the tooth and tame,
too slow to hurt the herd. We shield our eyes

and stare at lakes a mile away, past higher
mountains we no longer climb. In gusts,
we hold each other under vast outcroppings

of rocks, and pitch the tent and light the stove,
a bounty of new devices insulated and cozy,
home-like and warm, and ours, for now.

[Previously published in *The Poet's Canvas* 19 (Summer 2002).]

The Mating Season

Caliph, a giraffe in the London zoo, fell
splay-legged while attempting to mate with one
of his three females. Attendants will try
lifting him tomorrow before he dies of shock.

How dumb to be
sprawled,
my
crushed
tool
drooling
under my
gut.
If I
didn't
hurt
I'd laugh
like people.
I wonder how they mate with no flat back
to mount. It's hell
the way they parade
my wives past me.
Don't they know
I'd rise if I could.
My groins are killing me, my heart
drums on the ground
like people
starting
a hunt.

[Previously published in *The New York Quarterly* 40 (1989): 101.)]

On Sons and Sleeping Dogs

BEWARE OF THE DOG appeared
one noon on our boy's locked door,
new teenager sleeping in. Fool that I am,
I listened for a growl, ears tuned
to imagine anything those years.

Big orange words on black
warned something vicious
would snarl, clamp down on my throat
and rip. "Cute," I thought, one more
rebellious gesture to ignore.

I passed his dog-barred door
six times for coffee, and frowned
but didn't knock, didn't break it down,
trusting the fabled walls of Jericho
and the seventh time around.

[Previously published in *Windhover* 3 (1999): 28–29.]

May All Our Babies Have Angels

Killing takes timing, leading a deer
with arrows. Hold the bow taut
and release, knowing steel arrows zip
till they fall or something stops them,

even a body softer than barbs.
We never aim into shadows. Steel flies
wherever we point, even if fingers slip.
May all of our babies have angels.

If our son's out of work some month,
he's a target. Or maybe he's driving home
and a drunk runs a red light.
Assume our son's healthy for decades

and life is a romp through a forest.
DNA may launch cancers
like steel-tipped darts through shadows,
not wobbling, and razor sharp.

[Previously published in *Windhover* 6 (2001): 60.]

Aunt Emma's Garden

Opened, her back door showed why Aunt Emma
kept no scrapbooks. Fourteen abandoned cars
like flowerpots, blue grass and cactus sprouting
from bumpers and hubcaps. Seen from the porch,

her junked cars made a low-tech topiary garden—
loblolly Pontiacs, Cadillac vines, and wild-rose Fords.
Aunt Emma loved them all, decades of journeys
and memories her sons and husband drove rattling

to the back. What else could she see from the window
scrubbed kitchen-clean as her sink and threadbare rugs?
Uncle Fred's Edsel told what the Fifties meant,
no reason to fix it. Repairs and travel shared a name—

someday—like her stubborn cousin's common-law
husband before the man tucked tail or died. Aunt Emma's
children suspected mischief, but back-seat secrets
were safe in coupes and pickups rusted shut. Snakes

oozed like evidence, lazy guards between steel coils.
My wife and I were only kinfolk—grand-nephew
and niece-in-law named in her will to execute
her estate, uncles long gone, leaving snapshots

in five-and-dime picture frames in her hall. What's left
to execute? No bank account, no rubber tires,
not one car not on blocks. Wreckers would
have to jerk them through mud to load them,

roots and vines trailing like entrails, like digging up
scandals to have them drawn and quartered—for what?—
dumped in a river of steel with Emma's other secrets,
the dogs and lovers buried there, even the snakes.

[Previously published in *Southern Humanities Review* 35, no. 3 (2001): 224–25.]

In the High-Country Medical Center

His death is a hawk gliding high in the hard wind,
quickly gone. He almost died five times last night.
Thumped back by doctors' paddles, he gasped

like a baby's first blind breath. Grandfather
loved hawks as a boy when the Rockies were forests,
not tunnels and ski slopes. Grandmother's hair

looks black in pictures, not white like a child
the riveters scared on a school trip to Denver.
He was four grades ahead, but all the school was there

the month the century turned, 1900 a marvel—
a hospital with electric lights, a faster train
for the Rockies. Now, Grandmother rocks by his bed

in a chair that never squeaks. The room's so still
it's soundproof, nothing but an old man's breath
she can't quite hear. When they were kids

twenty miles from here, bald eagles soared
over their parents' ranches, falcons,
red-tailed hawks. Little girls and boys

rode horses to school under thousands
of widespread wings. Old men broke trails
for them each winter through snowdrifts,

riders keeping watch after school
until the last kid left, no doctor for miles,
no broken arms their parents couldn't set.

[Previously published in *Southwest Review* 87, no. 1 (2002): 73.]

Father and the Sad Soap Operas

"Don't cry!" my daddy said, slapping that razor strap.
How that man could hit and hold. His daddy taught him
respect with a belt and the back of his hand. For years,
I thought God gave him that arm, no fistfights
like Daddy's calm-faced licks. I wished I'd find him
someday in a wheelchair, maybe on a lake,
tumbling in with a fishing pole, no one but me

to save him. After Vietnam, I found him healed,
clumsy the ways he tried to hide his passion
for soap operas, crossing his sock feet on the lounger,
squeezing back screams and trembling, blowing his nose.
I'll never know what happened while I was gone—
maybe his first grandchild, my mother's cancer,
his own first stroke that flipped him to the floor.

I've seen that look on others—tears for dogs run over—
but never saw my father cast down by demons
like a man. I wondered what to do—scowl
and walk away, switch channels or slip outside for a smoke.
I thought of fields where he fought in Flanders,
the body bags and burning huts I saw around Saigon,
and held that man and held him while he shook.

[Previously published in *Literature and Belief* 18, no. 2 (1998): 33.]

Angelica's Banjo and Karate

Aunt Angie taught banjo and karate
after her last boy left for boot camp.
Firemen signed up when she flipped
the big guy off the platform, a tag-team
match of songs and self-defense. Angelica
raised four Marines like their father, a banjo

the first thing she tried after Uncle Eddy
stepped on a mine outside Da Nang.
Her coach swore a banjo's twang and jangle
made any blood dance, too busy picking
to brood. So she married a Marine,
why not? Angie had boxed since high school,

and threw the discus farther than most men.
Karate was natural after the pain of babies
with broad shoulders. Her first day at the mall,
Aunt Angie and I played "Dueling Banjos"
faster than local girls could dance. She circled
the college coach and dumped him, dumped him

five more times for a crowd. Off-duty cops
signed up for karate and banjo, the whole package,
young couples who hoped they could save each other,
mothers in sweats who knew about drugs
and teenage rage, boys my age waving their fists
with dollars for karate, eager for the Marines.

[Previously published in *The Dalhousie Review* (Canada) 80, no. 3 (Autumn 2000): 422–23.]

Uncle Carl and the Purple Heart

Uncle Carl scratched his haunches,
tilting the porch swing sideways,
banging the wall like a dog's paw

thumping the floor. "It's all right,"
Aunt Martha sighed, "he's been healed
for years, no Mekong jungle rot

in his crotch, no fungus in his toes."
We watched him tilt and lift
a skinny thigh and scratch

like lighting a match on his pants.
"Habit," she told us nephews
sprawled on the porch, Popsicles

dripping. Uncle Carl flew home
from Saigon dwarfed in a uniform,
duffel bag hoisted, scratching

like a madman. Aunt Martha screamed
and ran to meet him, squeezing him
so fiercely they fell. Even when

she led him to the door, Martha
wouldn't stop sobbing or let go.
Nights when we slept over, we

bounced on the beds and shouted,
loud pillow fights until Aunt Martha
shushed us, or Uncle Carl cried out,

another nightmare, all quiet except
Uncle Carl sobbing and Martha's
muffled voice across the hall.

[Previously published in *Michigan Quarterly Review* 44, no. 1 (Winter 2005): 11.]

A Time to Keep Silence

The stone wall holds its ears.
Trees are talking out of season,
trying to remember bud, and blossom,
the xylem needing to swallow.

The first frost only weeks away,
stone walls feel winter in their knees,
Like children, this far south
they never learn not to fall.

Trees refuse to listen, having heard
it all before. Birds flutterer down
like clowns, chittering, the orchard
heavy, weary with peaches,

then one night, frost again, and fruit
dropping like hail. All summer,
trees have nothing but limbs at ease,
unless wind brings back the storms.

[Previously published in *The Laurel Review* 17, no. 2 (1983): 49.]

Retired Pilots at the High School Track

No one jogs by before dawn but old men
and widows much younger than us.
They knot flowing scarfs over iPhones

and trot. Heart is monitor to old men
pleading "easy, easy." Decades ago,
I jogged with friends around tracks

before flying. Jets were the birds we flew,
and luck was the pulley bone. We panted
and barked like dogs as halters and shorts

strolled by, but softly–some other guys'
daughters or wives. After miles of old jokes
and lies, someone broke hard,

and we followed, faster than old lungs
should go, chasing those nobody caught,
maybe jocks from West Point or Navy,

sure to make General or die early, all of us
pilots, pounding the same free track going
nowhere but back, a sprint to the finish line.

[Previously published in *The Poet's Canvas* 19 (Summer 2002).]

What Do You Wish They Could Do?

The brain crouches behind trees,
through caverns, reading books,
willing to share words we love.

All the brain hears it believes,
healing news for the wicked, yodels
echoed by canyons and cliffs.

Words can be wine and cheese
for sweethearts, for hermits
miles from Geneva, keeping watch

on their flocks after midnight,
fatigued and sleepy with chilled
mountain air and cheese, tearing

tough sourdough bread and eating
by firelight, reading everyday
words strung like perfect pearls.

[Previously published in *The Devil's Millhopper* (1996): 32–33.]

Wars and Rumors of War

I strummed, but music wouldn't come,
my thumb and fingers numb with numbers
in summer school, my last math class

before the draft. Call it romance
that didn't last, the rash decision of a kid
to enlist, simpler than admitting he wanted guns.

I was sure we'd win, heirs of uncles who fought
at Normandy, grandfathers who whipped the Kaiser.
While we humped on hikes and crouched

on firing lines, the truce hit Korea
like a typhoon, refugees and tons of rations
stacked like rubble, Red Cross trucks and clerks

directing traffic back to the States. Years later,
I flew off to war in Vietnam, flanked by rockets
and thoughts of family, and sappers at night.

Our Army son flies Black Hawks overseas,
as old as I was dodging rockets outside Saigon.
Nights, counting time until our son's return,

I think of the black-granite wall in Washington,
wondering where young soldiers will fight
other wars, if grandsons will have to go.

[Previously published in *The Oklahoma Review* 2, no. 2 (2001).]

My Wife's First Day of Class

I stopped by during her break. "Yes,"
she whispered, "yes," and shoved me
back to work. All morning, my wife
watched tiny scissors cut,
and she was a kid again, how lucky
could a teacher be? Her tongue

tasted sweet as lipstick. She shrugged,
she couldn't help it, the scent of paste
and crayons was enough. Her twenty children
turned pink papers around and upside down
and cut, and stubby fists colored
Valentines for friends and parents later.

Twenty first-grade tongues twisted out
and around and licked to teach
their clumsy scissors how to snip.
She watched those agile tongues contort,
and she was a child again, cutting sails
to make a boat, her own teacher tongue

turning somersaults along her lips,
licking her lipstick. "Yes," she whispered,
and hugged and shoved me toward the door,
she loved it, needed children of her own,
twins to start with, or triplets or more,
details we could talk about tonight.

[Previously published in *U.S. Catholic* 67, no. 10 (October 2002): 47.]

Father after the War

He bolted the last oily plough-blade home
and waited, down on his knees and knuckles.
I offered to help, but Daddy waved me away,

shaking his head like a boxer down for the count.
He shoved to one knee, then up, like an old man,
but only forty. I remembered him magically down
on one knee, looking up where he lifted me

proudly at arm's length. When he swung me
down, Mother clung to him without a word
before he hefted the duffel bag and boarded
the bus with other soldiers. After the war,

after troops set him and other POWs free,
he came home stooped over and slow, on crutches.
Father looked short as Grandpa, hobbling down
off the bus, old and bony in his uniform.

I was taller than him, teenager on the tractor,
the boy our dogs followed barking into the fields,
sniffing for rabbits and rattlesnakes. Hawks kept
watch on what dogs caught and all they missed.

Fifteen, I would have killed for Daddy that day.
He was slumped on the lawn swing, in awful pain
I couldn't stop, leaned over while I bawled and spun
the tractor around and gunned it down another row.

[Previously published in *The Listening Eye* (2002): 6.]

The Right to Bear Arms

Out here, men toss dry cow chips up
and draw, and let the chips fall
where they will. Eight out of ten

is only fair shooting. Sunday's
the Lord's Day, no killing. Back home
after church and beans and cornbread,

we rest under the only oak and whittle,
hats low, boots crossed in the sand.
Buzzards glide by on thermals,

biding their time on wide bent wings
and eagle eyes. We take turns squinting,
picking them off with our fingers.

We pass an oil can around like communion,
cleaning our pistols inside and out—
hammer, bore, and chamber—

spinning cylinders like hands
of mechanical clocks that have lost an hour,
winding them tight for tomorrow.

[Previously published in *Brooklyn Review* 4 (1987): 36.]

After the Random Tornado

The herd kept having calves. Sewers backed up,
and power failed randomly in five counties.
Aunt Edna, making soup and cornbread, swears

the oven baked, but soup on the stove stayed cold.
Nobody died, but south of Slaton the sundown sky
rained blood. Next day when the sheriff arrived,

the pasture was only mud. Outside the county seat,
four barns collapsed. Two teenagers missing
since March were still gone. Their parents swore

their babies would never elope. One father
kicked the sheriff's car again and again, led finally
by deputies back to the porch and eased down,

the sheriff silent all the way back to the car,
sunglasses on, glancing around the horizon,
sliding inside without his hat and driving off.

[Previously published in *The Drunken Boat* (Winter 2002).]

Midnight at Dillon

This far out, no other boats,
a mile from shore. My son
clicks a penlight off and on
like code. Far under us
dark lunkers cruise deep troughs.

I close the throttle. Silence,
a million stars. We gild our hooks
with sunfish filets smooth as suede,
splash them over the side
and count. Invisible lines snick

down to bass needing no moon,
no fragile boat to support them.
Watching for bobbing, we brace
for whatever our fists find
leaping and dying at midnight.

[Previously published in *Connecticut River Review* 5, no. 2 (1984): 24.]

Temple of the Lame, the Grateful

Bundled in fancy pants and backpacks
designed by Dallas bachelors, we're here,
skiing away from grandbabies

kept by nannies packaged with the slopes.
Grandparents in baggy pants, we flock here,
temple of the lame who stumble to the lifts

in clumsy boots, our wrinkled cheeks
pink as cherubs. We slide off at the top
on wobbly legs and plant our poles

like family flags on mountaintops, and tug
wide goggles down, almost graceful
all the way downhill, our children sliding by

and waving, far from cities where smog
turns snow to sludge and Porsches
jockey and honk in fast lanes racing home.

[Previously published in *The Drunken Boat* (Winter 2002).]

The Last Pullman to Houston

Sometimes we see them when we're back
hiking to the pond, spikes rusted dark,
the color of smoke, in this silence

since the last train rolled away to Houston
years ago. No work, no flattened pennies
on the rails, no roar or rattling windows.

Old Uncle Bubba claims he saw the Duke
of Windsor's private car one year,
three movie stars whose films I never saw,

a hundred Pullman cars a week. The tracks
are gone, the crossties buried somewhere.
It curved here where the weeds are high.

One year, digging for spikes, we filled
four buckets and waddled home.
We lined up spikes by size and shape

of their points, how bright we could buff them
on Grandfather's grind wheel in the barn,
and hung them like silver ingots on the wall.

[Previously published in *America* 156, no. 23 (1987): 481.]

Cousin Roy's Gold Star and Market

Uncle Earl hauled off tons of dung a month
in World War Two. When the breeze was in the east,
feedlots rolled their methane over us, a town of thousands
holding our noses and hurrying back inside,
most with lucky jobs in offices or the one munitions plant.
In school, we pooted and blamed the stink on windows,

breeze almost always dry and from the east.
Girls fanned with their hands and their lips turned down.
We thought they secretly admired us, often in trouble
with the substitute. Often, the rattle of Uncle Earl's
iron wagon wheels clattered by, windows raised
except for those few days it snowed, and sometimes then,

a blizzard better than stink of boys and sometimes girls.
How they found me out I never heard, but Billy Ray up front
or Carl would crane above the windowsill and whisper loud,
"It's him, Walt's uncle," and later in the year, "It's him,"
and the whole room knew. All of them, even Cousin Martha,
called me "Wagon man, Mr. Fertility,"

a mistaken nickname that stuck, switching the word
for *fertilizer*, a tag turned lucky in junior high
when we learned to swagger like studs. Uncle Earl never heard,
or ignored us, scratching me roughly on the head
at family gatherings, fried chicken, corn bread
and beans, the whole family old or only kids like me,

all cousins out of high school overseas in foxholes
or battleships, even Uncle Earl and Aunt Martha's oldest,
blown up on Guadalcanal, an artillery shell,
my sister said, splattered on the island,
not even a corpse, just bits of bloody flesh
and intestines some soldiers had to bury.

Aunt Martha's gold star was always in the window
with the shade up and a light on every night.
There wasn't a coffin, not even a marker
in the cemetery until after the war when Aunt Martha
and Uncle Earl bought the finest marble coffin
and had it hauled from Dallas on the midnight train.

[Previously published in *Brooklyn Review* 15 (1998): 92–93.]

Ranching at Ridgeway

Elk in the meadow,
a tan-green cover of field
with only spots of snow.

The hill slopes 10 degrees,
but elk graze Spring
as if it's easy, big-bellied,

not worried about cougars, yet.
They're grazing for today.
Next month, when calves come,

will be time enough.
They wander across a mile
of grass below aspens

and Douglas fir. They know
they're being watched,
not by us with binoculars,

but cougars like midwives
timing their progress,
and wolves among boulders.

[Previously published in *Front Range Review* (Spring 2002): 71.]

Dawn on the Telephone Wires

Busy old crow, black-hearted
and foreign, but somehow like me
up there, all business and cawing,
bored or blessed, bird in a billion,
a bit hoarse, choking on your tongue,
hunching forward at every caw,
hacking, barking to cough it up,
berry or feather stuck in your craw,
bawling because you can't stop
the noise crows make, boasting
or calling for help, love song,
warning, or poem.

[Previously published in *The Cape Rock* 31, no. 2 (1997): 45.]

Uncle Giuseppe and the Razor's Edge

All night Giuseppe wept, trimmed fingers
trembling through his hair, sobs with a broom

shoving clumps of limp, snipped curls
and customers' cigarettes. Gossip

for beauty shops: the barber takes a wife
and loses her, but to which of the men

he clicks sharp scissors to, to keep them
fashionably neat for wives? How many nights

alone with that woman, and now alone? How many
heads has he held in his hands and pampered,

how many men's throats were exposed
to the straight steel edge of his razor? Which one

could have done it? Which head of trimmed
tapered hair, razor-cut, goes home with her tonight?

[Previously published in *The New York Quarterly* 32 (1987): 108.]

Nobody Dead or Missing

The year Uncle Bob left Texas, he set fires
in weeds to help cousins take back the plains.
He'd done it for decades, but this burn was big,
ranch pastures infested by noxious weeds
and beetles. Smoke kicking up at dawn

should have warned us, but calls about the burn
went unnoticed, the rowdy west wind
throwing its glove down. Wind follows
nobody's orders. Uncle Bob thought
four hundred acres would do, the weeds gone

and springer calves born. Fire starters torched
dry grass and weeds in the wind. Cactus
and bear grass popped, smoke swirled
and green mesquite trees flashed, a prairie fire
nothing stopped. Thousands of acres blazed,

bonfires of oaks for miles along the creeks.
Firetrucks rolled too late to save five houses
and a hundred cattle. Insured, Uncle Bob
retired and moved to Arkansas where fields
are flooded for bass boats, ducks, and rice.

[Previously published in *Connecticut River Review* 22, no. 1 (2002): 36–37.]

Home Movies

Caught, a black squirrel freezes. His stare
says these pecans are his, our fence no border.
Hops, flicks his tail and listens, takes it

out of his mouth and cracks it, gnawing
rapidly back and forth, jaws furiously fast,
tiny paws tilting the pecan so teeth can strip it.

Lacking a dog, we're stuck with rodents
flicking their bushy tails like peacocks,
using our roof as a racetrack, scrambling

around and around at night, at dawn,
cracking nuts and bird eggs on the roof.
Our children fed red squirrels long ago

in Yellowstone, but never big bears that waddled
fat and begging to our car. Hiking trips
come back in videos that whir for an hour

without rewinding, but fading and dim
as if we need new glasses. We take ours
off and clean them, to watch our kids climb aspens

like bear cubs—clumsy, loveable seconds
and hours shot almost as afterthoughts,
watching them now long after they're gone.

[Previously published in *Windhover* 2 (1998): 61.]

Granny Hedy and the God Called Fine

Drought would break on Hedy's ranch.
The county's high school teams would win,
the cost of feed go down. When neighbors
warned the railroad spur might close,

Grandmother scoffed, "Don't bother, cattle love
riding in trucks to Dallas, and drivers always
need work." *Fine* should have been her ranch's
brand, *It's fine*. Granny kept the ranch

after Granddaddy died. Hand her a lancet, she'd cure
an abscess or canker, just hold the horse hoof up
or pry the cow's mouth wide. If the cow died, fine,
it would have died sometime—"Move 'em out,"

she'd say, "alfalfa's ready." She worshipped
another god called *If*—God's will, if it rained,
if the stock market rallied, if Hedy's dog came back.
She spoiled my sister and me as toddlers, rocked us

and made us call her "Hedy," not even "Granny."
She tucked herself into bigger bras and let her Levi's
out, the better to hug us. No end of grandchildren
when we weren't there, waifs from the church

who rode her ponies on Sundays. Once, when we hugged
her hard, she winced, then laughed to show it's all right,
soft belly jiggling. When her foreman hinted about
doctors, that fire in the belly, Hedy said, "It's fine."

The night he rushed her to the clinic, before she died
in the hall on a gurney, Grandmother said "Don't bother
calling my daughters in Montana and Dallas,
they'd only worry, and I'm fine, I'll be home tonight."

[Previously published in *Magma* (UK) 22 (Winter 2002): 42.]

Ranching in the San Juan

Shelter the colt and let the wolves
be wary. Never a mother dies
but woods and men are angry.
Busy yourself with dust

and shake stiff muscles loose
in cold wind whipping from the north.
Only a mare lies down and delivers
in darkness, then runs for miles

until a neighbor finds her,
wild-eyed, bleeding and alone.
Some months make any man angry,
digging and pitching out stones

for a burrow wide as a grave.
Owls fly over in the night,
inquiring. Shelter the colt
and let the wolves be wary.

[Previously published in *Weber Studies* 4, no. 2 (1987): JJ-35.]

What Old Pilots Never Did but Once

We bellied up to the bar
with buddies calmed
by a coating of rum, boasting
war stories—one hand,

us; the other, the bad guys—
dogfights we always won
back at the bar. Any landing
you walk away from is good,

even slamming down so hard
your teeth rattle. No one with wings
hasn't landed badly in thunder,
poor judgment, or fatigue,

fog on the field or the brain,
glitches we confess only in bed,
wide-eyed at midnight—What if
a landing strut had snapped

or a wing tip clipped the runway,
your wild life tumbling
in flames and swearing "Never,
I'll never do that again."

[Previously published in *Great River Review* 41 (Fall/Winter 2004): 39.]

Marching Through Georgia

Punching holes in hot Georgia skies,
we buried our hopes in loops and lazy-eights,
welding ourselves to forces we'd never known—
hard turns and rolls, spins and Immelmanns
inverted in jets, blinded when blood flooded
our heads like sex. Sundays, we scoured the town,
hoping for dates with local girls hoping for us.

Mondays, cramped in crash helmets in jets,
some of us hungover, we frowned and squirmed
from instructors' curses teaching us touch and trim,
how to pitch and hold a ten-ton plane inches away
from wing tips of other planes in bumpy air, in dives,
how to tighten our guts and come level, how to climb
in combat formation and if we had to, how to die.

[Previously published in *Confrontation* 68/69 (1999): 248.]

Uncle Leland and the Laws of Boulders

Uncle Leland saved drivers' lives from landslides,
sun-burned widower on a tilted bulldozer.
Boulders rubbled his talk, steep cliffs of curses
boys like me believed more than switchbacks

he showed pictures of. He swore the plains
where I grew up were mountains pounded flat.
His cigars snowed ashes on the floor, the uncle
who rescued me from boredom at fourteen.

After childless Aunt Norma died, he came home
often to help my mother, his baby sister.
I worshipped his muscles and girly tattoos.
He taught me tricks of friction with baseballs,

the bluff and fulcrum of wrestling, balance
in worlds of risk. Drunk, he pounded walls
and wept about boulders that broke loose
last month when his back was turned. How

could a man in fits of coughing keep climbers
safe? Wrecks rusting below bore witness
to risking mountains without a net. Thousands
lived because of his bulldozer's brakes

and blade, but he took the blame for his wife,
who wanted babies but died in childbirth.
Tight-lipped, he heaved huge stones from cliffs,
risking slopes to shove them tumbling.

He made steep mountains shudder and break,
his bulldozer's rumble and tilt, belching diesel
regret, gnashing into reverse to back away
from the cliff then roaring fiercely toward the edge.

[Previously published in *Art/Life* 11, no. 8 (1991): 34.]

Tactics

Early in World War II, old men out of work
and always broke haunted the draft board
by the news stand in the courthouse.
Blind Uncle Oscar with his wobbling eyes
knew exactly what candy cost, what time

it was, how many cigars he had in boxes.
He slipped us sticks of gum, a sack of popcorn
to share, asked how our daddies were,
when they'd be coming home. Later on,
every boy's daddy was gone, churches

like old folks' homes with worried aunts
and mothers and big boys begging to enlist.
Eddy's dad was a carrier sailor, the Pacific
only a name to us on maps. We launched
a navy on a pound of water, our carriers

bottle caps, our cruisers toothpicks to make
a fleet. Teachers made us gather tin cans
and rubber by the highway, haul scrap iron
and bottles on wagons to town. Eddy and I
found pennies and toothpicks by benches

at the county square, amen corner of old men
whittling and spitting, stabbing their sticks
at each other, shouting about navies and battles,
our best airplanes and ships, the quickest way
to peace, too many boys already killed.

[Previously published in *The Pacific Review* 21 (2003): 112.]

After the Monsoon

Our stock tanks offer the only water for miles,
ponds we're never stingy with. I'd sell all we own
for a cloudburst, trade sleep for a day of rain.
At dawn, we rock on the back porch, counting stars.

Doves dive out of purple skies to drink. If we talk,
we drive them off, skittish as colts Grandfather herded
a hundred years ago. We count the doves and wonder
how many breed in a pasture. Dust clings to our eyes,

grains of grit in our teeth. If this flat land is all mirage,
at least we're home. I came back after Saigon to burn,
heat waves shimmering for years. Grandfather's herd is gone,
even his windmill, which pumped sweet water to pastures.

The wolves are gone, the buffalo, the last game warden bored
with nothing to patrol. We're here far from war,
on a porch swing. The day's first siren calls
the neighbors' dogs. Ears back, they mourn the void

no dog calls father. It comes to this: our dogs are dead,
our children gone to cities we visit twice a year,
our pipedreams vanished. Parents we thought immortal
trembled for years in rockers, brittle as frost.

They learned to shake their heads, their plastic lips.
We taught them to listen for our footsteps on visits, lie back
and sleep without weeping, trusting lullaby good-byes,
and one by one they learned. Today, we'll seed puffy clouds

with faith and plow real fields for grain. The way to move
through nightmare is to sit up, pretending it's dawn.
Rocking, mugs of hot coffee in our fists, we watch the sky
light up like a lantern, slowly at first, then burning.

[Previously published in *The National Forum* 77, no. 1 (1997): 9.]

Keeping Up with the Joneses

When my wife and I go jogging,
Mr. Parr hobbles out and points.
His mouth drops, and he shouts
"You're back!" as if buying a car
was a two-month cruise.

All down the block, they're talking,
"Carl has a new car," like a heart attack,
as if an ambulance is parked
on our grass, lights flashing
and siren winding down,

me on the gurney gasping
and calling, "Lock the car!"
Edward's waxing last year's
Cadillac, his wife's good Buick
already two. He bends down,

frowning, staring for dents.
The Johnsons' Maltese sees us
and stops, one paw raised,
then goes on covering it up.
Al's door is down, his Honda gone.

Tomorrow, he'll have new cars
in his drive, buffing them both.
We jog past sprinklers on lawns,
glancing both ways for cars.
The Rookers' poodle yaps

from the sidewalk, her shrill bark
frothy, too mad to swallow.
She struts to the corner and follows
until we reach the school
two blocks away and turn.

[Previously published in *Apples & Oranges Poetry Magazine* (December 18, 2001).]

In Times of Plenty

These are the years of plenty,
fields without locusts, rain
for the roots of saplings

already budding. Fat cattle
are in our barns, all fences tight,
a litter of lambs each week. Last night,

I dreamed the dream of Pharaoh,
though, lean years in store like bones.
I saw starved Lazarus

lying in rags. Quick,
find the fired hired hands
and retrain them. Don't tear down

bulging barns. Feed doves and pigeons,
watch stingy cirrus clouds
for signs. Pray that our gates

bring strangers. Give away grain
overflowing the silos,
press beggars in from the roads

and clothe them, send riders
to warn our cousins
beware of angels seeking work.

[Previously published in *Poetry Durham* (UK) 23 (1990): 26.]

War Never Stops until All Vets Are Dead

The fields are calm tonight, not one wild coyote howling.
The windmill is still, not creaking, no restless banging
against the fence by billy goats. How many nights
have we lain like this together since our children aged
and moved away? I hear the ticking of Grandfather's clock,
the far-off barking of dogs, the pack maddened by blood,

the whir and clatter of the roof in blizzards. Dreams
take me back to a war long ago, most records closed,
engraved on stones in towns around the states.
I think of Harper and Don, names on a wall in Washington.
I picture children, some missing arms and eyes
outside Da Nang, shells exploding decades later

in fields turned into schools, playgrounds
surrounded by jungle growing back, the sudden
burst and smoke. Then I get up and go to a window
and look out, knowing I'll see only the moon
and silhouettes of trees, not soldiers crouching
through shadows, not fire or smoke or children bleeding.

[Previously published in *Sulphur River Literary Review* 15, no. 1 (1999): 127.]

Summer with Dakota

Dakota Jones came west at seventeen.
After her daddy died, the ranch was hers,
and she learned. When Dakota called,
we all trotted, tiny with a massive tongue.
The summer I signed on, she looked me over,

a maverick bony enough to fill out
after enough roundups and flapjacks.
When Dakota called, I flicked the tip of the reins
to turn the roan. She sent me for strays
under black wings wheeling in the east.

She gave me the easy tasks, the best saddle
from her daddy's tack room, my pick
of the palominos. The foreman told me
the son she lost in a car wreck
looked like me. She never wasted daylight,

often coughing and breathless, handkerchief
always bloody, a crew of bachelor cowboys.
She made me the scourge of the bunkhouse,
the boss's darling, and they made me sweat,
threatened to dump me in tar and cactus.

That summer, Dakota died after high school
called me home. I handed the palomino back
and she nodded, coughing, and closed the door.
The driver clicked his tongue and the wagon jerked,
the strong mares clopping, hauling me away.

[Previously published in *Borderlands* 22 (Spring/Summer 2004): 48.]

Trusting in Women Who Fly

Wind sways the plane. All aboard keep reading
as if nothing could happen. We ignore static
in earphones, things that go bump in clear air,
the roar and whine of turbines. Our flight attendant
with lovely smiles leans near, reaching a drink

to a man by the window. She rises, mating
another glass and napkin for the man on the aisle
who breathes her perfume like oxygen. She is
our hired canary. If there's trouble in this tunnel,
this mine of gold and diamonds in the sky, she'll be

the first to notice. The wings can sway and shudder,
an engine whine higher than any pitch we've heard,
our heads bounce on our necks like rubber balls,
no bother. We sip, and flip magazines, rainstorm
streaking the windows like a fuel leak. Turbulence

can shove us side to side, popping oxygen-mask
doors open up the aisle, like cobras dangling over
the scalps of children. Even that won't stress our faith
to breaking, if she's calm. Even if she passes by faster
than before, lurching from seat to seat, collects our

empty cups and dumps them unstacked in her cart
and disappears, we go on turning pages, believing
if there's danger she'll sing out, "Fire," or "Bend over,
hold your pillow tight to your head and listen to me
for instructions, listen only to the sound of my voice."

[Previously published in *Orbis* (UK) 64 (1987): 18.]

The B-25 and Bombs

Mine was the last pilot class to fly them,
loud as a steel mill, old rivets failing in mid-air
and crashing. Doolittle flew those planes
to Tokyo, twin-engine bombers designed
for mile-long runways. With boys he took

them off a carrier to bomb Japan, years
before bombers reached that far again.
My friend Joe Heller flew B-25s in combat
as a bombardier in World War II and wrote
Catch-22 about it, a popular comic novel

with horrors. Now, pilots young as my sons
cruise at Mach 2 on swept wings dark as night,
stealth fighters invisible to radar, each bomb
ten thousand times more deadly than all
Doolittle's squadron dropped. Computers

rule the cockpit, fly-by-wire, pitch and bank
controlled by sensors in the stick. If pilots
are the heart and hand, computers are the brain
and brawn. Pilots still fly loops and barrel rolls,
and drop bombs, and where the blue sky starts

is earth, where women and men in smocks
devise the square root of lasers and missiles,
where all of us in school were taught thirty
goes into two, that decimals are possible,
that wars are a simple way to stop wars.

[Previously published in *The New Criterion* 12, no. 8 (1994): 33.]

Wishing for Friends from Childhood

Start fire with sticks and tumbleweeds—
that's all we meant to do when we were ten
with wires and wieners at a rock pit,
a puny Stonehenge keeping no flames

from spreading—Billy Joe and Ray and me,
cooking hot dogs in the dark, winking
and telling lies. Tumbleweeds popped,
horse-nettle berries burst, and the grass

caught fire. We stomped and shouted,
but the Ryans' house blazed, a *whoof*
of flames that torched the roof and wall.
God and a garden hose saved the neighbors,

and mercy of a judge saved us. Our parents
paid for lawyers and the Ryans' new house
across town. Ray died after Vietnam
in a car wreck. A rugged Green Beret,

Billy Joe was bold, big-shouldered
even in high school. Many times, he bought
our coffee in Saigon. We talked about our wives
back home. Already, he'd had two.

He lifted his mug and frowned "Three,"
he smirked, "maybe four when I get home."
I saw him with a white mustache at our class
reunion, winking, a new blonde on his arm.

[Previously published in *North American Review* 290, no. 1 (2005): 47.]

Tommy and the Appaloosa

Weeks after chemo, our nephew bounced
in the saddle on our rail fence, cowboy
of five, with boots too big and a western vest,
bald laughing boy with dark, deep eyes.

Spurring the fence with his boots,
Tommy galloped after the bad guy
toward the gate twenty feet away.
In make-believe, the hero always wins.

His mama risked her allergies to watch him
riding the wind. Sneezing, she dabbed
at her eyes and applauded. Our burly son
propped Tommy up by both shoulders,

taught him to twirl a rope and not fall,
wrap it twice around the saddle horn
and let his brand-new hobby horse
do the work, jerking the rustlers down.

[Previously published in *The Pacific Review* 21 (2003): 113.]

Joe Bubba's Grandpa's Barn

Mr. Nall kept a barn of antlers, peacocks
and hawks he stuffed with sawdust. Buzzards
kept watch over decades of dust. Joe Bubba
his grandson charged a penny to let me in

to the odor of mold and rat dung. Big bears,
grotesque, erect, had almost freed themselves
from rods and wires that were their spines.
Shedding chests sagged with wadded sawdust

like tumors, once fierce but now pathetic,
needing a vet, mastectomies, a decent decay.
An amateur's wax museum, but fur, real fur
and eyes and tongues in some. Real eyes,

Joe Bubba swore, no plastic beads for Grandpa.
Whatever embalming jam Mr. Nall injected
had parched, West Texas a desert. Joe Bubba confessed
the eyes of antelopes were raisins, no way to see

that coyote a foot away, tail drooped like a whipped dog's.
He bragged his grandpa shot them all, even tarantulas
and snakes. Joe Bubba grinned and grabbed a rattler
like a hammer and shook the tail to make it birr,

then thrust the fangs at the Johnson boy, who screamed
and fell back into a Grizzly, showering hosannas
of dust, bear arms and paws reaching out
as the boy ran bawling toward the door.

[Previously published in *Reed: A Journal of Poetry & Prose* 55 (2002): 55.]

Boys and Girls by the Brazos

After rains, boats floated away, ropes cut, or loops
simply lifted. Boys, usually, high schoolers like us
with something to prove. Night watchmen
were usually retired, armed with flashlights.
Old watchmen had old bladders, so timing

was everything when we took somebody's dares,
especially if our dates waited to witness,
back in the pickups. At midnight, we picked
the easy ones at first, tempting the limits
of hearing aids and toilet flush, jogging down docks

past bass boats with outboards, sleek speedboats
big as yachts, houseboats with no one home. By dawn,
some boats bumped ashore downstream, beached
like obedient pets. Some wedged under limbs of oaks,
bows crushed or cracked. Some boats would go

with the flow of the Brazos, end up in Glen Rose,
ranches, who knows where. Sometimes, rewards
went out, and someone squealed–no jail time,
but fines, boys sweating in our daddies' fields,
dropping post-hole diggers down and squeezing out

rocks from hardpan. Sometimes a pickup stopped
nearby, and some girl waved at a big, bare-chested
boy as he slammed the digger down with a thud,
wet muscles bulging, cocking his sweaty head
and winking, the promise she was hoping for.

[Previously published in *The North* (UK) 29 (2001): 25.]

Gehenna and the County's Tires

Uncle Oscar burned all junked tires he found
until the county ruled "No pollution, no rubber fires."
Hell was that black canyon, that stench

the devil's breath. Oscar dragged dead wolves
and antelopes off the school ground and graveyard
when he was a boy, wherever he found them,

a quarter from his daddy for every carcass, his habit
by World War I. When he came home with a cane
and Purple Heart, he found the county trashed,

abandoned cars by the fence, fenders, blown-out tires.
Forget the rules, he hated junk, hauled tons of tires
and burned them. I hunted coyotes around the canyon,

hoping for cougars and bobcats. At the rim,
I dismounted and coughed, pinching my nose
and sneezing. Down there, thousands of black tires

boiled, the canyon mushy with bubbling rubber smoke.
Heaps of coals blazed hot like lava, about to burst.
At times, coming home at dusk, I saw a glow

like a man beyond every cactus, gone when I got there,
but the horse saw. His hind hoofs cantered sideways
until I coaxed him hard toward home, then had to hold him

back while his iron shoes clattered on the highway
in darkness, ears up and sweaty, about to gallop,
the raging fire behind us, the good dark barn ahead.

[Previously published in *William & Mary Review* 41 (2003): 72.]

Search and Rescue

Slopes with mountain goats are below us while we climb
over tundra onto cliffs that warn harm to climbers,
even mountain goats that slip, or doomed airplanes that crash.

Help is here when we need it, we hope, although some days
nothing can save us. Even Jesus, who could cast whole
mountains into seas, knew what little time we have.

If we never climb again, what is that to rocks that tumble,
and geese that fly a thousand miles back to arctic lakes
to breed? We pound steel pitons into stone and loop the ropes,

insert our boots and stcp out into space and swing across
to a ledge by faith, where the town saw fire on the mountain
last night, nothing now but seared and twisted metal

that looks nothing like a plane. For hours, we photograph
and tag, and scoop a human into sacks of plastic that last
longer than blood and breath we cling to, and ropes

that lift us spinning off the cliff, over chasms thousands
of feet straight down, nothing above us but one helicopter
throbbing like salvation's heart, bolts and computer chips

installed by human hands. Waiting for a cable, dangling
and spinning above this seared, sheer millennial cliff,
we know we are not immortal angels, not even goats.

[Previously published in *Literature and Belief* 18, no. 2 (1998): 101.]

What We Wouldn't Give

Someday, he might remember a thousand bees
he wore on his back like barbed wires twisted tight,
stings driving him clawing and screaming from the shrubs,

cast like Adam and Eve out of Eden, after his game
of catch in the back yard, the ball bouncing sideways
to honeybees' corner of the garden. Fleeing to the street

was the hour his head hit the car, what stars, what utter,
delicious honey numbing his brain and tongue.
All fall, a feeling of silence or songs of the spheres,

our son out there among them all—sun, moon, even the stars
forgotten. Brought back at times when we tap, he may
hear someone thumping his arm and calling, probing

another vein to stick with needles, not nearly the sting
of a thousand bees, and done by a grim-lipped lady
he should know, needles she sticks into something

oddly like arms. Still has no clue about a car that hit him
and disappeared. He might be listening to us
like pranksters pulling a fast one, hiding his shoes

or swapping his furniture for ours, His back and skull
are shattered, but he smiles, almost, as if nothing hurts.
He makes no effort to rise or roll on his elbows, to crawl

or walk again. His dark eyes stare and flutter shut. Oh
my son, take my place—let my thin gray hair turn white,
let steel posts hold me down. Take my eyes, see the bees,

let them sting me. Take Mom's arm and dance on the lawn
while there is light. Laugh with Mom like you did
when you were ten, when we still sang and played until dark.

[Previously published in *Defined Providence* 5 (1997): 12–13.]

Cougars and Uncle Bob

"Back off," Uncle Bob cautioned,
"that cougar's wounded."
I lifted the tip of the reins

and the gelding stiffly stepped back
until I could turn him,
the trail too narrow, there.

I saw the stick in the ribs
a hundred yards off, arrow
wagging as it tried to rise.

If the cat had been a calf,
Uncle Bob would track the hunter down,
broker or good ol' boy with a toy.

Whoever pulled the bow and shot
was bragging back in his pickup,
would have heard the *thunk*,

plenty of blood at the spot
to prove he didn't miss.
If he tracked it, he'd find it

down in the canyon–dangerous,
maybe, although almost a carcass.
Black wings wheeling

could lead him, if he wasn't afraid
of what might wait for him,
maybe growling and gut-shot

behind cactus and barbed wire.
If he believed in signs,
if he cared enough, he'd find it,

down on its side, sprawled
in cottonwood shadows,
a long shaft through the heart.

[Previously published in *The Louisville Review*.]

Approaching the Condo

We're at the gate of the very old. It's locked,
a combination we jotted down, somewhere.
Our parents in their eighties passed it down.

Not even fifty, we tucked it away like recipes
for gruel only the old would eat. The gate sags
like jowls of fat guys slouched, not like our home

with a picket fence, brass hinges bright, not locked,
no reason to lock it in our friendly neighborhood
near the base. The planes I flew roar grandly by

in peacetime and in war. This street's so quiet
I hear a TV blaring a block away. Look at this
cracked sidewalk, the wobbly, muddy bricks.

Old people here should dig them up and mate them
evenly again. This warped board porch is filthy,
one porch step smashed, the *Welcom* doormat

jagged, the *e* missing, the mud caked hard.
This isn't where we meant to live. And what's that
awful odor, those moans beyond the door?

[Previously published in *The Devil's Millhopper* (1996): 32–33.]

Believing Every Word

I was three or four, no more than five:
Grandmother lay in bed, propped up,
telling tales about Samson, Daniel
in the lions' den, and a boy called
David who grew up to be king–

and I was hooked on language
long before I learned Grandmother
was lying there dying of cancer.
First grade was cookies for all,
and rhythm band, until Miss Crump

brought to class a man in buckskin,
in moccasins without socks, a feather
headdress that sprawled all the way
to the floor. That man told stories,
and I sat there hearing the most

amazing tales, thrilled out of my skull,
believing every word. I don't remember
his face, his name, but I'll never forget
the splendor of it all. It seems only months
since I propped on elbows and heard

Grandmother read magic in words
I barely understood. Wasn't it days ago
a chief told stories so thrilling all kids
that winter shouted and clapped
till our hands stung? What writer

doesn't long to move us to tears
or chills and hugs, or laughter? For those
who love words, before the golden bowl
breaks and the silver cord snaps, who
wouldn't want to give us thrills like that?

[Previously published in *Windhover* 8 (2003): 120.]

Grandmother and the Lions' Den

Grandmother taught us
to sing, my sister and me
propped by her pillows
in bed. She whispered
about angels and maidens,

a man in a den of lions,
a girl named Mary
and a baby and a boy
who danced for God,
fought giants, real giants,

and played the harp.
It was hard for Grandmother
to talk, and hard to hear
her gravelly cancer voice
with wobbly folds

of throat we stroked,
holding a book she hadn't
read to us yet, and said
she'd read that afternoon,
but never, never did.

[Previously published in *Sunstone: Mormon Experience, Scholarship, Issues, & Art* 141 (April 2006): 14.]

What Saves Us

Slumped on the sofa, my uncles griped how stupid
they'd been, how damned unlucky. They bragged about
deals they nearly pulled, cheap land they almost bought.

Uncle Carl swore Rockefeller tossed him a dime
when he was ten, eye to eye with the old man with the derby
and sunken cheeks, who whispered to him, "Buy cheap."

Uncle Carl paused for a laugh—"I thought he meant
shop DISCOUNT stores!" Nobody listened. Uncle Bob
bragged he always bought stocks cheap but lost a fortune

when the market dropped. Uncle Don snorted, fat arms
on his belly, the bald, family buddha with a head plate
after the parachute dragged him bumping across France.

These old men were boys who won the war and griped
about college kids sniffing it away. Uncle Don bragged
about General Patton patting him on his bloody skull

in a field hospital. The General asked Don what he would do
to Hitler. "Smash him!" Uncle Don said and slammed a fist
in his palm. "Destroy his panzers and you'll win the war,"

Uncle Don said, as if Patton had never thought of that.
Don leaned back with forearms that would hardly cross,
as if we'd ask to see his Purple Heart, the steel in his skull.

I remember him in tears after Aunt Martha died, milk
buckets empty in both big fists, and cows lined up at dawn,
stomping the straw floor to dust, tight udders bulging.

Uncle Carl and Bob followed me down, taking the buckets
from Uncle Don, leading him slowly back to the house
to call the preacher, to ask that good man what to do.

[Previously published in *Silverfish Review* 29 (1998): J.]

Keeping Time by the Clatter of Horseshoes

My uncle and dad rode great Appaloosas,
bold men, like sheriffs again, clopping
through sagebrush and cactus, right hands
by their hips always balanced, though neither
wore guns anymore. The mustang I rode

trotted slowly, reins loose in my fist just for me.
It knew where to turn, and we turned.
Uncle Carl owned the world that he wanted,
hardscrabble he bought for his heart.
My father leaned forward, fists crossed

like counting the cattle of neighbors
grazing beyond Carl's miles of barbed wires.
Alone after Aunt Martha died, Carl wanted
no man's land, only thousands of acres to ride.
Years after Saigon fell, Dad died, and my uncles,

many cousins and in-laws and friends. I waged
war often at night, like a child on the back
of a stallion, pale horse that needed no reins.
Tying barbed wires tight around fence posts,
I hear steel on steel of the Amtrak, and hawks

as constant as war. I smell gas of the jungles at night,
even now with the wind at my back. I keep time
by the clatter of horseshoes, raising cattle
and mustangs for children, grown, now, and parents
raising four by the grace of God's hand.

[Previously published in *Connecticut Review* 26, no. 1 (Spring 2004): 145.]

Grandchildren Tumbling from Cars

Whatever perfume's made from
oozed on my darling's tongue,
dark-purple grapes that dripped
when I lifted clusters glistening

to her lips, sweet sherry confection
dribbling down her chin. I patted
the juice, the wrinkles by her eyes,
sparkles of silver in her hair.

For years we tilled Grandmama's
vineyard, knew every inch.
We learned where field mice hid,
designs spiders spun upside down

on the vines. Her mules plowed the fields
for decades, for Christmas and birthday
wine and communion cups, hauled
by buggy to churches miles downhill.

Her neighbors feasted like pilgrims
from England. We watered her hobby
acre by acre, some land left fallow,
carefully pruned, saving the best

for grandkids who leap running from cars
and squeezing us sticky with kisses,
playing hide and seek in the vineyards,
gobbling Grandmama's grapes.

[No previously published information available.]

Mercy Was a Plate of Peas and Cornbread

Before widows built the town's food bank,
Uncle Croom's legumes fed cows and families
out of work. My brother and I crawled rows
with cousins, picking and filling buckets
of black-eyed peas for neighbors and strangers
at the door. No post-hole diggers, there,
no fences. In the 1930s, anyone could come.
Even dogs wouldn't drive them off.

Uncle Croom kept gourds on thongs at the well
so hobos could wash their supper down, cornbread
and peas, and carrots for their pockets. Aunt Elzie
shelled tons of peas on the back porch, rocking,
humming old gospel songs, bushels of peas
for the poor, the almost starved. In gold October
when the last peas were picked, Uncle Croom
pulled up the plants like stumps, silage for cows.

Nights, our cousins taught my brother and me
how to climb magnolia trees' slippery limbs.
Wedged between top branches, we swayed,
chewed waxy leaves and whispered, searching
the dark for barking dogs we never saw,
believing whatever we heard, thrilled by the long
mournful whistle of the night train to Amarillo
like coyotes or ghosts of hoboes going home.

[Previously published in *Southern Humanities Review* 35, no. 3 (2001): 227.]

Anniversary Waltz

A year since you flew away. Often, I pictured you
married, a villa in Tahiti. One afternoon I turned,
and you were there on the stairs before the opera started,
dangling "Maybe" across the lobby for me, for me.

Or was it only "hello," a civil greeting? If the cashier
had hitched her girdle, fumbled the bills or sneezed,
you might have disappeared forever, carried along
by the throng. Friends would say "They missed each other

by seconds." The cashier had a diamond, tiny as an eye blink,
and she dealt my change like black jack. I turned,
glanced up at Madonna Destiny with a happy face
at an opera in Texas, darling, not a strip show.

There you were, at ease, watching me stumbling
on the stairs, watching your dazzling smile and lips,
those fabulous eyes. The dashing American sailed back
in the opera, but with a bride, and Madame Butterfly

would die by her own knife, after the purest aria
ears can hear. Love's a dangerous game at best,
but Darling, you stood your ground, you knew
what I offered. You had time to turn and disappear

before I turned with a ticket, before I could bump my way
politely through the crowd. In seconds, step by step,
decades of ecstasy and children we might have rose up
and swirled like sugarplums in my head. You saw,

you bet it all. Straw turned to silk and pots of gold,
like Rumpelstiltskin's fairy-tale magic—then
we were together on the stairs, you without a ring
or villa in Tahiti, laughing and eager to say yes.

[Previously published in *King Log* 6, no. 1 (Summer 2003).]

Walt McDonald
(1934–2022)